INTONATION

D0218148

INTONATION

ALAN CRUTTENDEN

SENIOR LECTURER IN PHONETICS
UNIVERSITY OF MANCHESTER

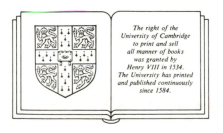

The right of the
University of Cambridge
to print and sell
all manner of books
was granted by
Henry VIII in 1534.
The University has printed
and published continuously
since 1584.

CAMBRIDGE UNIVERSITY PRESS

CAMBRIDGE

LONDON   NEW YORK   NEW ROCHELLE

MELBOURNE   SYDNEY

Published by the Press Syndicate of the University of Cambridge
The Pitt Building, Trumpington Street, Cambridge CB2 1RP
32 East 57th Street, New York, NY 10022, USA
10 Stamford Road, Oakleigh, Melbourne 3166, Australia

First published 1986

Printed at The Bath Press, Avon

British Library Cataloguing in Publication Data
Cruttenden, Alan
Intonation. – (Cambridge textbooks in
linguistics)
1. Intonation (Phonetics)
I. Title
414   P222

Library of Congress Cataloguing in Publication Data
Cruttenden, Alan, 1936–
Intonation.
(Cambridge textbooks in linguistics)
Bibliography; p.
Includes index.
1. Intonation (Phonetics)   I. Title.   II. Series.
P222.C78   1986   414   85-11393

ISBN 0 521 26028 0 hard covers
ISBN 0 521 27805 8 paperback
ISBN 0 521 26058 2 cassette

BS

CONTENTS

v

Contents

Contents

Contents

ACKNOWLEDGEMENTS

My principal acknowledgement for any knowledge I have about intonation must be to my teachers Gordon Arnold and Doc O'Connor; the influence of their teaching and of their book pervades large chunks of this book. If the study of intonation is now developing a body of theoretical discussion, this is only happening because of the existence of prior and thorough basic descriptions, and of these O'Connor and Arnold's *Intonation of Colloquial English* is pre-eminent. It should also be apparent that the two recent writers on the theory of intonation who have influenced me most are Bob Ladd and Carlos Gussenhoven; while in the area of universals, the chief influence has been that of Dwight Bolinger. I must also acknowledge a debt to various colleagues with whom I have discussed intonation over many years and who have provided me with many examples: David Allerton, Edward Carney, Alan Cruse, Martin French, and John Payne. Postgraduate students have also supplied me with examples: in particular I mention Mangat Bhardwaj, Madalena Cruz-Ferreira, Eric Jarman, and Graham Low. My thanks to John Trim, who has provided helpful criticism of the whole manuscript; to David Faber, who has critically dissected almost every sentence both for content and for style, besides being the most fertile of all sources of examples, and who has also compiled the main index; and to Penny Carter, who has always been a most helpful in-house editor. And my final thanks go to those who provided the secretarial assistance, principally Eunice Baker, and, to a lesser extent, Patricia Bowden and Irene Pickford.

PREFACE

This is the first textbook on intonation for linguists and the first text-book which attempts to widen the discussion of intonation to include languages other than English. There have been a number of excellent textbooks which have been pedagogically oriented to the needs of speakers of English as a second or foreign language (see in particular Palmer, 1922; Armstrong and Ward, 1926; Kingdon, 1958a; O'Connor and Arnold, 1961 and 1973; Halliday, 1970; and Pike, 1945, as the sole American book of this sort). Such textbooks have all included at least some (and often a large amount of) practice material. The present book is not intended as a practice book; those whose ears and mouths need to practise the skill of recognising and producing intonation patterns should use one of the above books, preferably one which uses the same tonetic-stress marks as the present book (e.g. O'Connor and Arnold, 1973). Among previous books on intonation the nearest approaches to the present volume are Bolinger (1972b), Crystal (1969a), and Ladd (1980). Bolinger (1972b) is a book of readings with the selective coverage which that entails; Crystal (1969) is the most thorough bibliographic survey in print, but covers essentially only English; Ladd (1980) gets to grips with many of the difficult theoretical problems in intonational analysis, but is nevertheless selective and limited to English. The present book differs from any predecessor in attempting to give thorough descriptive and theoretical coverage and to extend the database to languages other than English. In this attempt to achieve wider coverage, it is inevitable that there are many areas which are near-virgin territory and where what is written is almost entirely my own point of view based on my own long interaction with theory and analysis in intonation; where this applies I have clearly said so in the text.

For many linguists the content of this book will represent a curious mixture of the analytic, the descriptive, the typological, and the theoretical. Linguists tend to belong to one of these categories and to regard those belonging to one of the other categories as at the very least doing a different sort of linguistics. But if this book is to be used as a textbook it seems to me important that students should be introduced to (i) the sort of difficulties involved in setting up the formal units within which an intonational description is to be made; (ii) a certain amount of descriptive detail about the actual forms and meanings of tunes (see in particular chapter 4, sub-section 4.4.1); (iii) a discussion of the theoretical issues which have been and/or still are in the forefront of intonational argumentation (see in particular chapter 2, sections 2.5 and 2.6; chapter 3, sub-section 3.8.1 and section 3.9; chapter 4, sub-sections 4.4.2–4.4.4; and chapter 5, sub-section 5.4.3); and (iv) some sort of cross-dialectal and cross-language survey to show dimensions of variation and putative universals (see in particular chapter 5). It follows therefore that, according to the persuasion and interests of any particular reader, sub-sections of the book can be skipped without necessarily impairing understanding of later sections.

I have written the book in such a way as to keep references in the text to the absolute minimum. At the end of each chapter there is then a very full listing of any sources I have used, together with guidance on further reading.

All the transcribed examples in chapters 3 and 4, which are the ones principally concerned with the theory and description of intonation, are read aloud by me on an accompanying cassette.

TRANSCRIPTIONS

Systems of intonational transcription fall into two categories, roughly analogous to the broad and narrow transcriptions of segmental phonology. A narrow transcription uses some sort of continuously varying line or series of dots (either through or alongside the basic text) to represent the continuously varying pitch of the speaker. The type of narrow transcription preferred in this book is often referred to as 'interlinear tonetic' and looks like this ● ·   ● ·   ● . In this type of transcription the top and bottom lines represent the top and bottom of the speaker's pitch range and each dot corresponds to a syllable, the larger dots indicating stressed and/or accented syllables (for a discussion of the terms stress and accent, see the beginning of chapter 2).

A broad transcription of intonation represents some level of phonological analysis of the pitch patterns used by a speaker. One such type of transcription common until fairly recently in North American writing indicated one of a number of pitch levels (usually four) at crucial changepoints in an overall contour (see in particular Pike, 1945; and Trager and Smith, 1951). Another type of broad transcription, this time common in British writing, indicates the tune of an intonation-group by the use of a number at the beginning of the group, with various diacritics following and underneath the number to indicate particular varieties of the basic tune (see in particular Halliday, 1967 and 1970). However, the type of broad transcription preferred in this book is of the type which involves what have often been called 'tonetic-stress' marks. This type of transcription has a long history of British usage with roots going back to Walker (1787), Sweet (1878 and 1892), and Palmer (1922); it has been used in a number of well-known pedagogical textbooks of British English intonation (see in particular Kingdon (1958a), Schubiger (1958) and O'Connor and Arnold (1961, 1973)). In a full system of tonetic-stress marking, a mark is placed before each stressed syllable and the differences between the marks indicate the type of pitch movement beginning on that syllable.

Transcriptions

In this book only a limited number of marks are used, as follows:

/ for an intonation-group boundary
ˋ for a fall from high to low (a 'high-fall')
ˎ for a fall from mid to low (a 'low-fall')
ˊ for a rise ending high (a 'high-rise')
ˏ for a rise ending mid (a 'low-rise')
ˇ for a fall-rise
ˆ for a rise-fall
> for a mid-level
ˈ for a high pre-nuclear accent

All these marks (with the exception of the last) indicate the pitch pattern involved in a following 'nuclear tone' (see chapter 3, section 3.6). The last mark indicates a high pitch accent in a pre-nuclear position. These tonetic-stress marks are explained again as they arise up to chapter 3, section 3.7, in which section they are given a full explanation; thereafter they are not usually explained.

It is sometimes necessary to refer to stress with no indication of pitch: this is done by placing the mark over the vowel (whereas all the tonetic-stress marks precede syllables), e.g. *áccent* and *tálking about áccent*. It is also sometimes useful to refer to the nucleus or nuclear syllable (or 'primary stress') of an utterance without indicating pitch movement: this is done by capitalising the nuclear syllable, e.g. *talking about ACcent*. Syllable division is occasionally indicated by a hyphen, e.g. /eks-trə/.

The context of particular intonational examples is indicated as follows:

Preceding utterance spoken by same speaker: no overt indication but intonation not usually marked
Preceding utterance spoken by different speaker: (   )
Situational context: [   ]
Pauses are indicated by three dots: . . .
Omitted portions of utterances are indicated by five dots: . . . . .

I
Preliminaries

1.1 Prosodic features

Phonetics, in the mind of the 'man in the street', nurtured on *Pygmalion* and *My Fair Lady*, generally consists of sounds and the transcription of sounds: he thinks, for example, of the word *nice* being transcribed as /naɪs/. Such a transcription might be made for various purposes including, for instance, showing the varying relationships between sound and spelling, or indicating how to pronounce a particular word in a language or dialect. This sort of transcription is usually limited to sounds (which are represented as discrete) that follow one another in a fixed order: in the case of *nice* an /n/ is followed by an /aɪ/ which in turn is followed by an /s/. Such sounds are usually referred to as segments and the sort of transcription that represents them is consequently referred to as a segmental transcription. But there are clearly other features involved in the way a word is said which are not indicated in a segmental transcription. The word *nice* might be said softly or loudly; it might be said with a pitch pattern which starts high and ends low, or with one which begins low and ends high; it might be said with a voice quality which is especially creaky or especially breathy. Such features generally extend over stretches of utterances longer than just one sound and are hence often referred to as suprasegmentals (and a type of transcription which indicates how any of them are used is therefore called a suprasegmental transcription). Alternatively, the shorter term PROSODIC is sometimes used and I shall generally prefer this term in this book. Prosodic features may extend over varying domains: sometimes over relatively short stretches of utterances, like one syllable or one morpheme or one word (the tones of tone languages are generally relatable to such shorter domains); sometimes over relatively longer stretches of utterances, like one phrase, or one clause, or one sentence (intonation is generally relatable to such longer domains). Of course this distinction is not always as clear-cut as it first appears: a sentence, for example, may consist of one word. Since this book is principally about intonation, I shall for the most part be concerned with features relating to the longer domains.

1.1.1 Pitch, length, and loudness

The prosody of connected speech may be analysed and described in terms of the variation of a large number of prosodic features. There are, however, three features which are most consistently used for linguistic purposes, either singly or jointly. These three features are pitch, length, and loudness. Pitch concerns the varying height of the pitch of the voice over one syllable or over a number of successive syllables; length concerns the relative durations of a number of successive syllables or the duration of a given syllable in one environment relative to the duration of the same syllable in another environment; loudness concerns changes of loudness within one syllable or the relative loudness of a number of successive syllables. The terms pitch, length, and loudness refer to features perceived by listeners; before we go on to consider the linguistic functions of these features, we must spend a little time considering the physiological and acoustic correlates of these perceived features.

1.1.1.1 **Length.** LENGTH is in one way the simplest of the features: it makes little difference whether we view it as the length of time a speaker decides to continue to produce a linguistic unit, as the duration of the acoustic correlates of the unit on a spectrogram, or as the length of time during which a listener hears that unit. But in other ways it is the most complex feature. If, for example, we wish to measure the duration of particular syllables in order to judge whether varying degrees of accent involve varying degrees of lengthening, we will initially have to make some decisions about syllable boundaries which are to some extent arbitrary. Where are we to place the boundary between the two syllables of *extra*? While the solutions /éks-trə/ or /ék-strə/ may seem the most likely, the decision between these two solutions is not easy. Again, where are we to place the boundaries of the accented syllable in *potato*? If we decide that the first /t/ belongs with the accented syllable but the second does not, do we then include the compression stage of the first /t/ in the duration of the accented syllable? The relevance of length as a prosodic feature is also difficult to assess because there are often many different influences on the absolute duration of a segment or syllable. If we wish to show that accented syllables are longer than unaccented syllables, we have firstly to discount such influences as the 'innate' length of vowels (e.g. the vowel of *peat* is generally longer than that of *pit*) and the fact that the last syllable before a pause is often lengthened.

1.1.1.2 **Loudness.** LOUDNESS as perceived by the listener is related to the breath-force which a speaker uses. A famous theory concerning the phonetic basis of syllables once asserted that speech is divided into syllables by the ebb and flow of increasing and decreasing breath-force on vowels and consonants. Later, more sophisticated equipment (the earlier equipment was balloons in stomachs, the later was electrodes in muscles) showed that increases in breath-force were only regularly present in the case of accented syllables; and even this has been called in question by experiments showing that accented syllables are more regularly indicated by length and pitch than by loudness. The acoustic correlate of loudness is intensity or the amount of energy which is present in a sound or sequence of sounds, variations in intensity being produced by variations in the pressure of air coming from the lungs. The relevance of intensity or loudness as a prosodic feature, like that of length, is often difficult to assess because there are often different influences on the absolute intensity or loudness of a syllable or sequence of syllables. For example, open vowels are acoustically of greater intensity than close vowels and listeners must in some way allow for this when interpreting relative loudness for other purposes. Again, the relationship of absolute intensity to perceived loudness is by no means linear (a sound has to be much more than doubled in absolute intensity before it will be heard as twice as loud) and moreover the relationship is different at different frequencies. Additionally, loudness may be used for a variety of linguistic purposes, some of which apply to single syllables, and some to sequences of syllables. I may shout because I am angry or I may make my accented syllables much louder than my unaccented syllables as an emphatic device.

1.1.1.3 **Pitch.** PITCH is the prosodic feature most centrally involved in intonation and it is with this feature that I shall be principally concerned in this book. Physiologically, pitch is primarily dependent on the rate of vibration of the vocal cords within the larynx (it is nowadays more usual to use the spelling 'cords' although the spelling 'chords' has often been used in the past). How such variation in the rate of vibration is brought about has been a matter of some dispute: at the moment the majority opinion is that such variation is principally produced by the length and tension of the vocal cords, which factors are themselves controlled by the intrinsic (and possibly the extrinsic) muscles of the larynx. Pressure of air below the larynx is regarded as a secondary influence on the rate of vibration.

Rate of vibration of the vocal cords is reflected in the acoustic measure-

3

ment of fundamental frequency. This term refers to the number of repetitions of the regular waveform within one second, such a regular waveform being typically produced when the vocal cords vibrate for voicing. So the number of times that the vocal cords completely open and close in one second is directly related to the frequency of the waveform. Fundamental frequency among male speakers varies between 60 Hz and 240 Hz and among female speakers between 180 Hz and 400 Hz. The average fundamental frequency for men is approximately 120 Hz, for women 225 Hz, and for children 265 Hz.

While fundamental frequency involves acoustic measurement measured in Hz (or the number of cycles of vibration in one second), pitch is used as a perceptual term, relating to listeners' judgements as to whether a sound is 'high' or 'low', whether one sound is 'higher' or 'lower' than another and by how much, and whether the voice is going 'up' or 'down'. Such judgements are not linearly related to fundamental frequency. For listeners to judge that one tone is twice as high as another, the frequency difference between the two tones is much larger at higher absolute frequencies, e.g. 1000 Hz is judged to be double 400 Hz, but 4000 Hz is judged to be double 1000 Hz. This is also demonstrable from musical scales where, for example, a difference of a semitone at the bottom end of a piano keyboard is much less in terms of Hz than a similar difference at the top end. Fortunately, fundamental frequency values in speech are all relatively low (i.e. usually less than 500 Hz), and for most practical purposes pitch can be equated with fundamental frequency.

There are certain local characteristics of fundamental frequency which a listener must allow for if he is listening to an utterance and extracting meaning from its pitch pattern. Firstly, only voiced sounds have a repetitive waveform and hence a fundamental frequency. Around a quarter of the sounds in a connected English text are voiceless consonants and hence have no fundamental frequency; an ear listening for an overall pitch pattern learns to ignore these gaps in voicing. Whether or not consonants are voiced affects the fundamental frequency of adjacent voiced sounds: in particular vowels have a higher fundamental frequency when preceded by voiceless consonants than when preceded by a voiced consonant. Moreover, the fundamental frequency peak will be at the beginning of the vowel following voiceless consonants but in the middle of the vowel following voiced consonants. It is also true that different types of vowels have inherently higher and lower fundamental frequencies: all other things being equal, open vowels will tend to have a lower fundamental frequency than close vowels. All such characteristics of fundamental frequency are in some way allowed for and discounted when listeners are listening to the semantics of an overall pitch pattern. However, they can complicate the extraction of such an overall pattern from an instrumental acoustic record of an utterance.

A slightly different sort of influence that the composition of individual segments and syllables may have on an overall pitch pattern is illustrated by the following words said with the same 'tone':

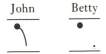

This tone is sometimes called a high-falling tone and semantically it represents a straightforward unadorned statement of someone's name. But notice that the tone is in fact 'realised' differently in each case. *John* consists of one syllable, which is voiced throughout: the fall is more or less continuous throughout the word. Whereas *Betty* consists of two syllables including two short vowels interrupted by a voiceless consonant; in this case the fall is realised as a step between a level high pitch and a level low pitch. As we shall see in chapter 3, some people actually consider the 'essence' of the pattern to be a sequence of high and low tones, rather than considering it a fall. This is a dispute between levels and contours as primes which has been argued for many years, has not been resolved in a principled way, and indeed may ultimately turn out to be a trivial question (see chapter 3, sections 3.3, 3.8, and 3.9). For the moment, however, all the reader need know is that what is essentially the same pattern will actually look rather different depending on the number and make-up of the syllables which go with it.

1.1.1.4 **Summary.** Sub-sections 1.1.1.1 to 1.1.1.3 have considered the prosodic features of length, loudness, and pitch. In each case we looked at the way in which speakers physically controlled the feature, at the acoustics of the feature, and at listeners' perception of the feature. We noted that there is no one-to-one relation between acoustics and perception. In particular, different types of segment directly influence the acoustics of a prosodic feature and such segmental effects have to be discounted by listeners interpreting the meaning of a longer prosodic pattern, e.g. the different effects of close and open vowels on fundamental frequency have to be discounted when listening for the semantics of a longer pitch pattern. Moreover, some prosodic features may be used for two linguistic effects simultaneously, e.g. some syllables may be loud because accented syllables are being made louder than unaccented syllables to give an emphatic effect, while at the same time a whole stretch of syllables is louder than usual because the speaker is angry. It was also mentioned that of the three prosodic features considered, our chief concern will be with pitch, this being the principal perceptual correlate of intonation.

1.2   **Auditory and instrumental**

The previous section discussed the disparity between acoustic records and perception. This disparity has been reflected in a duality of approaches to the study of prosodic features, in particular to the study of pitch patterns. The most common labels attached to the two approaches are the AUDITORY and the INSTRUMENTAL. There has been a long history of auditory analyses of pitch patterns and their meanings. Very detailed studies have been made of the meanings involved in English intonation, using auditory methods on large bodies of data. Critics of such auditory analyses often claim that the methods are unscientific, that they are too impressionistic, that even those trained to listen to pitch patterns in language will hear only what they have been trained to hear, and that in this way myths are propagated. It is said that such impressionistic listening will be even less reliable in listening to a foreign language, which will be filtered through the listening habits developed in a mother-tongue. Such criticisms are of course made by those who prefer a wholly instrumental approach to prosodic features. Instrumentalists claim that their methods, unlike those of auditory analysts, involve precise and verifiable measurements and are consequently more scientifically respectable. The response of auditory analysts is that such precise instrumental measurements can only by their very nature be carried out on small amounts of data. It is also pointed out that such methods usually involve a very crude approach to meaning: typically a speaker may be asked to read a sentence with a 'statement intonation' and a 'question intonation'. Moreover, it is said that we know too little about perception to rely entirely on acoustic records.

In this book I shall try to use the best of both approaches. In explanation, an analogy with segmental description may be helpful. Phonologists operate with consonants like English /p/, /t/, /k/ and vowels like English /i/, /æ/, /u/. If we look at acoustic records, we find very complex, inconsistent, and sometimes even intangible correlates of such sounds. Not only would we have difficulty in isolating such sounds if we relied entirely on acoustic records, but even with the benefit of many years of acoustic analysis, we cannot always tell what 'sound' has been uttered just by looking at the acoustic records. The essential point is that all linguistic units are in varying degrees abstractions and are perceptual rather than acoustic realities; because we cannot find invariant acoustic counterparts, we should not, on such grounds alone, discard such units. On the other hand, acoustic research has made considerable contributions to our understanding of sounds. One of the most famous contributions involved the acoustic nature of [p], [t], and [k]: the place of articulation of a plosive is principally indicated by the transition phase between the plosive and an adjacent vowel. There is no reason to regard the analysis of prosodic patterns any differently from the analysis of segmental patterns; both auditory and instrumental analysis have something to offer.

1.3 Prominence

The physical bases of three prosodic features have so far been considered. There are a number of other prosodic features of speech which have not been discussed, in particular TEMPO and PAUSE. I shall consider pause in some detail in chapter 3, sub-section 3.2.1 and tempo more briefly in chapter 6, sub-section 6.1.1. The reasons for the initial emphasis on length, loudness and pitch are twofold. Firstly, the relationship between their measurable attributes and their linguistic function is often complex; some examples of this complexity have already been given. Secondly, these three features conspire in varying degrees in many languages to give some syllables PROMINENCE when compared with other syllables. Such prominence (variously called stress or accent by different authors – I define my own use of these terms more precisely in chapter 2) is on one level a feature of words as stored in our mental lexicon (word-stress or word-accent) and on another level a feature of connected speech (sentence-stress or sentence-accent). Such prominences are often themselves linguistically important: they may be involved in distinguishing different lexical meanings, cf. *belów* and *bíllow*, or different grammatical classes, cf. *ínsult* and *insúlt*; or they may be involved in making certain syllables stand out in sentences, and hence make the word containing those syllables stand out as more important: cf. *John didn't dó it* and *Jóhn didn't do it*. Not only are the prominences produced by some combination of length, loudness, and pitch themselves linguistically important, they are also important because sequences of prominent and non-prominent syllables form the framework of connected speech. In many languages such patterns of prominent and non-prominent syllables produce a particular rhythmical effect. Additionally, and most important of all for this book, such patterns are the backbone of intonation. Intonation concerns which syllables are prominent, how they are made prominent, and to what extent they are made prominent; it also concerns how the movement from one prominent syllable to the next is accomplished. In chapter 2 I shall deal with matters of accent and rhythm, since it is impossible to describe and discuss intonation without first establishing a descriptive framework for accent and rhythm. In chapters 3, 4 and 5 I deal with intonation 'proper'.

1.4 Tone languages

Before proceeding to more detailed discussion of accent, rhythm, and intonation, a brief survey must be made of the linguistic functions of pitch in language. I have already said that, while the three prosodic features of length, loudness, and pitch may be involved in prominence generally, it is pitch which is the principal exponent of intonation. However, pitch is also used for differences of tone in tone languages. So we must discuss the differences between intonation and tone. Languages are also sometimes described as pitch accent languages (as opposed to stress accent languages) and these terms must also be briefly discussed.

Basically TONE is a feature of the lexicon, being described in terms of prescribed pitches for syllables or sequences of pitches for morphemes or words; whereas intonation is a feature of phrases or sentences (as we shall see in chapter 3, some linguists now speak of an 'intonational lexicon' which stores overall contours or sequences of pitches with their own meanings, which are at some point mapped onto phrases or sentences). Tone, then, concerns the pitch patterns of words. In the simpler type of case, a change of meaning is produced if one tone is exchanged for another on one syllable, while keeping the segmental composition unchanged. This situation results in sets of words distinguished only by tone and applies to many languages of the Far East. One variety of Chinese, Szechuanese, has four tones, producing four different words when combined with the segmental sequence [ta]:

[ta] + [⁄]: 'imitation of trumpet noise'	(Tone 1)
[ta] + [＼]: 'to answer'	(Tone 2)
[ta] + [\ ]: 'to beat'	(Tone 3)
[ta] + [◡]: 'big'	(Tone 4)

In the more complex cases involving the use of tone, words have prescribed tonal patterns, although minimal pairs are not always easy to find. For example, in Ganda, verbs fall into two tonal classes. Verbs in Class I have a high pitch on all syllables of the stem, e.g. *ku-seka* [· ˙ ˙] 'to laugh'; verbs in Class II have a falling pitch, generally on the first syllable of the stem, e.g. *ku-tambula* [. ↘ ..] 'to walk'. This type of use of tone is often called 'characteristic tone'. It often involves a complicated build-up of the overall pitch pattern of a word by the use of affixes which may not only have their own inherent tone but also produce changes of tone in the stem or in other affixes. Because the changes of meaning brought about by these affixes often involve the sorts of modifications signalled by inflectional morphology alone in other languages (e.g. case in nouns and tense in verbs), it is often said that such a use of pitch involves a grammatical function of tone. Indeed in some languages (e.g. Efik, Igbo) modifications of meaning may be produced by change of tone alone, without the use of affixes. As implied by the languages mentioned, grammatical use of 'characteristic tone' is typical of many languages of Africa. But whether we are thinking of 'lexical tone' as in the case of Szechuanese, or of 'characteristic tone' as in the case of Ganda, such uses of pitch apply at the word level and produce changes of meaning quite unlike those of intonation.

1.5 Intonation languages

INTONATION involves the occurrence of recurring pitch patterns, each of which is used with a set of relatively consistent meanings, either on single words or on groups of words of varying length. Grammatical constituents of any level up to at least the sentence may be treated as separate intonation-groups having their own meaningful tune (and indeed some features of intonation may even link such groups together into 'paratones', a word meant to indicate an analogy with paragraphs in the written language). For example, a common tone in English is the fall-rise, and one of its common meanings involves a contrast within a limited set of items either stated explicitly or, more usually, just implied. This tone is used on all the following examples:

(a)   (Isn't his name Jim?) No/ ˇJohn
(b)   The old man didn't come/ whereas the ˇyoung man/ did come and actually enjoyed himself
(c)   ˇJohn didn't do it

(/ indicates an intonation-group boundary, although boundaries are not marked at the beginnings and ends of examples, nor where a change of speaker is involved; they are automatically present in such cases. The ˇ mark indicates a fall-rise tone spread over all syllables before the next boundary.) In example (a) the fall-rise occurs just on the single-word response *John*; in example (b) on the two words *young man*; and in example

(c) on the whole sentence. Intonation-groups (which are sometimes also called intonational phrases) generally correspond with constituents of sentences in a somewhat loose way. For example, it is not uncommon for the noun-phrase subject of a clause to be given a separate intonation-group in English as in (b) above, but notice that the conjunction *whereas* has been incorporated into the group. Notice also that the fall-rise tone does not begin until the word *young*, indicating the focal point of the group. Such matters will be discussed in detail in chapters 3 and 4. The examples and explanation given so far are simply to illustrate how the domain of intonation differs from the domain of tone.

Intonation also differs from tone in the sorts of meanings it conveys. While tone is used for contrasts in lexical meaning or to produce modifications of meaning of the sort conveyed by case or tense, the meanings conveyed by intonation are often less concrete. Intonation may indicate a discoursal meaning like inviting a listener to make a contribution to the conversation, or an attitudinal meaning like being condescending. If I were to say to a colleague *I'll* 'show *you how to* ⁄*do it* (the ' mark indicates a high level pitch beginning on *show* and the ⁄ mark means a rise starting low on *do*, i.e. ‾•‾·‾·‾·‾•‾·‾), that colleague might well feel that I was being condescending, such a tune being frequently used to children. In some languages (not English) the meanings associated with intonation may come nearer to the grammatical use of pitch in tone languages: this is the case where the use of particular tunes is closely tied to functional sentence-types, e.g. where statement, yes/no question, and command regularly involve certain tunes. From most of the descriptions of intonation in languages other than English, one might imagine that this was the principal use of various tunes in intonation languages. It may indeed be true that many languages do use intonation less for attitudinal purposes than English, but the suspicion exists that an alignment of tunes with sentence-types is merely the easy way to investigate intonation and often more sophisticated attitudinal and discoursal uses remain undocumented.

1.6 Intonation in tone languages

Tone and intonation are not completely mutually exclusive in languages. Languages with tonal contrasts may nevertheless make use of a limited amount of superimposed intonation. Such superimposed intonation may be manifested in four different ways: (i) the pitch level of the whole utterance may be raised or lowered; (ii) there will usually be downdrift in the absolute value of tones but downdrift may be suspended;

(iii) the range of pitch used may be narrower or wider; (iv) the final tone of the utterance may be modified in various ways. Some of these are present in Szechuanese (previously mentioned in section 1.4): emphatic statements are produced with a higher pitch; various attitudes are expressed by a wider pitch range; and questions involve utterance-final tonal variants as follows: for Tone 2, low-fall becomes low-level; for Tone 3, high-fall becomes high-level; for Tone 4, low fall-rise becomes simple low-rise.

Some languages which are predominantly intonational languages may also make a limited use of tone. By limited use I mean that a limited number of words are distinguished by tone alone. This is the case in Norwegian and Swedish. In Swedish about five hundred minimal pairs distinguished by tone alone can be found: some well-known ones are ´*buren*, 'the cage' v. `*buren* 'carried'; ´*tanken*, 'the tank' v. `*tanken*, 'the thought'; ´*anden*, 'the duck' v. `*anden* 'the spirit'. The two marks are those traditionally used in studies of Swedish; words with ´ are said to have Accent I and words with ` are said to have Accent II. The actual pitch patterns associated with the accents vary in different dialects of Swedish, although Accent I is commonly associated with a single-peaked falling tone (the mark traditionally used for this accent is misleading) while Accent II is commonly double-peaked, e.g. [⌣⌢]. Accent I is in fact the common accentual pattern for words in Swedish and is not limited to words where the accent is on the first syllable, whereas Accent II is the 'marked' pattern and limited to word-initial accent. The tonetic patterns described refer to the citation forms of the words. Some indication of the different accents is regularly maintained in connected speech: any accent which occurs at the focal point of an intonation contour will generally appear in a form similar to the citation form; and, even occurring in a non-focal position, each accent will produce a different type of minor deviation from the overall contour. This sort of incorporation of tonal distinctions into an overall intonation contour can be illustrated from another language, Panjabi. Two 'marked' tones occur in Panjabi, both in different ways corresponding to the voiced aspirates [bʰ], [dʰ], [ɖʰ], [dʒʰ], [gʰ] and [ɦ] present in other north Indian languages. A 'low' tone corresponds to a syllable-initial voiced aspirate and a 'high' tone to a syllable-final voiced aspirate; and an 'unmarked' tone corresponds to positions where no voiced aspirate was present. A minimal triple is /kɑɭɑ/ (low tone) 'mess' 'fraud'; /kɑɭɑ/ (high tone) 'impatient'; /kɑɭɑ/ (unmarked tone) 'black'. In connected speech a low tone will lower the unmarked intonation pattern where it occurs whereas a high tone will raise the intonation pattern, cf.

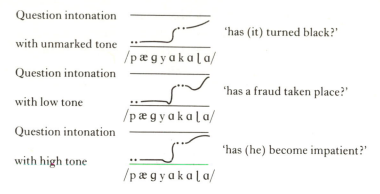

Question intonation with unmarked tone /pægyakala/ 'has (it) turned black?'

Question intonation with low tone /pægyakala/ 'has a fraud taken place?'

Question intonation with high tone /pægyakala/ 'has (he) become impatient?'

To sum up what has been said in this section: languages where pitch patterns are produced primarily by lexical tones will have a limited potential for intonational variation; and languages where pitch patterns are governed primarily by intonation may have some perturbations produced in intonation patterns if the language makes a limited number of lexical distinctions by means of tone. There is of course a difference between the two cases which should by now be apparent: the intonational variation in tone languages will always be present in some degree whereas limited use of lexical tone in intonation languages occurs in only a very few such languages.

1.7 Pitch accent languages

While the distinction between tone and intonation is a relatively clear one, the distinction between so-called 'stress accent' languages and so-called 'pitch accent' languages has never been very clearly defined. The term 'stress accent' is usually used to refer to languages, like English, using pitch primarily for intonational purposes. It is, however, an unfortunate term since it implies that prominent syllables in such languages are produced primarily by 'stress' which in this usage seems to mean breath-force or loudness. It has never been clearly shown that any non-tone language produces prominences primarily in this way and it seems certain that pitch is in some way used for accentual purposes in all languages which are not tone languages. What does however seem to be characteristic of intonation or 'stress accent' languages is that, although prominences or accents will commonly involve pitch, the actual type of prominence involved will be determined by intonational factors. In a sentence like *It's Johnny*, the first syllable of *Johnny* is likely to be accented and hence given some sort of pitch prominence, but the type of pitch prominence may, for example, be high, as in:

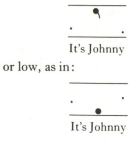

It's Johnny

or low, as in:

It's Johnny

Intonation or so-called 'stress accent' languages like English are generally contrasted with 'pitch accent' languages, of which the best example is Japanese. In the standard Japanese of Tokyo words fall into two classes: accented and unaccented. Words with an accent realise the accent by a high pitch on the accented syllable followed by a low pitch on the following syllable, e.g. *óngaku* [● . .] 'music'; *toshókan* [. ● .] 'library'; *tama-négi* [. ˙ ●.] 'onion'. The pitch of unaccented syllables is predictable by rule: an initial unaccented syllable is low, any other unaccented syllables before the accent are high, and all unaccented syllables following the accent are low. The examples above involved initial or medial accent; words may also have a final accent, e.g. *musumé* [. ˙ ●] 'girl', or may be unaccented, e.g. *sakana* [. ˙ ˙] 'fish'. The difference in these two accentual patterns is only explicitly realised by the pitch of an unaccented syllable at the beginning of the next word or particle, cf. *musumé wa* [. ˙ ●.] and *sakana wa* [. ˙ ˙ ˙]. Clearly, in Japanese accents are realised by pitch as they are in English; but the Japanese accents, involving high pitch and following low pitch, cannot be reversed by intonation as English accents can. Indeed the use of intonation in Japanese is limited in much the same way as it is in a tone language, involving, for example, only some limited modifications of pitch patterns before pause.

Just to complicate matters still further, those languages which are primarily intonational but make a limited use of tone, like Swedish and Panjabi, have sometimes also been described as using 'pitch accent', on the grounds that these languages, like Japanese, have no more than one accent per word and that this accent is realised by pitch prominence. The fact that Japanese uses one type of pitch prominence, whereas Swedish, for example, involves two alternative types of pitch prominence (two lexical tones), is seen as relatively insignificant in comparison to their differences with fully-fledged tone languages on the one hand and the so-called 'stress accent' languages on the other. Indeed the difference between Swedish and Japanese is reduced further by saying that a high pitch will apply to a 'mora'. A 'mora' is said to equal the full length of a short syllable or half the length of a long syllable. The two different tones on Swedish syllables are then said to be produced by putting the high pitch on the first or second mora of a syllable, thus producing a rise or a fall. More generally the difference in tones is thus said to be one of phase, i.e. the exact point in a syllable where the high pitch occurs. Ascribing the difference in tones to phase in this way is also useful in that it can be used to explain differences in the exact realisation of the tones in different dialects.

So Japanese and Swedish can be said to have one high pitch on each accented word if we use some notion like the 'mora'. What I think this sort of argumentation shows is that any taxonomy of the use of pitch patterns in language can never really involve absolutely discrete and clear-cut categories. Different classifications will emphasise different types of similarity. Personally I prefer to regard Swedish as principally an intonation language making a limited use of tone, because it has the possibility of tonal contrast on one syllable, and to regard it as very different from Japanese, which does not have this possibility.

Japanese does not allow the type of intonational variation permitted in English and is hence not an intonation language. Nor does it involve tonal contrast on one syllable and in this sense is not a tone language. It comes rather closer to those languages using 'characteristic tone', as many Bantu languages do. Many of these languages, like Japanese, can be analysed as having a high or a low tone at various points in a word. But these Bantu languages can change the highs and lows under the influence of surrounding affixes and where modifications of grammatical meaning are involved. Japanese does not do this. It is therefore necessary to have a separate category for languages like Japanese. Since the term 'pitch accent' has been used so often for Japanese, I propose to keep it (although I find no use for the related term 'stress accent'; indeed I find it positively misleading).

1.8 **Summary**

Thus a taxonomy of the use of pitch divides languages into three types:

(1) Intonation languages
(2) Tone languages
(3) Pitch accent languages

Type (1) includes all European languages. Some intonation languages, like Norwegian, Swedish, Serbo-Croat, and Panjabi, also make some limited use of tone. Type (2) includes languages which use tone almost exclusively for lexical purposes, like Chinese, Vietnamese, and Thai; and languages which use 'characteristic tone', like most Bantu languages. The label for type (3) is used by me in a more restricted way than it is by some other writers. It refers to languages like Japanese which have one immovable high-pitched accent for each accented word. Little more will be said in this book about types (2) and (3) since I am principally concerned with intonation. But it should not be forgotten that a majority of the world's languages are tone languages.

Sources and further reading

For detailed exemplification of the prosodic uses of length and loudness, see Lehiste (1970); for priorities among pitch, length, and loudness in the perception of stress and accent, see Fry (1955, 1958), and Mol and Uhlenbeck (1956).

For the acoustics of intensity and fundamental frequency, see Ladefoged (1975), chapter 8; for the physical mechanisms involved in the production of pitch, see Ohala (1978).

For tone languages, see Pike (1948) and Fromkin (1978); for the tone-system of Szechuanese, see Chang (1958).

For the interaction of intonation and lexical tone in Norwegian, see Haugen and Joos (1952); and in Swedish, see Gårding (1977a, 1977b).

For pitch accent in Japanese, see Martin (1952).

2
Stress, accent, and rhythm

2.1 Stress and accent

In chapter 1 the articulatory and acoustic correlates of the perceived phonetic features of pitch, length, and loudness were discussed. The justification for concentrating on these three features was that they are all used to make some syllables more prominent in words and in sentences. Perceptual experiments have clearly shown that, in English at any rate, the three features form a scale of importance in bringing syllables into prominence, pitch being the most efficacious, and loudness the least so. The importance of length varies in fact across languages, depending on whether a language uses length for phonemic contrasts on the segmental level; if it does, then loudness will take over from length as the second most important indicator of prominence.

The terms 'stress' and 'accent' were also introduced in chapter 1, although no systematic difference was made in the use of the three terms 'prominence', 'stress' and 'accent'. In the past the word 'stress' has been used in different and confusing ways. It has sometimes been used simply to refer to syllables (or vowels) made prominent for linguistic purposes, either in words or in sentences. But stress has also often been used to mean 'breath-force or loudness' the implication being that this is the principal means whereby syllables are made prominent. This second type of usage is misguided since, as indicated in the last paragraph, loudness generally plays a minor role in producing prominences. The term 'accent' has also been used to refer to syllables made prominent for linguistic purposes: it commonly implies that such prominence is principally associated with pitch (hence the common term 'pitch accent').

In this book I shall use the term STRESS to mean 'prominence', however such prominence is achieved. The term ACCENT will be limited to prominences where pitch is involved (hence it is equivalent to PITCH ACCENT). 'Stress' is therefore being used in the more general, less specified, way. In particular I will continue the traditional use of the word 'stress' in three areas. Firstly, the term 'word-stress' will be used to refer to those syllables which would be marked as stressed if stress were marked in a lexicon or dictionary and which therefore have a potential for 'accent' in utterances (see following section 2.2). Secondly, studies within the tradition of generative phonology (and metrical phonology) have preferred the term 'stress' even for sentences. This has been justified by saying that even stress rules for sentences are an abstraction, since they say nothing in detail about the phonetic realisation of stress or the types of accent which occur or how these are united into an overall intonation contour. I shall consequently use the term 'stress' in this way in the sections of this book which deal with generative phonology (see in particular section 2.5 below). Thirdly, it has been suggested that the rhythm of certain languages (the so-called 'stress-timed' ones) is dependent upon the regular occurrence of stressed syllables in connected speech. In my account of this theory I shall, of course, make use of the term 'stress' (see section 2.4 below).

Before going on to more substantive matters, it must be made clear what this chapter is doing. It is intended to show in this chapter how a framework of stress is built up on sentences. This representation of stress is then used as a basis for an intonational pattern. I am dealing with word-stress and sentence-stress only insofar as they are a prerequisite for intonation. They will not, therefore, be dealt with in the sort of detail which a book primarily on stress would contain. This is particularly true of English word-stress, where no attempt is made to give a systematic detailed coverage.

2.2 Word-stress

Many languages have word-stress regularly in a certain position on almost all words: Czech and Finnish have the stress on the first syllable; Spanish and Welsh on the penultimate syllable; and French and Turkish on the final syllable. Compare, for example:

> Finnish – týtar 'daughter'; líkainen 'dirty'; mérimies 'sailor'.
> Spanish – bastánte 'enough'; mañána 'tomorrow'; múchos 'many'.
> French – compagníe 'company'; bagáges 'luggage'; maláde 'ill'.

The stress marks on the above words are not, of course, included in the ordinary orthography of these languages. Nor do the examples given tell the whole story for the languages concerned. In Spanish most words end in a vowel and such words do have penultimate stress as stated; but words ending in a consonant more usually have final stress, e.g. tomár 'take'. In addition there are a number of absolute exceptions like próximo 'next' (in these cases Spanish orthography does actually mark the stress). Most languages with so-called 'fixed' word-stress are not usually as simple as that term implies; nevertheless it is true that word-stress is at least fairly easily predictable in such languages. Because it is predictable stress takes on a strong DELIMITATIVE FUNCTION in such languages. If I know that words generally begin with a stressed syllable in Finnish, my ear will easily segment the stream of speech into words. However, once again, the real situation is often not quite as simple as this. While French words, for example, regularly have their stress on the final syllable, many words will lose their stress in connected speech and hence stress will only occur at the end of a group of words, e.g.

> Les múrs de votre maisón sont trop nóirs

Hence the occurrence of an accent delimits a word group rather than a single word in French.

Other languages hardly use word-stress in a delimitative way at all. In particular, this is true of languages like English which have no fixed word-stress. Only occasionally will some combination of stress and segmental pattern suggest the presence of a word boundary in English, e.g. /-éɪʃn̩/ or /-éɪʃn̩z/ suggest a following word boundary. English does, on the other hand, use stress to indicate differences of lexical meaning or of grammatical class cf. *defér* v. *díffer* and *ínsult* (noun) v. *insúlt* (verb). In fact, in English there are only a very few words which are differentiated solely by stress, and this seems to be universal in languages, i.e. the use of word-stress with a DISTINCTIVE FUNCTION (e.g. in Russian and Greek) never carries a high functional load. It is also true that the delimitative and distinctive functions of word-stress are not necessarily mutually exclusive. We saw above that Spanish is a language with word-stress which is more or less fixed. But we also saw that there were exceptions even in Spanish, and such exceptions can lead to distinctive pairs, e.g. *allá* 'there' v. *hálla* 'he finds' (initial *h* not being pronounced in Spanish).

There are, then, languages which do not use word-stress delimitatively and use it distinctively only to a very restricted extent. In such languages word-stress may be largely predictable but only by a set of complex rules. Such a language is English and a great deal has been written about the rules necessary to predict word-stress in English. In the next section I give a brief introduction to English word-stress; in section 2.5 a more formal framework is introduced for generating stress in English words.

2.2.1 English word-stress

As a prerequisite for the description of intonation, we have to know which syllables are stressed in words so that we then know which syllables are potentially accentable in utterances; we have to know which syllables are accented in utterances because accented syllables form the framework for intonation. A large part of our intonational description will be exemplified from English; as a start, therefore, we need to know a little about English word-stress. Any description of English word-stress rules inevitably involves a large number of exceptions. However, the fact that there are a large number of exceptions does not defeat the object of the exercise; a general rule with exceptions is more economical than listing every word with its own unique pattern (i.e. listing everything as an exception).

English words may be divided into STEMS and AFFIXES. Stems include not only single free morphemes like *blood*, *survive* and *chloroform* but also that part of a word remaining when an affix is removed, even though such a part cannot stand on its own, e.g. *ephemer-al*, *tremend-ous* and *kaleido-scope*. A very simplified set of informal rules for stress placement in stems can then be stated as follows:

(i)   **Verbs and adjectives**
        (a) stress on the penultimate syllable when final syllable has a short vowel in an open syllable or is followed by no more than one consonant, e.g.

             surrénder, pólish, astónish, rígid, explícit.

        (b) otherwise, stress is on the final syllable (subject to rule (iii) below), e.g.

             reláte, maintáin, sublíme, sevére, rejéct, defénd, abrúpt.

(ii)   **Nouns**
        (a) if the final syllable has a short vowel, disregard it and apply rules under (i) above, e.g.

             élephant, móment, compléxion, surrénder.

        (b) if the final syllable has a long vowel, it is stressed (subject to (iii) below), e.g.

             políce, machíne, dispúte, campáign, catárrh.

(iii)   **Words of more than two syllables with a long final vowel:** stress on the antepenultimate syllable, e.g.

             ánecdote, fáhrenheit, pédigree, órganise, éscalate, móribund, érudite.

As has already been indicated, there are a large number of apparent exceptions to these basic rules for stems, e.g. *posítion*, *wíndow* (with British pronunciation involving an unreduced vowel in the final syllable), *kangaróo*.

Since most sets of rules for the stressing of English words involve counting the number and type of syllables working backwards from the end of the word, the influence of suffixes on the stressing of words is particularly important. Suffixes fall into three classes:

(a)   Suffixes which leave the stress on the stem unaffected, e.g. *fulfíl/fulfíl-ment*; *úsual/úsually*.

(b)   Suffixes which themselves take the stress, e.g. *límit/limitátion*; *pícture/picturésque*; *Chína/Chinése*.

(c)   Suffixes which shift the stress on the stem, e.g. *ecónomy/económic*; *cúrious/curiósity*; *applý/ápplicant*; *maintáin/máintenance*.

There are a large number of complex words in English, i.e. words composed of two stems, and indeed frequently composed of two free morphemes. In the more common type of combination a relatively large amount of paradigmatic variation is possible in each half of the combination and the meaning is clearly derivable from the two elements. Such combinations usually involve adjective plus noun or noun plus noun, e.g. *red bóok*, *old búilding*, *grass skírt*. These combinations are labelled PHRASES and the primary stress is on the second element except in cases where an emphatic contrast is intended on the first element. But another type of combination of two free morphemes admits of rather less paradigmatic variation for each element and the semantics of the combination is often less obviously derivable from the two elements, e.g. *bláckbird*, *mátchbox*, *líghtning conductor*, *blúe stocking*. These combinations are labelled COMPOUNDS and the primary stress is on the first element. Like other areas of word-stress there are many inconsistencies, e.g. *central héating* and *full móon* seem semantically akin to compounds yet are stressed on the second element; also cf. *Óxford Street* v. *Oxford Róad* and *Chrístmas cake* v. *Christmas púdding*.

Two additional points need to be made about the rules presented above. Firstly, they have only been concerned with the principal (or 'primary') stress in words (including compounds). Clearly some of the other syllables in words are more stressed than others, i.e. there are degrees of stress, e.g. in *pedigree* the primary stress is on the first syllable but the last syllable is more stressed than the second. Clearly, also, the less a syllable is stressed, the more likely it is to have a reduced vowel, e.g. in *kangaroo* the least stressed syllable is the second syllable and this has a vowel reduced to [ə]. I shall have only a limited amount to say about lesser stresses and reduced vowels since it is mainly primary stresses which are relevant to the intonational framework. Secondly, it should now be apparent that rules for stressing apply in an ordered way. The rules given for verb, adjective, and noun stems are subject to modification by the antepenultimate rule (iii). Stems are in turn subject to modification by the addition of suffixes and also when put together in compounds. In the case of compounds, although a compound rule will tell us which element to stress, the rules for stems will already have told us which syllable of that element is stressed.

2.3   Degrees of stress/accent

Every word has at least one stress in its citation form, e.g. *I said 'the', not 'a'*, where the words 'the' and 'a' are pronounced /ðí/ and /éɪ/. But some types of words most commonly occur in an unstressed form in connected speech, e.g. the articles cited above typically occur without a stress and with a reduced vowel as /ðə/ and /ə/. Other types of word most commonly occurring without a stress (and with reduced vowels) are auxiliary verbs, personal pronouns and shorter prepositions and conjunctions, whereas the majority of nouns, main verbs, adjectives and adverbs commonly occur with a stress. The exact syllable on which the stress occurs will, of course, be determined by rules for word-stress like those outlined in the preceding section.

Stresses in connected speech occur with varying degrees of prominence. In English we need to distinguish four such degrees of stress/accent within 'intonation-groups' (the definition and delimitation of intonation-groups is discussed in detail in chapter 3: for the moment it is sufficient to know that intonation-groups correspond typically with major grammatical constituents like simple sentences, or noun-phrase subjects, or predicates):

(i)   PRIMARY STRESS (or PRIMARY ACCENT), involving the principal pitch prominence in the intonation-group.

(ii)   SECONDARY STRESS (or SECONDARY ACCENT), involving a subsidiary pitch prominence in the intonation-group. (The notions of principal and subsidiary pitch prominence will be subject to further clarification in chapter 3.)

(iii)   TERTIARY STRESS, involving a prominence produced principally by length and/or loudness (and hence we cannot refer to this as 'tertiary accent' because the term 'accent' has been reserved for pitch prominences).

(iv)   UNSTRESSED (the term UNACCENTED covers both (iii) and (iv)).

These degrees of stress/accent are illustrated in the following sentence (= one intonation-group on this occasion):

I ran all the way to the station

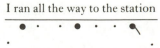

The primary stress/accent is on *sta-*, the prominence being mainly produced by the fall in pitch initiated on *sta-* and completed on *-tion*; a secondary stress/accent occurs on *ran*, the prominence being provided by the step-up in pitch from *I* to *ran*; and a tertiary stress occurs on *way*. Here is another example:

John decided to run all the way to the station

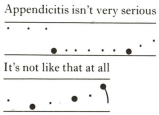

In this case the primary stress/accent is on *run*, and tertiary stresses are on *-cide-*, *way* and *sta-* (notice that two of these follow the primary accent and one precedes). I analyse *John* as having a secondary stress/accent, although a pitch movement does not precede or follow it. It is analysed as having a secondary accent because it is considerably higher than a presumed 'baseline'. As we shall see in later chapters, unaccented syllables at the beginning of an intonation-group will typically be on a pitch slightly above the bottom pitch used by a speaker; this level slightly above the bottom pitch is called the 'baseline'. A syllable is prominent in pitch at the beginning of a group if it is above this 'baseline'. As usual there is a further complication in that high unaccented syllables may also occur at the beginning of an intonation-group. However, these involve no syllables with word-stress and furthermore often also involve reduced vowels; hence their pitch prominence does not indicate accent (although it may indicate something about the intonational meaning). In the following examples the initial syllables are consequently best analysed as high but unaccented:

Appendicitis isn't very serious

It's not like that at all

In most languages it is not necessary, or even possible, to distinguish between four degrees of stress/accent. In French, for example, the final syllable of a word-group is accented (as already mentioned in section 2.2 above) and non-final syllables in a word-group are generally unaccented. No analyses of French distinguish two intermediate levels of stress/accent; at most some analyses distinguish one intermediate level, often called an 'accent d'insistance', indicated by high pitch and/or extra length and loudness, e.g.

C'est parfaitement stupide

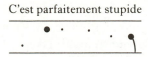

The accent on *par-* cannot be analysed as ending a word-group, since of course it actually occurs on the first syllable of a word; nor are there any other phonetic indicators of the end of a word-group, e.g. pause. French is a language which is often said to be 'syllable-timed', i.e. taking approximately an equal amount of time over each syllable ('syllable-timing' is discussed further in section 2.4 below); and vowels are not subject to reduction to [ə] as English vowels are. The only syllables which are longer than others in French are those at the end of a word-group and those having an 'accent d'insistance'. This means that there is sometimes a long string of unaccented syllables of approximately equal length, e.g.

Pourquoi êtes-vous allé là?

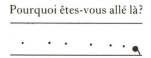

This is of course very different from English, which involves a rhythmic alternation of stressed and unstressed syllables, where the unstressed syllables are usually shorter and often involve reduced vowels. Syllable-timed languages like French (and Italian and Hindi) operate with fewer distinctions of stress/accent than languages like English, which are often called 'stress-timed'. 'Syllable-timed' and 'stress-timed' are discussed further in section 2.4 below.

In English (and in many other languages, e.g. German) unstressed syllables often involve reduced vowels like [ə]. In fact we can say that reduced vowels only occur in unstressed syllables. But the converse is not necessarily true, i.e. unstressed syllables do not necessarily involve a reduced vowel, e.g.

I got a large piece of wood

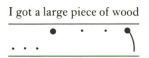

In this example *piece* is unstressed but keeps its full vowel; *got* is unstressed and may also keep its full vowel. (As is the case in this whole area of stress and accent, confusion is easily produced by varying terminology: some writers, particularly in generative phonology, use [± stress] to equal '[± reduced vowel]'; this is the case in one version of metrical phonology – see section 2.6 below.)

2.4 **Rhythm**

At the beginning of the preceding section we noted that in English some types of word are regularly unstressed in connected speech. Those words which are stressed will of course only have a stress on certain syllables – in many cases on only one syllable. Overall, in connected speech this means that there will be a large number of unstressed syllables together with a more limited number of stressed syllables. As we noted at the end of the previous section, English is often described as a STRESS-TIMED language. What this means is that a general rule of English rhythm is that we take an equal amount of time from one stressed syllable to the next, i.e. that English rhythm has an isochrony based on stresses. This is illustrated in the following example:

Whát's the dífference between a síck élephant and a déad bée?

I shall call the stretch of utterance from one stressed syllable to the next (including a stressed syllable with the unstressed syllables which follow) a RHYTHM-GROUP. (This term has been used in other ways by other writers, and the term 'foot' has sometimes been used for what I am calling rhythm-group.) Notice first in the above example that the number of syllables in each rhythm-group varies considerably: 2, 5, 1, 5, 1, 1. The theory of stress-timing holds that there is a tendency in some languages (English is one) for rhythm-groups to be of approximately equal duration. If this is the case, then the five syllables of the second rhythm-group in the above example will be said in roughly the same amount of time as the single syllable of the third rhythm-group. It should not, however, be thought that all the syllables within a rhythm-group are of equal duration – a stressed syllable is generally longer than an unstressed one, particularly if the latter has a reduced vowel. Here is another example:

There's a dréadful din cóming from Dán's wórkshop

Starting from *dréad-* there are 3, 3, 1 and 2 syllables in the rhythm-groups. But we have so far not taken account of any unstressed syllables at the beginning of an utterance. In this case there are two such syllables in *There's a.* I shall call such syllables an ANACRUSIS. The general tendency in English is to produce syllables in an anacrusis with greater speed than any unstressed syllables within following rhythm-groups; hence also such syllables are extremely liable to be reduced. In the example quoted the two syllables of *There's a* may even be reduced to one syllable and even pronounced with no vowel, i.e. [ðː drédful . . . . .]. We shall see in chapter 3 that these characteristics of an anacrusis may help to indicate the presence of a boundary between two intonation-groups. The rate of syllable production shows a marked increase as the boundary is traversed and the anacrusis of the new intonation-group encountered.

So far I have explained the theory of isochrony in English as if it were accepted as fact. However, although there has been a long adherence to this principle on the part of phoneticians, the theory has never been experimentally verified. Even the very rare experiments which have found some evidence for it have been forced to conclude that it is an extremely weak factor in determining the actual lengths of syllables (other factors include segmental composition, the presence or absence of stress, and extra length for primary accent and for utterance-final position). The most that can be said when viewing the experimental evidence is that there is a tendency to isochrony, e.g. it is true that a five-syllabled rhythm-group will not be five times as long as a one-syllabled rhythm-group, although it is not true that the five syllables in the former group will be compressed to equal the length of the one syllable in the latter group. So, in the first example above concerning the sick elephant and the dead bee, the five syllables of *elephant and a* may each be shorter than the one syllable *sick*, but the five syllables together will not be compressed into exactly the same duration as *sick*. It may be that the reduction in the lengths of syllables merely produces the perceptual impression of stress-timing in English.

The failure to find clear experimental support for such isochrony has been repeated for other languages which have also been claimed to be 'stress-timed' e.g. Russian and Arabic. Nor does a difference show up very clearly when such 'stress-timed' languages are compared with so-called SYLLABLE-TIMED languages like French and Yoruba, which, it is claimed, take an equal amount of time over each syllable. All the evidence suggests that both stresses and the number of syllables influence rhythm in all languages but particular languages have a tendency to give greater or lesser weight to the stress factor.

A different approach to English rhythm proposed by Bolinger (see, in particular, 1981, and forthcoming) suggests that the most important factor is neither the number of syllables nor the number of stresses but the pattern made in any section of continuous speech by the mixture of syllables containing full vowels with syllables containing reduced vowels. According to this theory, the basic unit of rhythm is a full-vowelled syllable together with any reduced-vowelled syllables that follow it. Each rhythm unit must thus contain one and only one full-vowelled syllable. This is reminiscent of the analysis of continuous speech by the stress-timing theory into rhythm-groups each containing one (and only one) stressed syllable and all the unstressed syllables that follow it. There are, however, fundamental differences between the stress-timing theory and the theory of what I shall call, for want of a better word, full-vowel timing. The following two examples will serve to illustrate the most crucial of these differences:

Those pórcupines aren't dángerous
F   F F F   F   F RR
The wallabies are dangerous
R F R R R   F R R

Stress-timed isochrony would suggest the same rhythm in both sentences, which are each divided into an anacrusis and two rhythm-groups. Full-vowel timing suggests that there are six rhythm units in the first example (with the three syllables of *dangerous* constituting one unit) while there are only two units in the second (one of four syllables and one of three syllables). The central tenet of full-vowel timing is that a reduced-vowelled syllable following a full-vowelled syllable 'borrows time' from it, so that together they are roughly equal to a full-vowelled syllable forming a rhythm unit on its own; however, any succeeding reduced-vowelled syllables do not 'borrow time' and hence add to the length of a rhythm unit. So in the second example above the second syllable of *wallabies* 'borrows time' from the initial full-vowelled syllable while the third syllable of *wallabies* does not 'borrow time' even though it also contains a reduced vowel. Full-vowel timing seems to account for the instrumentally measured facts of English syllable durations more successfully than stress-timed isochrony. It cannot, however, lead us to discount completely some tendency towards stress-timed isochrony, since without it there would be no reason for the reduction of some syllables and vowels in the first place.

2.5 Generative stress rules

We are now nearly at the stage where we can begin the study of 'intonation proper'. We have seen that stresses in words are converted into stresses/accents in utterances; it is the primary and secondary accents which will form the skeleton for intonation. We have also seen that stresses are said to be among the factors that affect rhythm, i.e. there is said to be a tendency towards stress-timing. At the same time there is perhaps another influence on rhythm, namely the occurrence of full and reduced vowels. Before we begin the study of 'intonation proper', we must first take a brief look at the ways in which the notion of stress has been formalised within generative phonology. This is, of course, interesting in its own right, but, more importantly for this book, the output of stress rules is potentially usable as an input for generative rules for intonation (see chapter 3, section 3.9).

The most influential formalisation of stress rules for English over the last fifteen years has been Chomsky and Halle's *The Sound Pattern of English* (1968) (henceforth SPE). The basic assumption of SPE is that stress in the majority of cases does not need to be marked in the lexicon but can be predicted by rule; and that, even though there are many exceptions, these do not invalidate the general rules. The stress rules of SPE apply to the output of the syntactic component of a grammar. More precisely they apply to a surface structure with a 'proper labeled bracketing of a string of formatives', i.e. to a sentence with a constituent structure marked and where each constituent has a category label like N (Noun), V (Verb), or NP (Noun Phrase). A certain 'readjustment' has to take place before the stress rules can apply: the surface structure has to be divided into 'phonological phrases' (roughly equivalent to what I shall be calling 'intonation-groups'). Such 'phonological phrases' are in many cases coterminous with sentences and SPE generally talks in terms of cases where they are equivalent. Stress rules then apply cyclically within sentences, i.e. a particular rule will apply first to the smallest constituents, e.g. stems or words without affixes, then to larger constituents, e.g. stems plus affixes, and so on to even larger constituents like compounds and phrases. Ultimately the rules will apply to 'phonological phrases', which, as I have already pointed out, are generally in SPE coterminous with sentences. In reality it is only at the higher levels that the rules are truly cyclical, since those parts of rules applying at the word level are marked as specific to N (Noun), V (Verb), and so on.

The procedure for stress assignment in SPE is that all segments (vowels and consonants) are marked initially as [−stress]. [1 stress] (primary stress) is then assigned to particular vowels by rule. Two conventions (i) weaken any previous stress assignments by one level each time [1 stress] is assigned, and (ii) weaken one level more all non-main stresses within a word (this latter is so that secondary stresses will appear only as reductions of primary stresses in constituents above the word). The stress rules applying to stems and words without affixes are basically a formalisation of those presented informally in sub-section 2.2.1 above. The stress patterns of such 'roots' may then be modified by the effects of affixes. Thus we have derivations such as the following:

$[_N[_V\text{regulat}]_V\text{ion}]_N$

27

On the first cycle the final vowel of [regulat] is assigned a primary stress because it is long. However, words which have a long final vowel and are more than two syllables long may be assigned a primary stress on the antepenultimate vowel; this occurs in this case and the previously assigned primary stress on the final syllable is downgraded to secondary stress. Because secondary stress cannot occur in addition to primary stress within one word, it is further downgraded to tertiary stress. These stress assignments on the first cycle would produce the stress pattern for the verb *regulate*. On the second cycle, the effect of the suffix *-ion* is to assign a primary stress to the vowel immediately preceding the suffix: thus the final vowel of the stem receives [1 stress] again and the stress on the *reg-* is downgraded to [2 stress] and then to [3 stress].

When we move to stress patterns above the simple word level a basic division is made into compounds on the one hand and all constituents higher than the word on the other. In compounds primary stress is re-assigned to the left of two primary stresses previously assigned (the Compound Rule) whereas in higher constituents primary stress is reassigned to the right element (the Nuclear Stress Rule). The compound *bluebell* is assigned stresses as follows:

```
[ [ blue] [bell] ]
NA     AN  NN
    1      1        Main Stress Rule (for words)
    1      2        Compound Rule
```

Whereas the phrase *blue bell* is assigned stresses as follows:

```
[ [ blue] [ bell] ]
NP A    AN   N NP
    1      1       Main Stress Rule
    2      1       Nuclear Stress Rule
```

The Nuclear Stress Rule not only assigns stress to the right element in phrases but cyclically to all higher constituents. So in the sentence *Óld Tóm gróws róses*, each word will first get a primary stress as marked; then the noun phrase subject and the verb phrase (predicate) will each be reassigned a primary stress on their right element (with consequential downgrading to stress level 2 of each left element) to give *Öld Tòm* and *gròws róses*; finally the noun phrase and the verb phrase are put together to make up the sentence and stress is once more reassigned to the primary stress in the right element to give *Öld Tòm gròws róses* (actually the pattern on *Old Tom* is not the most likely and I shall discuss this problem further below).

28

Such a brief summary only gives a very general feeling for the way in which SPE proceeds (many readers will already be familiar with the rules and those who are not should of course go to the original source if they wish to check on the details). Since its publication there has been a mass of criticism and emendation of SPE but nothing which supplants its descriptive detail. Here it is relevant to ask how the stress rules of SPE relate to intonation. Firstly, the rules predict word stresses, which of course tells us which vowels are potentially accentable in utterances (they prefer to say that stress is applied to vowels whereas I prefer to apply it to syllables). Secondly, they predict where the primary accent will fall in utterances. Here SPE admits that it is dealing only with 'normal' stress patterns. What constitutes a 'normal' stress pattern or a normal intonation contour is a matter of much dispute in intonation studies; indeed, many dispute whether there are any patterns which can be called 'normal' at all (see further discussion in chapter 4, section 4.3 and particularly sub-section 4.3.4). However, assuming we can judge a stress pattern as normal, SPE rules predict the occurrence of the primary stress on the rightmost lexical element in the sentence (e.g. on *roses* in the example above). They are not alone in this sort of prediction; linguists of totally different theoretical persuasions have often produced the same sort of rule for predicting the occurrence of the primary stress, or main accent, or 'nucleus', from which begins the principal pitch movement. But there are a number of classes of exception to this sort of rule. For the moment I shall mention only two: intransitive 'event' sentences seem regularly to have the primary accent on the noun phrase subject, e.g. *Your TROUsers are on fire* and final time adverbials do not usually take the primary accent, e.g. *I'm going to LONdon tomorrow*.

In considering the relationship of the stress rules of SPE to intonation, we have lastly to ask whether the various levels of stress produced are in any way correlated with pitch patterns. The levels of stress in SPE have been severely criticised because of 'indefinite lowering', i.e. because previously assigned stresses are downgraded each time a new primary stress is assigned, there is in theory no limit to the number of stress levels. I have already suggested in 2.3 above that we probably need to distinguish no more than four levels of stress/accent (principal and subsidiary pitch accents, a stress based on extra length and loudness alone, and unstressed). Most analysts would agree that certainly no more levels than this are required, and some would demand fewer. Moreover, it is often the case that the overall sentence pattern produced by SPE does not accord with the most likely pitch pattern. If we return to *Old Tom grows roses*, the 1 on *ros-* will typically correspond with a fall from high to low but any pitch prominence earlier in the sentence will almost certainly be on *Old* and not on *Tom*, which would produce a stress pattern $\overset{2}{Old}$ $\overset{3}{Tom}$ $\overset{3}{grows}$ $\overset{1}{roses}$.

In conclusion, the rules of SPE have the following applications and limitations for intonation: (i) they give us a set of word-stress rules which tell us which vowels (and hence syllables) are stressed in words (with many exceptions, of course, but any set of rules is bound to have many exceptions); (ii) they tell us where the primary stress (which we will be calling nuclear accent in the next chapter) is placed when sentence-stress is 'normal' (but there are problems with the term 'normal' and primary stress certainly does not always come on the rightmost lexical word even in apparently 'normal' sentences like *Your TROUsers are on fire*); (iii) they give us the potentiality of many more degrees of stress than can be shown to have tonetic or phonetic correlates (the problem of 'indefinite lowering'); and (iv) they do not apparently consistently predict the correct placement of secondary accent (as, for example, in the sentence *Old Tom grows roses*).

2.6 **Metrical stress rules**

Dissatisfaction with the SPE system has produced at least one alternative approach to stress which has almost supplanted it. This is the 'metrical phonology' initiated by Liberman and Prince (1977) (henceforth LP). LP reinterpret the basic descriptive data contained in SPE. They do this by eliminating the numbering of stress levels with its problem of indefinite lowering as in SPE, and replacing it by a system in which stress is defined on a tree structure in which nodes divide (only binarily) into *s* (strong) and *w* (weak) branches. Like SPE the system applies at both the word and sentence levels.

An English Stress Rule (ESR) assigns [± stress] to all vowels in words. This is done iteratively (i.e. by repeated application) beginning from the end of a word. Like SPE it involves skipping in certain cases over vowels which are short or which are followed by only one consonant. The English Stress Rule only involves giving plus or minus values to the binary feature [± stress]. It does not involve metrical values. On the basic framework provided by [± stress] a tree structure is erected which assigns strong and weak nodes in a hierarchy of relative prominences. All [−stress] vowels are associated with *w* syllables; [+ stress] vowels are most commonly associated with *s* syllables but may be associated with *w* syllables in certain positions, e.g.

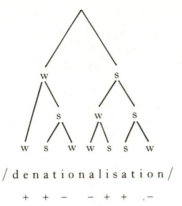

/ d e n a t i o n a l i s a t i o n /

  + + –   – + + ,–

The assignment of strong and weak nodes is governed by two rules: a Lexical Category Prominence Rule (LCPR) which covers words and compounds; and a Nuclear Stress Rule (NSR). The basic provisions of these rules are: in a configuration [X Y]:

> LCPR: Y is strong iff it branches
> NSR: Y is strong

The operation of the LCPR and the NSR is shown in the following example:

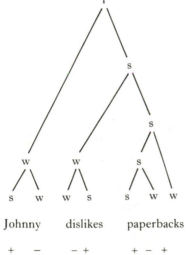

  Johnny   dislikes   paperbacks

  + –   – +   + – +

s occurs on the left branch in the compound *paperbacks* because the right branch does not itself branch (LCPR); whereas at the predicate and sentence levels *s*'s occur on the right branches (NSR).

Tree structures of the sort illustrated above represent the relative prominences associated with syllables: for example, the main stress is shown to be on the syllable not dominated by any *w*'s, e.g. *pap-* in the example above. But tree structures do not represent the timing and rhythm of utterances. To show the 'temporal reality' of metrical trees, they have to be transmuted into 'metrical grids'. A metrical grid for the sentence above would look like this:

$$
\begin{array}{cccc}
 & & 11 & \\
8 & & 9 & 10 \\
1 & 2 & 3\ 4 & 5\ 6\ 7 \\
\end{array}
$$

Johnny dislikes paperbacks

The rule for the construction of grids from trees is termed the Relative Prominence Projection Rule (RPPR) which I quote direct from LP:

In any constituent on which the strong-weak relation is defined, the designated terminal element of its strong subconstituent is metrically stronger than the designated terminal element of its weak subconstituent (p. 316).

'Designated terminal elements' (DTE) are found by following *s*'s down the tree: so, in the example given above, for the root node (R) at the top of the tree, the DTE of the *w* branch leads to *John* and that of the *s* branch leads to *pap-* (and hence *pap-* is metrically stronger than *John*).

As I have already said, metrical grids are seen by LP as a way of representing the rhythm of utterances. It was the problem of one particular rhythmic change which especially dominated the initial interest in such a grid system. This change is that shown in, for example, the word *absolútely* where the main stress in its citation pronunciation is on the third syllable; but, when put in a phrase like *ábsolutely trúe*, this accent moves to the first syllable (called by LP Iambic Reversal; by others the Rhythm Rule). Intuitively, the motivation for this move appears to be the avoidance of a clash of accents. LP show that this can be formalised in metrical grids. Elements are said to be metrically adjacent if they are on the same level and no other elements on that level intervene between them; adjacent elements are metrically clashing if their counterparts one level down are also adjacent. Thus the change from *absolútely* to *ábsolutely* can be represented as follows (where * represents the metrical clash):

$$
\begin{array}{ccccccccc}
 & & 11 & & & & & 11 & \\
 & *9 & & *10 & & 9 & & & 10 \\
6 & & 7 & & 8 & 6 & & 7 & & 8 \\
1 & 2 & 3 & 4 & 5 & 1 & 2 & 3 & 4 & 5 \\
\end{array}
$$

absolutely true → absolutely true

+ − + − +   + − + − +

It is claimed by LP and their successors that metrical grids can not only represent the avoidance of adjacent accents but that in doing so they represent how stresses are spaced out and hence ultimately that they can represent the notion of stress-timing in English.

Developments in the theory of metrical phonology have included the replacement of the feature [± stress] by an extra (lower) level on trees and grids, and, more relevantly for intonation, developments have also involved the labelling of nodes within the trees. Such labelling is carried out in one of two ways. Either particular tree patterns are regarded as the 'templates' of particular units: 'feet', for example, are represented by the following templates (where the bottom nodes are syllables):

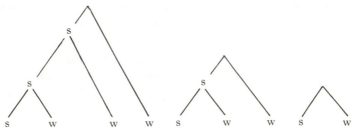

or, alternatively (and particularly for higher-level nodes), labels are assigned on syntactic grounds; this has generally been the suggestion for intonation-groups (or 'intonational-phrases' or simply I's), e.g. assign I's to clauses, noun-phrases, displaced constituents, parentheticals, and so on. In whatever way the labelling of nodes arises, it represents a hierarchy of phonological constituents, including at least intonation-groups, feet, and syllables. This type of metrical phonology thus includes two types of hierarchical structure, one involving constituents and one within each type of constituent.

Metrical phonology including labelled nodes is potentially more relevant to rhythm and intonation than an SPE type of approach to stress. Stress-timing and full-vowel timing can both be extracted: stress-timing by the occurrence of *s*'s at the beginning of feet and full-vowel timing (confusingly!) by the presence of the feature [+ stress]. Intonation-groups (or phrases) are represented in the hierarchy; as will be seen in the next chapter, some such phonological constituent is certainly necessary in intonational description (such a phonological unit having probabilistic relationships with syntactic constituents but not invariantly predictable by syntax).

The 'nucleus' of an intonation pattern coincides with the Designated Terminal Element (DTE) of an intonation-group (or 'phonological phrase' as LP call it), e.g. *pap-* in the example given earlier. The problem with nucleus placement remains the same as in SPE: both types of representation predict normal placement on the rightmost lexical item (counting compounds as lexical items) whereas there are in reality a large number of classes of exception to this prediction. Besides the nucleus, the second most important point in the pitch pattern of an intonation-group is likely to be the first accent and it is important that a theory of stress should predict this correctly. In some cases Iambic Reversal will predict the correct pattern, e.g. *Ábsolutely nóbody does thát* and this is an advance on SPE. In other cases LP, like SPE, makes the wrong prediction: so in a sentence like *The red book is on the table*, *book* will be represented as of greater metrical strength than *red* whereas in a reading of the sentence without any specially contrastive accents a pitch prominence will almost certainly be on *red* and not on *book*.

Nevertheless some version of metrical phonology, involving as it does the notion that stress levels are relative rather than absolute, appears easier than the SPE model to mesh to the units and meanings shown to be relevant for intonational representation in the next two chapters.

2.7 Summary

In this chapter, word-stress in languages, and particularly in English, has been briefly surveyed, because we need to know which syllable of a word is stressed when we assign accents in utterances; a summary has been given of rules for word-stress, particularly in English. Such word-stresses are converted into four degrees of stress/accent in connected speech. The relationship between stress and rhythm was then considered: it was suggested that 'full-vowel timing' generally explains the facts of timing in English rather better than 'stress-timing'. Finally, two formal treatments of English stress patterns were outlined.

Sources and further reading

For priorities among pitch, length, and loudness in the perception of stress and accent, see Fry (1955, 1958), and Mol and Uhlenbeck (1956).

For the varying importance of length as a cue to stress, see Berinstein (1979).

For word-stress generally, see Garde (1968, 1973).

For word-stress in English, see Kingdon (1958b), Chomsky and Halle (1968), and Fudge (1984).

For stress-timing, see in particular Lehiste (1977) and Roach (1982).

For full-vowel timing, see Bolinger (1981 and forthcoming). For instrumental data on English rhythm, see Thompson (1980).

For generative stress rules, see Chomsky and Halle (1968), and Goyvaerts and Pullum (1975).

For metrical phonology, see in particular Liberman and Prince (1977), van der Hulst and Smith (1982), Giegerich (1984, 1985), and Selkirk (1984).

3
The forms of intonation

3.1   **Intonation-groups, nucleus, and nuclear tone**

In this chapter I shall discuss the type of framework which can be set up to describe the forms of intonation; and the support that can be adduced for each one from phonetic reality. The descriptions operate in three different areas: firstly, the division of connected speech into INTO-NATION-GROUPS; secondly, the selection of one syllable within one word in each intonation-group to bear the principal accent or NUCLEUS in the intonation-group (this syllable is variously called the tonic, or main stress, or main accent); thirdly, the choice of tune within the intonation-group, that part of the tune beginning at the nucleus (the NUCLEAR TONE) being generally the most important. I shall now deal with the phonetic realisations and intonational resources associated with each of these three areas before going on to discuss the functions and meanings associated with these resources in chapter 4.

3.2   **Intonation-groups**

In this book I speak of INTONATION-GROUPS (in other places they have been variously called sense-groups, breath-groups, tone-groups, tone-units, phonological phrases, phonological clauses or intonational phrases!). Almost all analysts operate with some notion of intonation-groups although most writers have no explicit discussion of how the division between intonation-groups is signalled. Those who do discuss the subject vary considerably in their judgement of the ease with which an analyst can unambiguously divide a text into intonation-groups. Two quotations serve to illustrate this difference of opinion:

(a)   '. . . . . phonological criteria suffice to indicate unambiguously where a tone-unit boundary should go in connected speech in the vast majority of cases'. (Crystal, *Prosodic Systems and Intonation in English*, 1969a, p. 206)

(b)   '. . . . . we encounter constant difficulty in identifying tone groups in spontaneous speech . . . . .' (Brown, Currie and Kenworthy, *Questions of Intonation*, 1980, p. 46)

My own judgement is that the truth lies somewhere in between these two statements, although it is undoubtedly also true that the majority of linguists assume that the phonetic correlates of boundaries between intonation-groups are far more straightforward than they actually are. In reading, or in speaking prepared texts, most intonation-group boundaries are clearly marked. But even with the most experienced readers and speakers, there are many cases where it remains difficult to decide whether a boundary is present or not. And with inexperienced readers and speakers (adults' intonational competence is extremely variable) the difficulties are multiplied. When we consider spontaneous speech (particularly conversation) any clear and obvious division into intonation-groups is not so apparent because of the broken nature of much spontaneous speech, including as it does hesitation, repetitions, false starts, incomplete sentences and sentences involving a grammatical caesura in their middle.

Judgement that an intonation-group boundary is present would in an ideal situation be based on 'external criteria', i.e. on phonetic cues present at the actual boundary. But in practice such phonetic cues (e.g. pause) may be either ambiguous or not present at all. Therefore 'internal criteria' must also play a part: that is, our judgement that the application of the external criteria produces chunks of utterance all of which have pitch patterns which accord with acceptable 'whole' intonation patterns. The assignment of intonation-group boundaries is therefore something of a circular business; we establish some intonation-groups in cases where all the external criteria conspire to make the assignment of a boundary relatively certain; we note the sorts of internal intonational structure occurring in such cases and this enables us to make decisions in those cases where the external criteria are less unambiguous. And, in some difficult cases, we take grammatical or semantic criteria into account, i.e. when regular correspondences between intonation and grammar/semantics have been established in cases where boundary assignment is clear, we may lean heavily on such correspondences when assigning boundaries in the difficult cases. Before returning to this general issue, I shall now consider in detail what the basic external and internal criteria are.

3.2.1 **Pause**

The criterion most often mentioned in the demarcation of intonation-groups is that of pause. The forms of pause fall into two categories, the unfilled pause (i.e. silence) and the filled pause. In R.P. and in many other dialects of English the latter typically involves the use of a central vowel [ə] and a bilabial nasal [m], either singly or in combination, and of varying lengths. In other dialects of English and in other languages the sounds of filled pauses may be different: in Scottish English a sound in the region of the vowel in *gate* and *play* is typical and in Russian an alveolar nasal is more common than a bilabial nasal. The use of pause in general and the relationship between unfilled and filled pauses in particular is subject to a large amount of idiosyncratic variation and in the following discussion of the functions of pause all statements concern only general tendencies.

Reference is sometimes made to the fact that breaths are often taken at pauses and some writers even regard the taking of breath as the reason for pausing. It is indeed true that some people talk so much and so fluently that they are forced to pause for breath, but the vast majority of pauses cannot be accounted for in this way. Both male and female speakers can count reasonably slowly up to twenty without taking a breath and without any strain at all. Yet pauses almost always occur much more frequently than every twenty words in any form of speech. Even allowing that counting these low numbers involves mainly one- and two-syllabled words, the discrepancy is such as to suggest that we do not, except on rare occasions, pause for breath. Rather, we pause for other reasons and seize the opportunity to take a breath.

Pauses seem typically to occur at three places in utterances:

(i) at major constituent boundaries (principally between clauses and between subject and predicate). There is a correlation between the type of constituent boundary and the length of pause, i.e. the more major the boundary, the longer the pause. Moreover, pauses tend to be longer where constituent boundaries (usually in this case sentence boundaries) involve a new topic;

(ii) before words of high lexical content or, putting it in terms of information theory, at points of low transitional probability. So words preceded by a pause are often difficult to guess in advance. This sort of pause typically occurs before a minor constituent boundary, generally within a noun-phrase, verb-phrase, or adverbial-phrase, e.g. between a determiner and following head noun;

(iii) after the first word in an intonation-group. This is a typical position for other 'errors of performance', e.g. corrections of false starts and repetitions.

Pause type (i) is generally to be taken as indicating an intonation-group boundary, e.g. (boundaries are indicated by /)

37

> The Prince of Wales / is visiting Cardiff tomorrow
>
> Yesterday I went to London / and saw the Queen / outside Buckingham Palace

Although this type of pause will typically be unfilled, it may sometimes be filled, and in such cases the filling seems to be used as a turn-keeping device, particularly in conversation, i.e. it is used to prevent another potential speaker interrupting the current speaker. Also it cannot be assumed that every intonation-group boundary will have such a pause. Pauses at intonation-group boundaries, even where these occur at major constituent boundaries, may sometimes be obliterated rather than filled as an alternative method of turn-keeping. When such obliteration occurs, it is frequently followed by a pause-type (iii).

Pause types (ii) and (iii) are generally to be taken as examples of hesitation phenomena. Type (ii) indicates a word-finding difficulty, e.g. (hesitation pause indicated by . . .)

> The Minister talked at length about the . . . redeployment of LABOUR
> There was a . . . GOLDcrest in the garden yesterday
> I saw a BUGATTi in . . . Cross Street yesterday

A hesitation pause before the nucleus (for the moment this can be thought of as the accented syllable of the most prominent word in an intonation-group, transcribed above with capital letters) is of rare occurrence (e.g. the hesitation before GOLDcrest above) where it might be thought to be most likely (i.e. where the word is of high lexical content). But evidence from slips of the tongue indicates that the word carrying the nucleus is planned well in advance. For instance, the word carrying the nucleus is a prime cause of a slip of the tongue on a word earlier in an intonation-group e.g.

> The Chancellor has been outlining his plans to *f*light inFLAtion

Thus a hesitation pause of type (ii) will occur before a word of low transitional probability although it is unlikely before a word carrying the nucleus of the intonation-group in which it occurs.

Pause type (iii), occurring after the first word of an intonation-group, seems to serve a planning function, i.e. it is essentially a holding operation while the speaker plans the remainder of the sentence, e.g.

> I do like Elgar's violin concerto. / It's . . . quite the most perfect work of its kind
>
> Why don't you join an evening class? / You'd . . . be quite likely to meet some interesting people

Pause types (ii) and (iii), as has already been implied in talking of them
as internal to an intonation-group, are not taken as markers of intonation-
group boundaries, because they do not result in utterance chunks each
of which has a pitch pattern typically contained within an intonation-group
(this is discussed further under 'internal criteria' below). Pause types (ii)
and (iii) are more common in all types of unscripted speech than in reading
or prepared speech.

Instrumental measurements have not demonstrated conclusively a correlation between pause-type and pause-length (probably because, as has
already been noted, pausing is extremely idiosyncratic and because the
number of subjects in all experimental studies has always been extremely
low). Indeed the minimum threshold at which a pause is perceived has
been put at different levels, varying from one second down to one quarter
of a second. A better system for measuring pause may be to relate it to
the length of syllables or rhythm-groups in surrounding speech. Whichever
way of measuring is used, most investigators find boundary pauses to be
longer than hesitation pauses.

It should by now be apparent that the criterion of pause as a marker
of intonation-group boundaries cannot be used on its own. Despite its
explicit or implicit use as such in many studies and textbooks on intonation,
pauses do not always mark intonation boundaries, nor are intonation boundaries always marked by pauses. Pause can only be used as a criterion
for intonation boundaries if considered together with other external and
internal criteria.

3.2.2 **Other boundary markers**

Apart from pause there are three other external criteria which
may act as markers of intonation-group boundaries. Firstly, the presence
of an anacrusis (see chapter 2, section 2.4) generally indicates the beginning
of an intonation-group, e.g.

I saw John yesterday / and he was just off to London

The most likely place for the first stress in the second intonation-group
is on *just*; and the unstressed syllables before *just* are likely to be pronounced more quickly than unstressed syllables elsewhere in the sentence
(and, specifically, more quickly than those at the end of *yesterday*). The
sudden acceleration beginning at *and* indicates that these syllables are
anacrustic and hence that a new intonation-group is beginning.

Secondly, and regardless of whether it is stressed or unstressed, the
final syllable in an intonation-group will often be lengthened, e.g.

On my way to the station / I met a man

Here the second syllable of *station* may be lengthened and help to indicate an intonation-group boundary. The lengthening may be a by-product of two other things occurring at an intonation-group boundary: in the first place it may act as a sort of pause-substitute; indeed it could be regarded as a type of filled pause. At the same time this final syllable of an intonation-group will often carry a final pitch movement (in some types of analysis called a 'terminal'). As an illustration of this point, consider the following typical intonation of the above example:

On my way to the station   /   I met a man

(It should by now be clear that in interlinear transcriptions large dots indicate stressed syllables and small dots unstressed syllables.) In the first intonation-group, the primary accent (='nucleus') is on *sta-* and the tone from there to the end of the group is falling-rising. The second syllable of *station* carries the rising part of the pattern, and, for syllables to carry a pitch movement within themselves, they clearly have to be of a certain length.

Some of the reasons for final syllable lengthening may be language-specific, but nonetheless it does seem that the phenomenon itself may be an intonational universal. Cross-linguistic studies of final syllable lengthening have generally concentrated on syllables which are both at the end of a sentence and immediately followed by a pause (e.g. on *man* in the example above); since it occurs before a pause in such studies, the syllable concerned is clearly not acting as a pause-substitute. Nevertheless, even before a pause it may still be used as an additional boundary cue. Other reasons suggested for such lengthening include (i) that it is evidence of a natural relaxation before pause (which could not of course apply to those cases where the lengthening actually replaces the pause); (ii) that it provides time to check that the preceding group has been articulated correctly (the 'review' theory); and (iii) that the speaker is thereby given time to plan the following group (the 'motoric planning' theory). It is difficult to see how any of these last three reasons can in fact be distinguished from the use of final syllable lengthening as a boundary cue. The most clear function for final syllable lengthening is undoubtedly as a boundary marker, sometimes replacing pause, sometimes in addition to pause. This appears to be at least a putative universal, although the lengthening ratios reported for different languages vary considerably: there is said to be a high lengthening ratio in English, a low lengthening ratio in Finnish, and an intermediate lengthening ratio in Spanish.

Unfortunately both anacrusis and syllable lengthening may occur in positions other than at intonation-group boundaries. In particular, like a pause, they may indicate a hesitation, e.g.

> He's [z:] in the middle of doing it NOW
> I don't know what you [u:] arRANGed

In these examples the [z:] and the [u:] specially lengthen the syllables which they terminate, and the *in the* and the first syllable of *arranged* constitute syllables in anacrusis; nevertheless, because of internal criteria (discussed in the next section) the sentences above may each constitute only one intonation-group. So far, then, we have three criteria for intonation-group boundaries (pause, anacrusis and final syllable lengthening), all of which are ambiguous between boundary marking and hesitation phenomena.

The last external criterion concerns the pitch of unaccented syllables. Changes of pitch level and pitch direction most frequently occur on accented syllables. A change in pitch level and/or pitch direction among unaccented syllables is generally an indicator of an intonation-group boundary. After falling tones followed by low unaccented syllables, there will be a slight step-up to the pitch level of the unaccented syllables at the beginning of a new intonation-group, e.g.

John's not GOING tomorrow / But on FRIday . . .

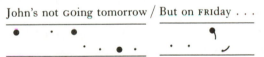

This change of pitch reflects the fact that low unaccented syllables at the beginning of an intonation-group are generally at a higher level than low unaccented syllables at the end of an intonation-group (I shall have more to say about this in chapter 5, when I talk about declination as a universal). Following rising tones there will be a step-down to the pitch level of any unaccented syllables at the beginning of the following intonation-group, e.g.

John's gone to GERMany? / I didn't think he'd have the NERVe

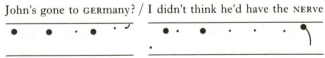

So a change in the pitch of unaccented syllables is a fairly clear boundary marker. At this point it might be objected that the argumentation here is illogical since I have already in chapter 2 noted that a pitch prominence

involving a step-up or a step-down in pitch is an indicator of an accented syllable. But it must be remembered that accents in connected speech normally fall only on syllables which are lexically stressed. Hence changes in pitch level or direction on syllables which are not lexically stressed generally indicate boundaries, not accents.

3.2.3 Internal structure as group marker

In the discussion of pause, anacrusis and final syllable lengthening, it was concluded that such phenomena are ambiguous between boundary and hesitation marking. It was suggested that a decision between these two functions could sometimes only be made on the basis of 'internal' criteria, i.e. on the presence or absence of a likely internal structure for an intonation-group. If the features of pause, and/or anacrusis and/or final syllable lengthening divide an utterance into two part-utterances either one of which does not have the minimum internal structure of an intonation-group, then any combination of those features is taken as a hesitation. But what is this minimum internal structure of an intonation-group? Firstly, it must contain at least one stressed syllable. Thus utterance fragments which contain only unstressed syllables are not taken as separate intonation-groups, e.g.

The [ə:] real point of the problem / is that . . . . .

Here *the* is not to be taken as a separate group since it constitutes an utterance fragment containing no stressed syllable. Secondly, there must be a pitch movement to or from at least one accented syllable. In the following *John* does constitute a separate group:

John [n:] / isn't going

whereas in the following *John* does not constitute a separate group:

John [n:] isn't going

In summary, one or both of the following criteria will in most cases delineate intonation-groups:

(i) change of pitch level or pitch direction of unaccented syllables

(ii) pause, and/or anacrusis, and/or final syllable lengthening, plus the presence of a pitch accent in each part-utterance thus created

42

3.2.4   **Problems in group delimitation**

In English (and for the moment our consideration of basic constructs is exemplified principally from English) there are a number of particularly difficult pitch sequences which present problems for any analysis into intonation-groups. (The observant reader will have noticed that phrases like 'taken as one intonation-group' and 'marks the presence of a boundary' have systematically been used ambiguously, i.e. they refer both to what an ordinary listener might be doing in the language and to how a phonetician might make an explicit analysis. This ambiguity is quite deliberate and is meant to imply that the phonetician is trying to formalise what an ordinary listener does unconsciously.) I shall now examine three types of pitch sequence which present particular problems for dividing utterances into intonation-groups in English (and, as we shall see in chapter 5, similar problems arise in other languages).

The first type of difficulty concerns sequences like the following:

He went away unfortunately

Here we have a falling tone starting on -*way* and a rising tone starting on -*fort*- and the overall pattern is one which is very typical with some types of sentence final adverbials. The problem is: are we to analyse this pattern as consisting of one or two intonation-groups? In terms of the criteria presented above, it is clear that if there is a pause, or anacrusis on *un*-, or lengthening of -*way*, this pattern must be treated as two groups (since there is a pitch accent in each half). It must also be taken as two groups if the syllable *un*- is on a slightly higher pitch than the end point of the tone on -*way*. But frequently none of these patterns will be present and thus by phonetic criteria alone we would have to consider the pattern as one group. However, I mentioned earlier that on some occasions it seems sensible and productive of a simpler analysis if we take syntactic or semantic factors into account. In this type of pattern it seems reasonable to take account of the fact that markers of a boundary frequently **are** present between final 'sentence' adverbials and what precedes them and to regard the 'basic' intonation as involving two groups. The pattern above, where no markers are present, can accordingly be considered a special instance of INTONATIONAL SANDHI (the word 'sandhi' was used by the ancient Indian grammarians (= 'joining together') and here indicates the merging of two basically independent intonation-groups).

A second difficult type concerns vocatives and reporting clauses in sentence final position as in the following examples:

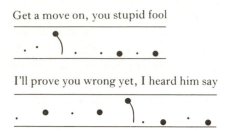

Get a move on, you stupid fool

I'll prove you wrong yet, I heard him say

Some analysts have considered that in such cases we have a low level tone within a separate intonation-group in such cases, since a pause is often present before the vocative or reporting clause. By the criteria presented here, however, such sequences consist of one group only, whether pause is present or not, on the grounds that there is no pitch accent in the vocative or reporting clause.

The third problematic case concerns instances where an adverbial on a low pitch may belong semantically either with the words in the preceding intonation-group or with the words in the following intonation-group, e.g.

He went to the States of course he didn't stay very long

(This example is deliberately presented without punctuation marks.) Here the low pitched *of course* could belong either with what precedes or what follows. However, in such cases markers of an intonation-group boundary usually are present in the relative pitch or rapidity of the unaccented syllables. In this particular example either the three syllables *of course he* are just above the lowest pitch and hence characteristic of beginning pitch rather than end pitch (in which case there is a boundary before *of* – as in the above transcription), or else the two syllables *of course* might be at the lowest pitch with *he* occupying a slight step-up (in which case the boundary would be between *course* and *he*).

The three problematic cases discussed in this section serve to show that the concept of intonation-group as a unit independent of any syntactic constituent (although with strong correlations with certain types of constituent, as we shall see in chapter 4) is, like many other units of linguistic analysis, essentially a theoretical construct. Sometimes there are clear phonetic markers of a boundary, sometimes a boundary 'seems' to be there, although the reasons why this should be so are complex.

It still remains to be shown that the boundaries of intonation-groups enclose a unit which is appropriate to the description of intonational meaning. In other words, does the establishment of intonation-groups enable us to describe intonation more effectively than if we regard intonation as simply a series of contours within some standard grammatical unit (e.g. the sentence)? The answer to this question depends very much on whether we can give relevance to the notion of 'nucleus', i.e. whether each intonation-group has one pitch contour which is more prominent than other contours in the group. I discuss the concept of 'nucleus' in section 3.4 below. At the moment, however, it is first necessary to establish pitch contours themselves as relevant and this I attempt to do in the next section.

3.3   Contours and levels

A basic difference between much British and American intonation analysis in the last forty years has been that, whereas British writers have preferred a 'contour' analysis, American writers have generally preferred a 'levels' analysis. Most such American studies have involved four levels (although a very recent departure has involved an analysis in terms of two levels only, together with a number of other variables, like pitch declination throughout the intonation-group and 'prominence', i.e. the extent of an upward or downward deflection at any point – I deal with this approach in section 3.9 of this chapter). Typically, such levels analyses also involve three terminal junctures (roughly characterised as the last pitch direction on the last syllable of an intonation-group): falling (marked by #), rising (marked by //) and level (marked by /). The following example of the combination of pitch levels and terminal junctures illustrates this type of analysis and marking system (underneath I show in interlinear tonetic transcription the pitch pattern which this represents):

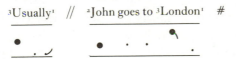

Notice that pitch levels (4 is the highest) are only marked at the beginning of an utterance and at the points where a change takes place to another pitch level.

This sort of analysis has been heavily criticised on a number of counts:

(a) Proponents of the levels theory have always claimed that it was relative not absolute pitch that was being discussed, but the question is 'How relative?' It is reasonable to assume that the four levels have at least the same absolute pitch within one intonation-group, for otherwise this type of analysis becomes wholly arbitrary, especially as no notion of declination (see this chapter, section 3.9 and chapter 4, sub-section 4.4.4.4, below) was ever built into any four-levels analysis. But experiments

45

dividing up the pitch range of intonation-groups have shown that sometimes very small pitch movements convey significant differences in meaning
whereas in other cases larger pitch differences carry no meaning. In other
words, there is no principled way of dividing the pitch range of an intonation-group into four levels if, that is, one wishes by doing so to capture
the meaning contributed by intonation to language.

(b) It follows from (a) that there is no real reason for having four levels
rather than, say, three or five. Certainly, most British 'nuclear tones' trans-
late easily into a system of three levels, yet at the same time there is
in British English a particular overall tone for an intonation-group which
sometimes requires more than four levels, a pattern which involves what
is sometimes called a 'stepping head' or a 'descending stress series':

Why are you always making so much noise?

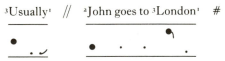

(c) The system does not make clear the tonetic details of the transition
from one pitch level to another. For instance, in:

⁴John didn't do it¹ #

where exactly does the fall from 4 to 1 take place? (The details of this
sort of 'tune-text association' have recently been taken up by the school
of autosegmental phonology and I discuss this further in section 3.8 below.)

(d) Terminals are only significant when they reverse the preceding pitch
direction, e.g. the terminal is significant in 41// (rising terminal) but not
in 41# (falling terminal). Simple falling tunes of the latter sort probably
account for at least 60% of terminals in British English (R.P.) and in
American English (G.A.). Some redundancy is allowable in any analysis
but this seems excessive.

The first example I gave in this section was:

³Usually¹ // ²John goes to ³London¹ #

In a contour analysis (marked with tonetic-stress marks) this would be
represented as follows:

ᵛUsually/ ¹John goes to `London

(Here / marks an intonation-group boundary; ᵛ marks the beginning of
a falling-rising contour which covers the whole of the word *usually*;
¹marks the beginning of a high level tune which covers that stretch up

to the next mark (i.e. *John goes to*); and `marks the beginning of a falling contour which ends at the end of the utterance.) Some of the arguments against a levels analysis apply equally against this sort of contour analysis. Contour analyses frequently make distinctions between high-falls and low-falls or between high-rises and low-rises and it can equally well be objected that we have no principled way of deciding how many types of rise or fall to differentiate in our analysis. Furthermore, the tonetic-stress marks in themselves do not directly tell us how the contour beginning at a certain point is actually associated with the words on which it falls, although in practice many systems of contour analysis do tell us the 'conventions' associated with certain marks; for example, a fall-rise will spread out according to the number and type of syllables available. On *Usually* in the above example, the fall takes place on the first syllable because it is long (a step down would occur between the first and second syllables if it were short) and the rise occurs on the very last (unstressed) syllable. But if there had been another stressed syllable after the fall, the rise would occur from that syllable, e.g. ᵛ*John didn't do it* where the rise would occur from *do*. These sorts of conventions which are usually associated with contour analyses could in principle just as well have been used with four-levels analyses.

So the arguments against levels analyses (with the exception of the criticism of terminals mentioned in (d) above) seem to be much weakened because many of the same problems apply to contour analyses as well. Also, the arguments do not really say anything about the basic question of whether listeners hear intonation patterns in terms of glides or in terms of the relative or absolute height at the beginning and end of the glide. Therefore, the decision to allow an analysis based on contours to predominate in this book remains to some extent an act of faith. But there is at least one factor which tips the balance towards a contour analysis: this is my conviction that there is some basic similarity of meaning in all falling contours as opposed to a basic similarity of meaning in all rising contours (this is discussed as a putative universal in chapter 5, section 5.5). An analysis in terms of levels does not capture this basic division between falls and rises. Proponents of a levels analysis might object that this is precisely what terminal junctures do. But it has been previously noted that it is impossible to isolate such terminals where they merely continue a preceding pitch movement, e.g. in cases like 3–1# (falling) or 2–3// (rising). So terminals may capture the basic difference between rising and falling but ascribe the difference to a portion of utterances which is difficult to isolate in many cases. It is more reasonable to say that the basic difference

47

is between intonation-groups whose last pitch direction is either falling or rising; this last pitch direction may extend over one or more syllables. In section 3.9 of this chapter I shall discuss a recent two-levels approach to a model of generative intonation but other than that I shall have no more to say about pitch levels analyses.

3.4 Pitch accents and nucleus

In chapter 1 I discussed how accents were realised principally by pitch, length and loudness; of these pitch is undoubtedly the most consistently used feature, with the other two factors playing a relatively minor role, at least in English, and probably in most other intonation languages. PITCH ACCENTS depend on some sort of obtrusion of pitch at the point of accent from the pitch of surrounding syllables. Such obtrusions depend on movements to or from the accented syllable, involving (i) a step-up, (ii) a step-down, (iii) a movement down-from, or (iv) a movement up-from. Accents may involve either a movement to or a movement from alone, or a combination of both types of obtrusion. Here are some examples of accents depending on various types of obtrusion:

He ought to have asked me first

Here there is a step-up on *ought* and a movement down-from on *me* (the other two large dots on *asked* and *first* indicate stresses only, realised by length and loudness alone).

I didn't say that

Here there is a step-down on *did-* and a movement up-from on *that*.

I don't agree with you

Here there is a step-up on *don't* and a combination of a step-down and a movement down-from on *-gree*.

He's not in the least intelligent

Here there is a step-down on *not* and a combination of a step-up and a movement down-from on *least* (with a tertiary stress on *-tell-*).

It has already been pointed out that such a series of accents dependent principally on various pitch obtrusions can only operate if we already know which words are likely to have an accent and which syllable in a word is likely to carry an accent. Otherwise, for example, in (a) above we would not know whether at the beginning of the sentence we were dealing with an accent involving a step-up to *ought* or a movement up-from on *He*. Hence the importance of the rules for word-stress discussed in chapter 2. Of course on some occasions we want to make a syllable prominent which normally does not have an accent, and, if there is then a potential ambiguity about which syllable is accented, we have to make the matter clear by extra pitch movement or extra length or loudness or some combination of these factors. For example,

I want some

In this case *want* as a lexical verb is more likely to have an accent than *I*, pronouns being usually unaccented. In order to ensure that the movement following *I* is interpreted as down-from rather than down-to, we have to ensure a longish glide starting from *I* and probably give that syllable extra loudness. If we simply have high level on *I* and low level on *want*, the latter and not the former will be heard as accented.

Almost all intonational analyses operate with some notion of NUCLEUS (alias 'tonic', alias 'primary stress'; also the term 'focus' is used, although this is usually more concerned with the function of nucleus placement – see chapter 4, section 4.3). NUCLEUS is used to describe the pitch accent which stands out as the most prominent in an intonation-group. In the majority of cases the pitch accent which stands out as most prominent is the last pitch accent. Looking back at examples (a)–(d) above, the nuclei are on *me*, *that*, *-gree*, and *least*. There seems to be some general psycholinguistic principle at work whereby the processing of intonational meaning takes place at the end of each group and the most recent signal carries the most meaning.

Although as a general rule the last pitch accent is the nucleus, there are a number of sequences of pitch accents in English where the last pitch accent may be downgraded because it is perceptually less prominent than the penultimate one, which becomes the nucleus. Two such sequences in particular will be mentioned because they are very common. The first concerns cases where a movement down-from with a very wide glide is followed by another movement down-from but with a narrower glide (both movements often preceded by a step-up), e.g.

49

But I want to go there

In these cases the pitch accent on *go* is only slightly more prominent than a stress dependent on length and/or loudness alone would be. When syllables are apparently stressed by length and loudness alone, it is generally true that the fundamental frequency will be slightly higher than on unstressed syllables for purely physiological reasons, i.e. producing syllables with extra loudness produces extra airflow through the vocal cords and pitch goes up accordingly. So it is sometimes difficult in cases like the above to judge whether there is a 'genuine' pitch accent (i.e. one where the speaker gives higher pitch over and above that produced simply by the physiological link-up with extra loudness). But even in cases where a pitch accent is fairly evidently present (e.g. when the height of the second fall is nearly as great as that of the first) it seems that the first fall is likely to be heard as more prominent.

The second type of sequence to be considered is that of an accent down-from followed by an accent up-from (what has in British contour analysis been called either a fall-rise or a fall plus rise). Let us consider first an example like the following:

Unfortunately / . . . . .

This sort of pitch pattern is very common on many adverbials occurring in clause-initial position. There is an accent involving a combination of step up-to and down-from on *-fort-*. A rise in pitch then occurs on *-ly* which is an unstressed syllable in the word and hence not potentially accented. The *-ly* is therefore not taken as accented but merely as part of the realisation of the tune following the accent on *-fort-*. But now consider a case like:

At ten o'clock / . . . . .

Here there are two potential accented syllables, both of which have pitch movement on them; hence it is logical to consider them both as accented. But the pitch pattern is the same as in the preceding example and its use on an initial adverbial is also the same. Hence it again seems logical to take the movement down-from on *ten* as the nucleus. It seems to be generally true in English that a final accent dependent on a rise following a fall is normally downgraded from its status as nucleus. Rises are in some way less prominent accents than falls. (This is confirmed by perception tests which ask people to say which is the most prominent word in sentences.)

In this type of case the situation is indeed further complicated by the problem mentioned in 3.2.4 above, namely, that in some cases of fall plus rise it seems sensible to analyse into two separate groups with intonational sandhi obliterating any potential markers of an intonation boundary. The problems of fall followed by rise in English may seem to readers new to the subject to have already taken up a disproportionate amount of space in this chapter; this is due to the fact that they do illustrate many of the problems of setting up a system of intonational analysis which is at least reasonably consistent and in accord with intuition; it also reflects the very considerable attention which has been given to this sequence in the history of English intonation.

Another, similar, sort of problem is presented by examples like:

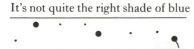

It's not quite the right shade of blue

In this sort of pitch pattern (which is common in southern Britain but much less common in North America), there is firstly a step-up, then a number of steps-down, the final step-down involving also a slight movement down-from. If asked which is the most prominent word in such sequences, some listeners say the initial step-up, while others say the final step-down. Also, the answers differ from one sentence to another, depending on factors such as the lexical weight of the items receiving an accent and the number of syllables in the rhythm-groups. In the example above most listeners do in fact judge *blue* to be the most prominent whereas in the following example they judge *face* the most prominent:

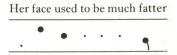

Her face used to be much fatter

I prefer nevertheless to continue to regard the final accent as the nucleus in such cases, while at the same time admitting that lexical and rhythmical factors can sometimes override intonation. But this type of pitch pattern and the two previous problematic patterns do illustrate areas where the concept of nucleus runs into problems. Some analysts indeed think that problems of this sort argue for abandoning the whole notion of nucleus and just settling for a series of pitch accents; this is an extreme view

51

and one which does not take into account the very large number of cases where nucleus assignment is straightforward. In any case, linguistic rules are rarely exceptionless. From now on I shall consistently use the notion of NUCLEUS to describe that pitch accent (usually the last) which generally stands out as most prominent in each of the typical tonal sequences within intonation-groups.

In section 2.3 of chapter 2 it was suggested that we need to distinguish four degrees of stress/accent in English. We are now in a position to define these degrees of accent more precisely:

(i)   PRIMARY STRESS/ACCENT involving the principal pitch prominence, i.e. the NUCLEUS

(ii)   SECONDARY STRESS/ACCENT involving a subsidiary pitch prominence in an intonation-group, i.e. a non-nuclear pitch accent

(iii)   TERTIARY STRESS involving a prominence produced principally by length and/or loudness. (This is not referred to as 'tertiary accent' because the term 'accent' is reserved for pitch prominences.)

(iv)   UNSTRESSED
(The term 'unaccented' covers (iii) and (iv).)

3.5   Accent range, key, and register

So far in this chapter I have dealt with the basic theoretical concepts of INTONATION-GROUP, PITCH ACCENT, and NUCLEUS. I have discussed how pitch accents depend on obtrusions involving movements to and from accented syllables. But I have not yet discussed the width of the movement to and from the accented syllable. This can vary in all four of the basic varieties of pitch accent. The width can vary in steps-up and in steps-down, cf.

In the first pair above, the second example involves an altogether more emphatic denial. In the second pair, the final accent with its step-down to a lower pitch is in some sense weightier (it is also felt to be very British by American speakers). The width of movement can also vary in the movements **from** the accent and this sort of movement (as opposed to steps) seems the more important for meaning. Clearly to some extent movements from an accented syllable depend upon the extremes (or not) established by the movements **to** the accent. In the pairs above there is more room for movement **from** in the second member of each pair. Movements down-from will all have in common the fact that the nearer they come to the speaker's baseline the more 'complete' they will sound. Movements up-from, on the other hand, will all sound more 'uncertain' the higher they go (meanings are discussed in detail in chapter 4, section 4.4.1), cf.

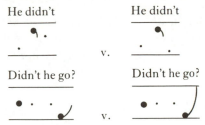

All such variations in the width of pitch movement actually occur in English, although the fall from high to mid pitch, i.e. is relatively uncommon in R.P. and in G.A. (but it is common in other languages – see chapter 5, sub-section 5.4.4.1).

A substantial majority of pitch movements in languages involve high-pitched accented syllables dependent on a step-up and/or a movement down-from. It is also true in English (and in many other languages) that most people speak in the lower third of their total pitch range, so that there is much more potential for varying the width of movements dependent on a high accented syllable than there is for those dependent on a low accented syllable. Thus variations in ACCENT RANGE (which I shall use to describe variations in movements-from) are most commonly associated with variation in the height of high-pitched accents.

In section 3.4 I talked about the sorts of pitch obtrusions which create accents. I discussed movements to the accented syllable and movements from the accented syllable. Movements **to** an accent usually involve steps-up or steps-down whereas movements **from** may involve either jumps or glides. The use of a jump rather than a glide or *vice versa* is often dependent on the make-up of the syllables over which they are spread. If there is only one syllable on which to place a downward movement, a glide is more likely to be used, as indeed it is if the pitch accent falls on a syllable with a long vowel, e.g.

Whereas if the pitch accent falls on a syllable with a short vowel (particularly if followed by voiceless consonants) and there is a following syllable onto which to spread the tune, the movement from the accent is more likely to be realised as a jump, e.g.

Patty

But such realisations are not obligatory and a speaker can, if he so chooses, use jumps on long vowels and glides on short vowels. In general the use of a jump where a glide might be expected sounds 'abrupt'; whereas the use of a glide where a jump might be expected sounds 'soothing' or 'reproachful', cf.

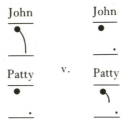

It is very likely that at least some of the distinctive intonational effects of particular languages and dialects are produced by preferences for jumps or glides (e.g. while English generally prefers glides, German prefers jumps). The reader might also like to refer to chapter 4, sub-section 4.4.4.3 where 'stylised' tones are described, which involve a sequence of two elongated levels, e.g.

Patty

In addition to differences of meaning which are produced by varying the width of the accent range on individual pitch accents, certain types of meaning can also be signalled by the overall width of pitch range of intonation-groups (once again differences in width will be signalled principally by differences at the top end). These sorts of differences are sometimes referred to as differences of KEY. They very often signal cohesion between intonation-groups. It is well-known, for example, that B.B.C. newsreaders indicate news 'paratones' (i.e. the spoken equivalent of paragraphs) in this way. The first intonation-group in the paratone will be wide, the last intonation-group will be narrow, and there will be a general narrowing of each group in between. The narrowing may of course be momentarily upset because of some local meaning demanding a wide accent range on an individual pitch accent, but the general tendency will remain clear.

Another type of modification which may affect longer stretches of utterances is variation in the height of the pitch range. This involves the overall shifting of the whole pitch range within which a speaker is speaking (i.e. both highest and lowest levels are moved upward or downward) and is, at least in principle, independent of pitch range width. Of course, some speakers always have a higher voice than others, but we are here talking of individual speakers moving their voice to a higher or lower REGISTER. Once again it is upwards that the register usually moves, because there is more unused pitch range available there. Such shifts are most frequently used for emotional or social reasons. Speakers may speak in a higher register when they are angry (this is often combined with extra loudness). In many languages (e.g. Tamil), a higher pitch than usual is associated with deference. If men speak with a 'high voice' they may be considered to be acting like women or children and hence subserviently. (For more detail on the meanings signalled by KEY and REGISTER, see chapter 4, section 4.5.)

3.6   **Whole tunes and nuclear tones**

This chapter is essentially concerned with setting up the units and variables within which the uses and meanings of intonation can best be described. So far, we have divided connected speech into INTONATION-GROUPS (which, as we shall see in chapter 4, very frequently coincide with major syntactic constituents); within each intonation-group we have a number of PITCH ACCENTS (which indicate prominent syllables and hence prominent words); among the pitch accents in an intonation-group, one is considered the NUCLEUS (indicating the most prominent syllable and hence most prominent word); pitch accents are indicated by an obtrusion of the pitch on one syllable from the pitch on surrounding syllables and the extent of such an obtrusion is varied by ACCENT RANGE (to give extra emphasis); the width of pitch range over whole intonation-groups is varied by KEY (principally for discoursal purposes) and the height of pitch range over whole intonation-groups is varied by REGISTER (principally for social and emotional purposes). Finally in this section we come to that part of pitch variation which is most central to intonation, namely the use of various pitch contours or 'tunes'. At this point I have to spend some space in justifying the sort of analysis I shall prefer. Section 3.3 above gave some explanation for the use of a descriptive framework that was formulated in terms of pitch contours rather than in terms of pitch levels.

But an even knottier problem concerns the syntagmatic divisions which are best fitted to the study of intonation. Some examples will be necessary to illustrate the various alternatives:

Why did you do that?

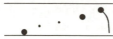

This example has a primary accent (pitch accent which is the nucleus) on *that*, a secondary accent (pitch accent which is not the nucleus) on *Why* and a tertiary stress (dependent on length and/or loudness alone) on *do*. One possible way of describing the meanings of tunes within intonation-groups is to describe 'whole tunes', that is, the contours produced by joining all the accents together. The pitch pattern in the example above has been called the 'surprise/redundancy' contour, because it is an overall contour which implies either that the speaker is surprised or that what the addressee has done is in some way unnecessary (actually this does not account for all the meanings of the contour but that is not relevant at the moment). Almost all intonational analysts agree that, at least for English and probably for most other languages, an analysis purely in terms of whole tunes fails because it misses important generalisations dependent on the occurrence of similar tones starting from the nucleus. Compared with the above example, a similar meaning could be conveyed by the following even though the overall pitch pattern is different:

Why did you have to do that?

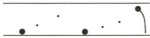

It might be contended that this is essentially the same contour with one part repeated, but this begs the question which asks 'within what domain does such variation or repetition occur?' Let us consider another example:

He hasn't gone

Here the pattern preceding the nucleus is more clearly different from that in the preceding examples; nevertheless, although the intonational meaning conveyed by the pattern (in this and other examples) is slightly different from that used with *Why did you do that?* above, a certain similarity of meaning remains because of the occurrence in each case of a wide fall (one on *that* and the other on *gone*) at the end. This similarity is clearly apparent if we compare the same sentence said with tones which rise from the nucleus:

Why did you have to do that?

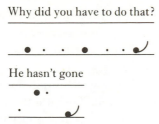

He hasn't gone

Both the sentences are gentler and more tentative when said with a rise than when said with a fall. What I am arguing is that the contour following the nucleus always carries the most important part of the intonational meaning of an intonation-group. This sort of assumption has been inherent in a long tradition of intonational analysis in Britain and is now implicitly accepted by much recent work in the U.S. (although some would wish to retain 'whole tunes' for some particular configurations like the 'surprise/redundancy' contour above). The relation between the contour following the nucleus (the 'nuclear tone') and what precedes is rather like the distinction between a stem morph and a prefix where the core meaning is carried by the stem and the effect of the prefix is to modify in some way the core meaning of the stem.

The previous paragraph has argued for describing the pitch patterns of intonation-groups by dividing them up into what precedes, and what starts at and follows the nucleus (the 'pre-nuclear tune' and the 'nuclear tone'). As has already been mentioned when discussing the question of contours versus levels, some analysts would wish to make a further division within the 'nuclear tone' by taking off the 'terminal' movements and describing them separately. Thus *Johnny* and *Johnny* would have a falling (or low) and a rising (or high) terminal respectively. As I have argued in 3.3 above, terminals are generally only significant where they reverse the direction of the preceding pitch, as in the second example. Terminals also obscure the similarity between certain patterns, cf.

Unfortunately   John didn't do it

In these two examples a terminal rise could be said to occur on -*ly*, but there is certainly no terminal pitch movement on *it* even though many analyses might mark a rising terminal. An analysis which ascribes a high (rather than rising) terminal in each case certainly fits the tonetic facts better but it still misses the essential similarity between the two examples which exists in the fact of the rise on unstressed *-ly* in one case and the rise between *do* and *it* in the other. So the last pitch movement is certainly important but it need not be 'terminal', i.e. it need not occur actually on the last syllable of the intonation-group.

I shall from now on talk of NUCLEAR TONES which begin on the nucleus and cover the stretch of utterances up to the end of an intonation-group. Remember that the nucleus is usually the last pitch accent (with certain exceptions discussed in section 3.4 above). A nuclear tone involves the major part of the meaning contributed by the pitch pattern of an intonation-group; this meaning may to some extent be modified by any pitch accents preceding the nucleus. In the next section I shall outline the ways in which we establish the number and shape of the nuclear tones operating in English, at the same time illustrating the use of the 'tonetic-stress' marking system, i.e. the system of shorthand marks which indicate the presence of stresses on the syllables marked and at the same time indicate the pitch movements following them (or 'tonetics'). This system will allow us to dispense with the somewhat cumbersome 'interlinear tonetic' transcriptions used so far in this book.

3.7   English nuclear tones

Three basic factors are involved in a taxonomy of nuclear tones in English (and almost certainly in similar classifications in all 'intonation languages' – see chapter 1, section 1.5):

(i)   the initial movement from the nucleus: fall or rise or level
(ii)   the beginning point of this initial movement: high or low; if there are syllables preceding the nucleus, a step-up will often signal high and a step-down will often signal low
(iii)   a second change of pitch direction following the nucleus: this produces complex tones such as rise-fall and fall-rise (and even rise-fall-rise).

If we permuted all possible combinations of these three basic factors, a very large number of nuclear tones would result, so in practice we limit ourselves to describing just those variations which most obviously carry major difference of meaning. This is an area where almost every analyst varies in his judgement of what constitutes a 'major difference of meaning' and hence in the number of nuclear tones which are set up. Nor are the arguments for any one particular set of nuclear tones ever very convincing or indeed explicit; in fact, given that intonational meanings are often so intangible and nebulous, it is difficult to see how a wholly convincing case for any one set of nuclear tones can be made. So the set of nuclear tones which I establish should not be regarded as 'God's truth'. In discussing the meanings associated with tones in the next chapter (with particular reference to R.P. and G.A.), I shall, by a combination of criteria (i) and (ii) above, distinguish between high-fall and low-fall and between high-rise and low-rise (indicated in tonetic-stress marking by ˋO and ˎO and ˊO and ˏO), e.g.

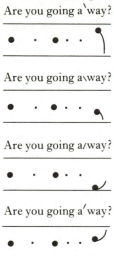

Are you going aˋway?

Are you going aˎway?

Are you going aˊway?

Are you going aˊway?

Notice that all four nuclear tones are quite possible on this yes/no question: there is no such thing as 'question intonation' although some tones may be more common on questions than others. The high-falling and low-falling tones both have rather 'serious' overtones, the higher tone being more 'involved' and the lower tone more 'business-like'; whereas the rising tones are altogether 'lighter' tones, the high-rising tone being the most casual. The high-rising tone on this sort of question is much more frequent in American English than in British English, which is one reason why Americans sound casual to the British; whereas the prevalence of the low-rising tone in British English is one reason why the British sound formal to Americans. The distinctions between high and low varieties of tones are of course not so clear when no syllables precede the nucleus, e.g.

ˋJohn   ˎJohn   ˊJohn   ˏJohn

In the case of the two falls the isolated forms seem to represent a pure gradient in form and meaning between a very narrow fall and a very wide fall, and indeed this is precisely how some analysts have viewed the matter (see further in chapter 4, sub-section 4.4.4.1). However, I myself prefer to set up the distinction on the basis of the clear-cut cases involving steps-up and steps-down. In the case of the two rises the distinction between high-rise and low-rise seems to be carried as much by the finishing-point as the starting-point: high-rises typically end at a very high pitch where the voice becomes 'squeaky' and this characteristic keeps the two tones apart even in isolation. Indeed this diagnostic value of squeaky voice contributes to a quite different problem, which is illustrated by the following intonation:

Are you going away?

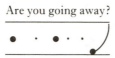

This has sometimes been called a 'full-rise'; it has the step-down and low starting-point of the low-rise but the high-pitched ending of the high-rise. By the basic criteria in (i) to (iii) above, it would be considered a low-rise (with a wide accent range as discussed in section 3.5 above); however, its squeaky ending seems to place it semantically with the high-rise. Again, analysts have differed in their solutions, some equating the pattern with low-rise, some with high-rise, and some setting up a third category. I prefer the solution which equates the pattern with the high-rise, since my judgement is that the above example with the full-rise is indeed closer semantically to the high-rise (and forced association tests carried out on adult listeners produce this result). So in this case a fourth factor has been introduced in the establishment of nuclear tones, i.e. the finishing-point. This was not initially mentioned because it is not regularly as important in English as the three basic factors mentioned.

The basic factors (ii) and (iii) lead us to hypothesise that there are also two bidirectional tunes, the fall-rise and the rise-fall, illustrated in the following examples (tonetic-stress marks being ᵛO and ^O):

I go there ᵛusually   He got a dis^tinction

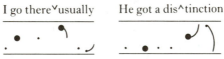

The fall-rise is sometimes even realised as a rise-fall-rise (although I shall not set this up as a separate nuclear tone because the meanings associated with it are not sufficiently distinctive), e.g.

I go there usually

In the examples of fall-rise and rise-fall above the change of direction within the nuclear tone is not taken as an accent because it occurs on a lexically unstressed syllable. In many cases the unstressed syllable will have a reduced vowel as in the example on *-tion* above. But the fall-rise tone has many forms, another common one being a sequence of two pitch accents, where the first (falling) accent is the nucleus and the second (rising) accent is downgraded (discussed more fully in section 3.4 above), e.g.

But 'I didn't fail the e/xam

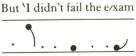

In this example the fall-rise has been marked with two tonetic-stress marks, indicting a 'split' fall-rise. This indicates clearly where both the accents occur. But the 'split' fall-rise does present another problem in that two distinct meanings are often involved, one of which does equate with the simple fall-rise and one of which does not. The point is illustrated by the following pair:

   I 'thought she was / married (and so she was!)
   I 'thought she was / married (although I wasn't certain and it turns out she wasn't)

I shall return to this problem when discussing the meanings of tones in chapter 4. For the moment, before leaving fall-rise and rise-fall, notice that I have not made distinctions between high and low varieties (dependent on steps-up and steps-down). Once again, the semantic differences do not justify it, at least at the level of delicacy which the present set of nuclear tones is aiming at.

So far I have set up six nuclear tones for English, all of which are 'moving' tones. But level nuclei can also occur, i.e. where the pitch accent is purely dependent on a step-up or a step-down. The choice between a step-up and a step-down does not itself seem to be significant, and the most common level is mid (this level tone being indicated by >), e.g.

When I went to > Africa . . . . .

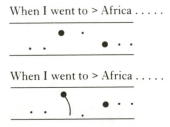

When I went to > Africa . . . . .

In the first example, the mid-level is approached from above; in the second it is approached from below. Yet the difference between the two examples seems to be carried by the difference in the first pitch accent, the extra movement down-from (in addition to step-up) in the second example giving the clause a more 'weighty' air.

I shall from now on (and mainly in chapter 4) principally refer to seven nuclear tones in English and use the tonetic-stress marks shown above. This is not to say that finer distinctions could not be made, but seven tones will suffice for the usual level of delicacy that is required. Where more subtle distinctions are occasionally required, or where other distinctions are needed for other languages, I shall revert to interlinear tonetic transcriptions.

3.8 Pre-nuclear pitch accents

Pre-nuclear pitch accents (which are by definition accents which are non-final in intonation-groups) will generally serve only to modify the meaning conveyed by the nuclear tone. A very common type of pre-nuclear pitch accent is level, and a common sequence of such accents will involve an initial step-up followed by a number of steps-down, e.g.

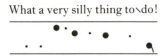

Particular sequences of pre-nuclear pitch accents are sometimes referred to as 'heads' (the example above is said to have a 'stepping head'), and in books which principally contain lots of practice material for students of English as a foreign language a further set of tonetic-stress marks are used to mark different sorts of head. As my purpose is different and as I shall not be dealing with pre-nuclear pitch accents in any great detail, I will not use the extra tonetic-stress marks. It is, however, worth illustrating some typical uses of pitch accents in pre-nuclear position:

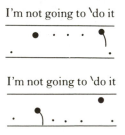

The first example above has a pre-nuclear step-up and level whereas the second example has step-up and additionally movement down-from. Pitch accents of the latter type are generally more emphatic. Pre-nuclear accents may also be low:

I don't think he⁄has

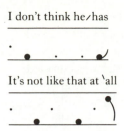

It's not like that at ˋall

Here the accent on *don't* is achieved by producing the first syllable *I* on a high pitch, thus 'making room' for a step-down. In the last example there is movement up-from indicating accents on *not* and *that*. Low-pitched accents have been called 'reversed accents' and their effect in pre-nuclear position is often that of a deliberate 'playing-down'; in particular, such accents will enhance by contrast the effect of a final high-pitched falling accent. I said at the beginning of this section that pre-nuclear pitch accents generally only modify the meaning associated with the nuclear tone. This sort of modification is at its greatest before a final low-rise; although a final low-rise always has the effect of 'something more to come' or 'something more to happen', there is a 'grumbling' overtone when no high pitch accent precedes whereas there is a 'soothing' overtone when a high pitch accent does precede the nucleus, e.g.

You needn't go a⁄way

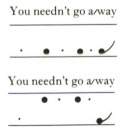

You needn't go a⁄way

But generally the modifications produced by pre-nuclear pitch accents are less marked than in this example. Preferences for different types of pre-nuclear pitch accent are characteristic of particular languages; English, for example, uses rising movements (i.e. movements up-from) rather rarely, whereas in Danish they seem to be the most common pattern.

3.8.1   Autosegmental intonation

In section 3.3, I compared an approach to tonal patterns in terms of contours with an approach involving four pitch levels. We saw that one of the major difficulties associated with four pitch levels was the confounding effect of the various distinctions of pitch range, i.e. those of accent range (whereby the width of the tone following an individual pitch accent is varied), key (whereby the range-width of a whole intonation-group is varied) and register (whereby the pitch range of a whole intonation-group is higher or lower, while the width remains constant). Recent work on intonation has begun to explore the possibility of giving a formal description of English intonation with the use of only two level tones, High (H) and Low (L), allowing for independent variation in the various dimensions of pitch range, and with a number of tonetic rules specifying the inter-actions between tones in sequence (for exemplification see later in this section and section 3.9 *in toto*).

Another criticism of the four pitch levels approach was that there was generally no explicit description of how the transition from one level to another was accomplished. For example, in

⁴John didn't do it¹#

most four-level descriptions did not show precisely how the fall from 4 to 1 was projected onto the sequence of syllables and segments. On the other hand, some of the textbooks using contour nuclear tones do give explicit descriptions of how such tones are realised, e.g. the rising part of a fall-rise tone is said to occur from the last stressed syllable following the nucleus or on the last unstressed syllable in the absence of a stressed syllable following the nucleus (e.g. the rise occurs between *pla-* and *-ces* on *In ˇsome places* whereas it occurs on *-ly* in *Unˇfortunately*).

However, the development of autosegmental phonology has shown that this sort of detailed specification of how a tone spreads over texts of varying length can be accomplished just as well, and sometimes even better, using a description in terms of levels together with explicit mapping rules. Auto-segmental phonology was first developed to provide mapping rules for African tone languages to show how any typical sequence of underlying level tones was mapped onto words and phrases of varying length. The segmental sequence constitutes one tier of language description and the tones a second tier of description. Rules which amalgamate the two tiers are called 'tune-text association rules'. Such tune-text association rules are now being applied to intonational representation.

So two developments come together in much recent formal (non-semantic) work on intonation: the re-analysis of contour tones into particular sequences of Highs and Lows and the explicit description of how such sequences are mapped onto various texts. So, for example, high-fall and low-fall are both $\overset{*}{\text{H}}$L (with a difference of range), fall-rise is $\overset{*}{\text{H}}$LH, low-rise and high-rise are $\overset{*}{\text{L}}$H (again with a difference of range), and rise-fall

is $\overset{*}{L}HL$ (although this last tone is often analysed as $\overset{*}{H}L$ plus a feature
of 'delay' – see chapter 4, sub-section 4.4.4.2). The asterisks (or stars)
indicate the level tones with which stressed syllables on the segmental
tier are to be associated. For example, *In sŏme places* and *Unfortunately*
would occur on the segmental tier with stressed syllables assigned (or,
more correctly, with degrees of stress assigned, probably by some version
of metrical phonology) and marked with a star. When $\overset{*}{H}LH$ is mapped
onto these phrases, the star on one tier is associated with the star on the
other tier and hence primary stress is associated with the level tone at
the beginning of a tonal sequence. A spreading convention (such rules
generally only apply to unstarred tones) would indicate that the L of HLH
spreads to the right to the last stressed syllable, or to the last unstressed
syllable in the absence of any stressed syllable. A formal autosegmental
representation would look like this:

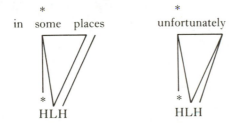

A major advantage of such autosegmental representations is that they
present various possibilities for capturing similarities between nuclear
accents and pre-nuclear accents. As was stated in the last section, a typical
approach to pre-nuclear pitch patterns within the nuclear tone approach
often involves the proliferation of many types of 'head', varying in number
in different analyses at least between three and eight. In fact it appears
that, in terms of semantic effect, the most important distinction in pre-
nuclear patterns is between the presence or absence of a high pitch accent.
In an autosegmental description nearly all Highs in pre-nuclear position
can be taken as basically the same underlying tone with varying transitions
to the following pitch accent. Gussenhoven (1983b:66) formulates an
optional Tone-Linking Rule which can account for three variations on
an initial High:

$$\text{Tone Linking } T(T)\overset{*}{T}\underset{\raise4pt\hbox{$\overset{\displaystyle\downarrow}{\emptyset}$}}{\longrightarrow}\overset{*}{T} \qquad (T = \text{any (level) tone})$$

If we apply this tone-linking rule to an $\overset{*}{H}L$ in pre-nuclear position (preceding another $\overset{*}{H}L$ in nuclear position), three variants are produced:

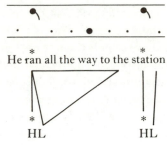

This variant has not had the tone-linking rule applied and H̊L is fully realised following both accents. The first L tone occurs on the same syllable as the preceding H̊ because of the length of voicing associated with the syllable *ran*, whereas the second L is not associated with *sta-* along with the preceding H̊ because *sta-* has a relatively shorter period of voicing. The first L spreads to the right because of the convention that an L will spread to the right between two H's (as it did in H̊LH in the earlier examples).

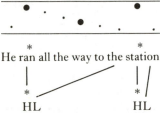

Here the tone-linking rule is partially applied: the L of the first H̊L is 'moved' to the right: the intervening syllables then (by convention) form a straight line between the H̊ and the L.

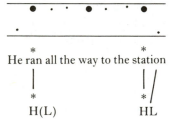

Here the tone-linking rule is fully applied: the L is not only moved to the right but deleted altogether.

There is a fourth way in which this sentence may be intoned:

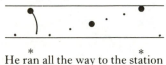

Semantically the uses and meanings associated with this sequence are more akin to fall-rise plus fall than to fall plus fall (it is, for example, a regular variant of a fully realised fall-rise on initial sentence adverbials and involves what has been labelled 'intonational sandhi' in sub-section 3.2.4 above and chapter 4, sub-section 4.3.1 below). This pattern therefore seems to be best regarded as a variant of pre-nuclear H̊LH before a nuclear H̊L.

The examples above show how tonal mapping rules can account for regularities in tune-text associations and how optional rules can bring together sets of variations which have something semantically in common. (i) to (iii) above have something in common which (iv) does not share: the pre-nuclear accent is semantically more subordinated to the nuclear accent in (iv) than in (i)–(iii) which indeed one would expect if it is to be taken as a fall-rise.

The next section will present a slightly different and more fully developed type of description in terms of only two tones, together with more complicated rules for tones in sequence. The ideas that have been presented briefly in this section and the model which is presented in more detail in the next section are together the beginnings of a theory of generative intonation.

3.9   Generative intonation

At the very end of chapter 2 we discussed two generative formulations of rules for English stress (that of Chomsky and Halle and that of Liberman and Prince). A major reason for discussing such formulations was that the generation of patterns of sentence-stress is taken as a necessary prerequisite for the generation of intonation patterns. As mentioned in chapter 2, it seems likely that explicit models for the generation of intonation will become a major focus of attention in the next decade; the model presented by Pierrehumbert (1980) is a first attempt at such a model (for English) and is already influential. I therefore spend the final section of this chapter giving an outline of this model.

The basic input to this model is firstly an LP-type metrical representation of the text (which indicates which syllables are stressed and which are unstressed) and secondly a tune represented by a sequence of high (H) and low (L) tones. This model takes no detailed account of the meanings of tunes. The model is concerned (i) with the tunes which occur in English and how they can be represented as a sequence of Hs and Ls and (ii) how tunes are variously mapped onto texts of varying length and make-up. Or, putting it in terms familiar in other parts of grammar, the model constructs an underlying representation for the tunes of English intonation and a set of rules which transmutes such tunes into actual patterns of fundamental frequency.

Each intonational phrase consists of a sequence of H and L tones. Each phrase involves H and L tones of three types: firstly, one or more pitch accents realised by a single tone (marked H* and L*) or bitonally (marked H⁻+L*, L*+H⁻, H*+L⁻, L⁻+H* and H*+H⁻ – starred tones indicating the centre of the accent and L⁻ and H⁻ indicating 'leading' or 'trailing' tones); secondly, a phrase accent (also marked L⁻ or H⁻) near the end of the word which contains the last pitch accent; and thirdly, a boundary tone on the very last syllable (marked L% or H%). The phrase accent takes care of any movement immediately following the last pitch accent and the boundary tone takes care of any movement on the final syllable. Neither phrase accents nor boundary tones can be bitonal. Phrase accents and boundary tones need not align with syllables marked *s*, but pitch accents may only occur on syllables marked *s* in the metrical representation of the input (see chapter 2, section 2.6) and the nuclear pitch accent (=last pitch accent) will align with the designated terminal element (DTE) of the phrase (= intonation-group), i.e. that *s* which is dominated by no *w*'s. I now discuss a number of examples to give a flavour of this type of representation:

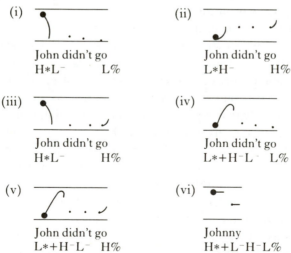

(i)   John didn't go   H*L⁻   L%

(ii)   John didn't go   L*H⁻   H%

(iii)   John didn't go   H*L⁻   H%

(iv)   John didn't go   L*+H⁻L⁻   L%

(v)   John didn't go   L*+H⁻L⁻   H%

(vi)   Johnny   H*+L⁻H⁻L%

These six examples are representations of tunes following the last pitch accent, i.e. they represent what I have been calling nuclear tones. In (i) the pitch accent on *John* is H* and the following phrase accent is L⁻, producing a fall between the two and the boundary tone continues the final downward movement. In (ii) the pitch accent on *John* is L∗, the following phrase accent is H⁻ and the boundary tone H% produces the final upward kick. (iii) is similar to (i) except that H% replaces L% and so the fall becomes a fall-rise. In (iv) the pitch accent is bitonal, its centre being low and its 'trail' being high; a low phrase accent then follows (giving an overall rising-falling contour). (v) is similar to (iv) except that the contour now becomes rising-falling-rising by the addition of an H% boundary tone. (vi) shows the representation of a common, so-called 'stylised', contour consisting of a high-level followed by a mid-level (often used as a calling tune – see chapter 4, sub-section 4.4.4.3). This representation is a little more complicated. First there is a high centre to the pitch accent. This is followed by an L⁻ 'trail'. However this L⁻ following a preceding H∗ is interpreted by rule as lowering a following H before being itself deleted (for those familiar with descriptions of downstep in African tone languages this mode of representation will be very familiar). The final L% simply indicates that there is no rise in pitch, the phrase accent H⁻ remaining level.

Pitch accents in pre-nuclear positions make use of the same inventory of accents as those in nuclear positions. Some more examples follow:

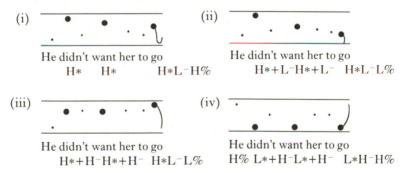

(i) He didn't want her to go
     H∗   H∗   H∗L⁻H%

(ii) He didn't want her to go
     H∗+L⁻H∗+L⁻ H∗L⁻L%

(iii) He didn't want her to go
      H∗+H⁻H∗+H⁻ H∗L⁻L%

(iv) He didn't want her to go
     H% L∗+H⁻L∗+H⁻ L∗H⁻H%

In (i) we have a succession of H∗'s: the convention for any sequence of H∗'s is that unstressed syllables in between will dip. In (ii) we also have a dip in the unstressed syllables of a sequence of H∗+L⁻'s, but the H∗'s themselves step down when compared with preceding H∗'s; Pierrehumbert's rules here state that a trailing L⁻ tone is present in the underlying representation and has the effect of lowering a following H before being itself deleted (as exemplified also in (vi) in the first set of examples). On the other hand, sometimes the H∗'s are maintained on the same level and any syllables in between do not dip; this is regarded as an H∗+H⁻ sequence as in (iii). Example (iv) shows a sequence of L∗+H⁻ tones in pre-nuclear position; if the syllables following the L∗'s had remained on the same level, we would have had merely a succession of simple L*'s. Notice the use of H% in this example as an initial rather than a final boundary tone; this use represents what in other analyses have been called 'high pre-heads'. Generally, H% in either initial or final position indicates a high excursion whereas L% indicates continuation of a level or a falling contour.

Pitch movement between tones is accounted for by phonetic rules for interpolating between tones. Unaccented syllables between accents will sometimes take the direct line between the two, e.g. where an H* follows an L* as in:

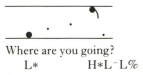

Where are you going?
    L*   H*L⁻L%

In other cases they will descend towards the baseline, as in the succession of H*'s in (i) above. But we also had the case in (iii) above where the trailing H⁻ maintained the high pitch; this was a case of 'tonal spreading'. Only L⁻ and H⁻ (trailing tones and phrase accents) can undergo spreading. The most common examples of this phenomenon involve L⁻ and H⁻ spreading before H%, as in (ii) and (iii) in the first set of examples above, which I recapitulate:

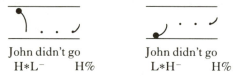

John didn't go   John didn't go
H*L⁻   H%   L*H⁻   H%

L⁻ spreads in the first example before the final rise; H⁻ spreads in the second example before the final upward kick of the H%.

If the terminal H% in the first example above is replaced by the low terminal L%, not only would the final rise not be present but the three syllables of *didn't go* would form a gradually descending sequence. This would be the result of 'baseline declination'. The 'baseline' is a construct which, most of the time, is only **inferable** from the values of tones; only L% following L⁻ at the end of an intonational phrase is necessarily on the baseline, although unaccented syllables at the beginning of a phrase may often be on the baseline. Pitch accents L* and H* represent deviations below and above this hypothetical baseline. How far each accent deviates from the baseline depends on 'prominence', that is the degree of emphasis given to each tone. Pierrehumbert suggests that 'prominence' (i.e. deviation from the baseline) is computed in 'baseline units' which become smaller as the intonational phrase proceeds. Thus not only does the baseline itself decline but equally prominent accents will be less distant from the baseline as the phrase proceeds. So a succession of equally prominent H∗'s can be diagrammed as follows:

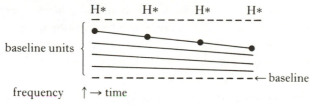

The H∗+L⁻ accent, which was to be interpreted as lowering a succeeding H∗ with subsequent deletion of L⁻, represents H∗'s which are downstepped beyond that implied by normal declination. L∗'s deviate below the baseline in similar fashion to H∗'s above the baseline although in a less obvious way because they are subject to the limitation of the bottom limit of a speaker's voice. (Remember that speakers tend to use only the bottom third of their potential pitch range.) The values of L⁻ and H⁻ depend only in part on the baseline, depending also on the actual phonetic values (i.e. the 'prominence') of the pitch accents to which they are attached. Baseline resetting normally takes place as the beginning of each new intonational phrase.

The very brief summary above does not do justice to the detail and explicitness with which Pierrehumbert puts forward her model, but it perhaps displays enough of its main tenets to enable some of the general issues raised by it to be discussed. Firstly, it follows American tradition and describes intonation in terms of levels rather than glides. But, as the author rightly points out, it avoids a lot of the problems encountered by previous descriptions in terms of levels (see section 3.3 above) by having only two levels. The actual height of any H or L is computed by reference to three things: its relationship to the baseline, the degree of prominence which the speaker opts to give it, and its relationship to preceding tones. (The model is in fact a finite-state model whereby any one tune is implemented with reference to what has preceded but not with reference to what follows.) By being context-sensitive in these various ways this model avoids many of the difficulties associated with previous descriptions based on levels. However, there are problems with Pierrehumbert's model. Firstly, the model involves the decomposition of what I have called 'nuclear tones' into sequences of pitch accent plus phrase accent plus boundary tone. The term 'phrase accent' is an odd terminological usage since no accent is involved additional to that identified by the preceding pitch accent; the term 'phrase tone' would seem more appropriate. Secondly, by relegating the degree of deviation from the baseline involved in L* and H* to a notion of 'prominence' (which of course might at times be syntactically or semantically predictable but at other times depends purely on speaker choice), the model to some extent pushes a large problem aside, i.e. at some stage the pragmatics of variations in prominence will have to be described. Thirdly, the use of the accent H*+L⁻ as a way of triggering a downstep in a following H* (with the L⁻ then deleted and given no surface realisation) seems unnecessarily abstract when compared with the remainder of the tonal representations. Clearly this sort of analysis was motivated by the occurrence of a downstepped high tone in some African languages where a low tone has in fact often been elided historically. A more consistent relationship would be kept between L in the intonational lexicon and its actual realisation in fundamental frequency if L⁻ were not used abstractly in the representation of downstep. Instead, as Ladd (1983) argues, downstep would be better accounted for by including a feature [+downstep] in addition to H and L (see chapter 4, sub-section 4.4.4.4 below). Lastly, I must repeat what was said at the beginning of this section: that Pierrehumbert's model completely ignores the problem of intonational meaning. It merely attempts to find a system for generating typical contours which occur in English.

Nevertheless, despite various shortcomings, it remains clear that the kind of representation of intonation used in Pierrehumbert (1980) is an important advance in intonational studies. The conversion of nuclear tones into sequences of H's and L's, which, together with various conventions and rules, serve as an algorithm for the generation of fundamental frequency, constitutes a first attempt at the explicit formal representation of the form of intonation.

3.10 Summary and preview

Throughout most of this chapter I have used exemplification from English to illustrate theoretical concepts. Comparative intonation will be dealt with in more detail in chapter 5 but it is worth looking forward a little at this stage and asking whether the theoretical concepts established in this chapter are likely in any sense to be universal. In the present state of knowledge about intonation in different languages, any reply is to some extent speculative. Some notion of INTONATION-GROUP is probably universal; more particularly, some of the characteristics which delimit such groups are likely to be universal, notably pre-boundary lengthening (mentioned in sub-section 3.2.2 above) and declination (suggesting, for example, that low unaccented syllables will commonly be lower at the end of a group than at the beginning). PITCH ACCENTS are a defining feature of intonation languages. (They are also a defining feature of the so-called 'pitch accent languages' – see chapter 1, section 1.7.) The limited evidence available suggests that variations in the pitch range of intonation-groups (KEY and REGISTER) are also universal. The concept of NUCLEUS is universally relevant in the sense that the principal (usually the last) pitch accent together with the following contour of an intonation-group will carry the major part of the intonational meaning. However, the concept of nucleus is less relevant for some languages where the last pitch accent is obligatorily attached to the last stressed syllable in the group (whereas in English the nucleus can fall on any stressed syllable – see chapter 4, section 4.3 and chapter 5, sub-section 5.4.2). But before dealing with comparative intonation, we must first look at the types of meanings conveyed by intonation. This will be the concern of the next chapter.

Sources and further reading

For pauses at constituent boundaries, see Goldman-Eisler (1972); for pauses before words of high lexical content, see Goldman-Eisler (1958); for planning pauses, see Boomer (1965).

For syllables in 'anacrusis', see Jassem (1952).

For final syllable lengthening, see Pike (1945), Oller (1979) and Vaissière (1983).

For intonational sandhi, see Trim (1959).

For the history of the study of English intonation, the most detailed treatment is Cruttenden (1981a). See also Pike (1945), Crystal (1969a), and Ladd (1979b).

For the standard exposition of pitch levels analysis, see Trager and Smith (1951). Pike (1945) also uses pitch levels (in reverse order of numbering with 1 as highest and 4 as lowest) but presents a semantic description in terms of glides ending at certain levels; so it is a sort of hybrid, but more convincing than Trager and Smith (1951), which hardly treats meaning at all.

For proportions of nuclear tones in English, see Davy (1968) and Gussenhoven (1985) (reprinted in Gussenhoven, 1984).

For the standard treatment of pitch accents in English, see Bolinger (1958), but the exposition in this book differs from his considerably, both in the number of types of pitch accent and in their definitions.

For sequences of falls and the judgement of nucleus, see Crystal and Quirk (1964) on 'tonal subordination', and Brown *et al.* (1980).

For a discussion of fall-rises, see Sharp (1958), Ladd (1977), and Gussenhoven (1984: 130–1).

For discussions of perceived prominence in sequences involving a descending series of accents ending with a low-fall, see Cruttenden (1981a) and House (1983).

For key, see Brazil (1975, 1978). For register, see, for example, Brown and Levinson (1978) on Tamil.

For 'whole tunes', see Armstrong and Ward (1926), Jones (1918), and Liberman and Sag (1974), this last especially for the surprise/redundancy contour.

For nuclear tones (and 'heads') in English, see in particular Palmer (1922), Kingdon (1958a), Schubiger (1958) and O'Connor and Arnold (1961, 1973).

For variations on the nuclear approach in which the nucleus becomes the 'tonic' and in which a different system of transcription is used, see Halliday (1967, 1970) and Brazil (1975, 1978).

For autosegmental approaches to intonation, see Leben (1976), and Gussenhoven (1983b).

For the generative model outlined in section 3.9, see Pierrehumbert (1980).

4
The functions of intonation

4.1 Introduction

In this chapter I shall take as the starting-point the formal framework established in chapter 3; in particular the concepts of intonation-group, nucleus, and nuclear tone. Theoretical issues will be discussed, once again mainly with reference to English. There will also be some semi-systematic description of the intonational system of English, more especially that of R.P., although the major part of the description applies to G.A. as well. Comparison with other dialects of English, like those in some northern British cities (which differ considerably from R.P.), will be postponed until chapter 5, as will more detailed consideration of languages other than English and the question of possible universals of intonation.

4.2 Intonation-groups

First to be considered is the question of intonational phrasing, or the way in which intonation-groups align with various portions of utterances. As speakers of English, we can if we wish give every syllable a separate intonation-group, although even for purposes of emphasis this is rare; what we are more likely to do in such circumstances is to begin a new intonation-group at each full-vowelled syllable, e.g.

/de/ /national/ /i/ \sation

But even this sort of phrasing is not common. Much more commonly, intonation-groups align with larger **syntactic** constituents, as in the following piece of transcription (only nuclear tones are marked, in line with the view presented in the last chapter, section 3.8, that pre-nuclear tunes are semantically less important):

> Most extra\ordinary / that Sandra Wheeler should have \asked that
> /question / because a \friend of /mine / actually suffers from a\cute
> absent-/mindedness / and he went to the \doctor / the doctor \told

me about it / he went to the \doctor / he said can you cure my
absent-\mindedness / and he said well when did you first \notice
it / and he said notice \what / Let's have another \question/

Most commonly of all (on 40% of occasions by one count) intonation-
groups correspond with clauses (using a traditional definition of clause
involving the occurrence of a finite verb in a surface structure). The clause
may be just a simple sentence (e.g. *Let's have another question* in the
above extract) or may be part of a compound or a complex sentence,
e.g.

He ran to the ⁄station / and caught the \train
Because he ran to the ⁄station / he \caught the train

But on many occasions intonation-groups correspond with something less
than a clause. They very often correspond with adverbials which are modifying a whole clause. Such adverbials include those labelled message-
attitudinal (e.g. *unfortunately*), message-likelihood (e.g. *obviously*), viewpoint (e.g. *officially*), speaker/listener-oriented (e.g. *seriously*), style (e.g.
briefly), validity (e.g. *broadly*), contingency (e.g. *nevertheless*) and con-
junctional (e.g. *incidentally*). Time and place adverbials (particularly in
clause-initial position), although by most classifications not regarded as
modifying a whole clause, are also frequently treated in the same way.
Here are some examples of various clause-modifying adverbials:

In \some ⁄cases / the in\ducements handed out to ⁄industry/.....
A∨pparently / from all the \evidence we ⁄get/.....
During the last four ∨years / private ∨enterprise / in the United
∨Kingdom/.....
> Therefore / because of ⁄this / and \other important ⁄evidence/.....
∨Seriously / it seems to ∨me / that the \crucial ⁄issue
Sur∨prisingly / he \passed the exam.....
Un∨fortunately / he hadn't much ex\perience at that sort of thing.....

All these examples have the adverbial in initial position and indeed this
is the most common position for this sort of modifier, but they certainly
occur in other positions, although less commonly; and in these other positions they again have the possibility of a separate intonation-group, e.g.

Richard has re\signed / o∨fficially
That \nursery / inci⁄dentally / grows very fine to\matoes

It should not be imagined that clause-modifying adverbials must have
a separate intonation-group; merely that they very commonly do. In very
general terms, it depends how prominent the speaker wishes the modification to be (see further discussion in sub-section 4.3.1 below).

One very common situation in which a clause modifier is given a separate group is where the remainder of the clause is itself subdivided into more than one intonation-group. Notice that this applies to the first five examples of clause modifiers given above. The earlier text illustrates another very common type of correlation between an intonation-group and something less than a clause: a correlation with a noun-phrase subject. Here are some more examples of this:

> A ˋfriend of ˏmine / actually suffers from a ˋcute absent-mindedness
> Mr. ˏWhite / wants to ˏknow / whether you would welcome an end
> to the ˏmyth / that private ˇenterprise / is always eˇfficient / and
> public ˏownership / means ˋinefficiency
> The first man on the ˏmoon / was Neil ˋArmstrong

Separate groups for subjects in this way are more typical of prepared and unprepared speeches, and reading, than they are of highly interactive conversations, although they certainly occur even in this register, e.g. in A's response below:

A.   I'm picking a few ˇroses / for that table in the main ˋentrance
B.   Always looks ˋlovely / / ˏthat does
A.   ˋMm. / One or two of the ˇbig ones / have ˋdropped

Separate groups for subjects seem common under two circumstances: firstly, where the noun-phrase subject is long, particularly where post-modification is involved; and secondly, where the subject is 'topicalised'. The subject of a clause is most usually the topic (or theme) of the clause, while the remainder is usually the comment (or rheme). So when I say that the subject is 'topicalised' it means that the topical nature of the subject is emphasised. Sometimes the purpose of this emphasis is obviously contrastive, as in the example above about private enterprise and public ownership.

Topicalisation also concerns other cases involving separate groups. The subject (topic) of a clause may be recapitulated or enlarged at the end of the clause, e.g.

> He behaved very ˋwell / ˏJohn did

These sorts of examples frequently involve omission of the subject before the verb and so can alternatively be regarded as 'moved' by a transformational analysis, e.g.

> Very ˋfattening / ˏbiscuits / ˋaren't they?
> (cf. Very ˋfattening biscuits / ˋaren't they?)

The object of a clause can also be fronted and topicalised, e.g.

> Well I like ˇher / but her ˇhusband / I can't ˋstand

Similarly, in passive clauses an agentive *by* phrase following the verb is commonly given a separate group, especially if post-modified, e.g.

> The murderer was ˋfinally arˊrested / would you beˊlieve it /by a man making a citizen's aˋrrest

Notice too that in the example about fattening biscuits above the tag at the end of the utterance is given a separate group. Most occurrences of tags do involve separate groups (with a choice between a rising or a falling tone – this is dealt with in sub-section 4.4.1 below).

A number of other grammatical structures which are parenthetical in nature commonly involve a separate intonation-group. Parenthetical clauses themselves will, of course, generally have a separate group, e.g.

> The ˋfact ˊis / and there are now books and articles ˋon ˊthis / the ˋfact ˊis / that an increase . . . . .

Other parenthetical structures commonly given separate groups are vocatives (particularly in initial position) and nouns in apposition (including appositive clauses as in the last example above), e.g.

> ˅Johnny / will you just shut ˋup
> Mr. ˅Green / the ˅butcher / 's become the new chairman of the Parent-ˋTeachers Association

In the latter example, involving apposition, notice that the tone on the noun in apposition is the same as the tone of the head noun. This is a regular instance of tonal harmony. Besides being one type of parenthetical structure, apposition might also be regarded as a type of structural parallelism, which is itself another frequent source of separate group assignment, e.g.

> . . . . . but above ˃all / in formal sessions at ˃Downing Street / in long private ˃talks / right through the ˃evening / lasting far into the ˃night / we discussed the problem . . . . .

In this example there are firstly two parallel locational phrases and then two parallel temporal phrases. Such parallelism is particularly characteristic of highly rhetorical public speaking, e.g.

> . . . . . tonight I'm ˃speaking to you / against a background of renewed ˋfighting / of aerial and naval bomˋbardments / of pitched ˃battles / and murderous guerilla ˋwarfare / of the slaughter of brother by ˋbrother / . . . . .

All the examples of separate intonation-groups so far quoted have involved cases where the group corresponded with a clause or with something less than a clause. But in some cases an intonation-group may encompass two clauses. This is particularly likely when both clauses are short; specific cases often involve a reporting clause followed by a reported clause or a conditioned clause followed by conditional clause, e.g.

> He said he couldn't ˋcome
> I will if I ˋcan

In some complex sentences involving embedding, an intonation-group boundary may be optionally shifted around a grammatical item (see section 4.3.1 below), particularly the verb *be*, cf.

> What I ˇwant / is a chance to ˋtry
> What I wantˇ is / a chance to ˋtry

It should by now be clear that there is a good deal of flexibility in the choice of intonational phrasing. Intonation-groups correspond with clauses more frequently than with any other grammatical unit. Correspondences with units smaller than a clause are most commonly with clause modifiers, with 'topicalised' items, and with parenthetical remarks. This is not to say that groups may not correspond with other units; under special conditions they may correspond with any grammatical unit – even with syllables (as illustrated at the beginning of this section). For example, while the noun-phrase subject of a clause is often given a separate intonation-group, a noun-phrase object or complement very rarely receives a separate group (unless of course it is fronted to the clause-initial position and hence 'topicalised'). But where there is a type of structural parallelism involving coordination, noun-phrase objects or complements may be 'remaindered' and hence receive separate group intonations, e.g.

> I quite like ˇhim / but I ˇloathe / and deˇtest / his ˋfather

What are the factors which determine the division into intonation-groups? Firstly, there seems to be an upward length constraint of some sort, although it is difficult to put a figure on this constraint in terms of syllables or words. Longer groups are tolerated in reading than in conversational or rhetorical speech. Also, the length constraint does not seem to be related in any simple way to breath control, since we can produce a far longer number of syllables or words on one breath than is ever used in intonation-groups. Secondly, there are probabilistic correlations with syntactic units, but they are only probabilistic. The strongest statement that can be made is that syntactic cohesion is generally stronger within intonation-groups than across intonation-groups.

Intonation-groups have sometimes also been called sense-groups or information-units and these labels suggest that intonation-groups are basically some sort of unit of performance. They may represent a unit of planning for the speaker (slips of the tongue most commonly occur within group boundaries); they may also represent a unit of presentation by the speaker for the listener, as if the speaker were saying to the listener: 'get this piece of processing over before we go on'. Because there is a large amount of speaker choice involved, we may never be able to **predict** intonational phrasing; the most that can be attempted is to put some limits on the range of speaker choice.

4.3 Nucleus placement

The previous section dealt with the division of connected speech into intonation-groups and the probabilistic correlations with syntactic units. Each intonation-group has by definition one nucleus (for discussion of the formal identification of the nucleus see chapter 3, section 3.4), the nucleus being the most prominent pitch accent in an intonation-group. Which of the syllables in a word takes stress was discussed in detail in chapter 2, sub-section 2.2.1 and section 2.5; this section now discusses which word in an intonation-group (and hence which syllable) takes the nucleus (and hence at what point the nuclear tone begins).

Nucleus placement is one device in language for showing FOCUS on some part of an intonation-group and hence of a sentence. It is not the only such device used in languages. Indeed any one language is likely to use a variety of methods for fixing the attention of a listener on some portion of an utterance. Besides intonational means of focussing, languages may use both lexical and grammatical means. Languages will naturally vary in the extent to which they use these various means: in a tone language the intonational means of focussing is likely to be much less used than in a non-tone language. In English the use of nucleus placement to indicate focus is more pervasive than the use of lexical and grammatical means. Lexical focussing in English involves the use of words like *alone*, *only*, *especially*, *even* and *too* and some of these words, as might be expected, have a fixed relationship with nucleus placement. For example, *even* regularly requires the nucleus to be on the constituent it governs, e.g.

Even JANE wouldn't be so stupid

Too, on the other hand, must take a nucleus itself, e.g.

He can do it TOO
cf. *HE can do it too

The principal grammatical means of focussing in English involve the use of passive, cleft, and pseudo-cleft constructions and it is of course also no accident that the items brought into focus by the use of these constructions frequently take the nucleus, e.g.

> The station was hit by a MORtar bomb
> It was the DOG that died
> What we want is WATneys

Nucleus placement is then the principal means of focussing in English. Sometimes single words (or even single morphemes or single syllables) are brought into focus, sometimes the whole of some larger syntactic unit, e.g.

> (I hope they send someone important)
> Well I was TOLD / they were going to send the head of the SCHOOL

In the second intonation-group above it is not just 'school' which is in focus but 'the head of the school'. The relationship between nucleus placement and 'being in focus' is a somewhat complex affair and is one of two particularly important questions which have to be discussed in detail in this section. The other especially important question which has to be discussed in detail is why we put words or higher syntactic units into focus at all.

Firstly, the matter of the scope of focus. This question can, as it were, be approached from either direction. We can either ask how different focussings (on units of different sizes within one intonation-group) produce different (or the same) nucleus placements. Or, alternatively, we can ask what unit (or units) can be brought into focus by different nucleus placements. I shall spend most of the following exposition on the first question, i.e. how a speaker, having decided what is to be focussed on, is then constrained to place the nucleus in a certain place.

A basic distinction has to be made between BROAD FOCUS and NARROW FOCUS. In broad focus the whole of the intonation-group is in focus; in narrow focus a grammatical constituent which forms only part of the intonation-group is brought into focus. Broad focus is related to what has often been referred to as 'normal stress'. A great deal of argument has been expended on the question of whether there is any such thing as 'normal stress'. I shall leave discussion of the details of this argument until later in this section; for the moment I shall assume that there is something which other people (and myself) prefer to call broad focus. Basically the sorts of intonation-groups which have broad focus can be thought of as 'all-new' or 'out-of-the-blue', or said in response to 'What happened?'; although this question 'What happened?' is only relevant to narratives. The problem for 'normal stress' really arises in those cases which must by their nature be heavily context-bound, cannot come 'out-of-the-blue', and hence are very unlikely to have broad focus. I shall return to this murky area when dealing later in this section with the matter of **why** the whole or some part of an intonation-group is focussed.

4.3.1 Broad focus

Assuming that the material in an intonation-group is in broad focus, we have to attempt to answer the question: where will the nucleus be placed in such cases? Section 2.3 in chapter 2 introduced the distinction between words which usually have an accent in connected speech (nouns, main verbs, adjectives, adverbs) and those which most commonly occur without an accent (the remainder, e.g. articles, auxiliary verbs, prepositions, conjunctions, pronouns). The distinction is sometimes labelled as between LEXICAL ITEMS (alias content words alias full words) and GRAMMATICAL ITEMS (alias function words alias empty words). This distinction has been around for a long time and is still often assumed as a basis for much discussion of matters of accent, rhythm, and intonation (and syntax), but is also regularly criticised as an unsustainable grammatical and/or semantic division. Although a lot of this criticism is no doubt just, the distinction nevertheless remains convenient as a descriptive device in intonation, simply to refer to items typically accented, and items typically unaccented, without any implications as to any absolute syntactic or semantic division. The word 'item' is preferred to 'word' because many of the lexical items referred to involve two or more orthographic words, e.g. phrasal verbs and nouns like *look up* and *fitness freak*.

Assuming then that we are dealing with broad focus and that we have a basic division between grammatical items and lexical items, the traditional rule for the placement of the nucleus has been: the nucleus falls on the last lexical item of an intonation-group (see earlier discussion in chapter 3, section 3.4), e.g.

> John ran all the way to the STAtion
> I don't know what to DO
> That performance really was suPERB

By this sort of traditional definition, it followed that any placement of the nucleus on a grammatical item or on a non-final lexical item represented some sort of narrow focus. Unfortunately for intonational description, things are not as simple as this. There are quite a number of identifiable exceptions to the rule of final lexical item for broad focus. I will exemplify these exceptions and then evaluate modifications to the final lexical item rule in the light of these exceptions. I group the exceptions initially under three headings: (i) 'event' sentences; (ii) final adverbials; (iii) adjectival wh objects.

'Event' sentences (sometimes called 'presentation' sentences) typically involve an intransitive verb which denotes (dis)appearance or misfortune. In such sentences it is commonly the subject which receives the accent though the whole sentence is in broad focus, e.g.

> Watch out! That CHIMney's falling down
> (What happened in the afternoon?) A WIND got up

This pattern occurs most frequently in cases where the subject is not human. Its occurrence with human subjects seems limited to verbs of (dis)appearance, e.g.

> (What happened while I was out?) The MILKman called
> (What's all the fuss about?) A CRIMinal's escaped
> cf. (Why can't I use the bathroom?) Because John's SHAving
> (Why was the teacher so cross?) Because a boy SWORE

It is occasionally even possible to have nucleus placement on the subject in cases where a transitive verb is involved, provided the semantic relationship between the verb and its object is very close, e.g.

> The TRAIN's run off the rails

Notice that if a pronoun occurs in the subject position, the nucleus will then be on the predicate (pronouns being grammatical items and at the same time indicating that the subject is no longer part of the focus – in other words, we are here dealing with narrow focus), e.g.

> It's falling OFF

Notice also that if the predicate is adverbially modified, an alternative and very common intonation pattern will involve two groups and hence two nuclei, cf.

> The DOG's escaped
> The DOG's unfortunately escaped
> The DOG's/unfortunately esCAPED

The pattern with two nuclei is also common on that type of event sentence mentioned above which has a human subject, e.g.

> Because the BOY/SWORE

The actual pitch pattern involved in the intonation with two groups may either be clearly marked as such by the use of pausal and/or rhythmic and/or pitch indications at the boundary, or intonational sandhi may occur between the two groups (see chapter 3, sub-sections 3.2.4 and 3.8.1). The two possible pitch patterns are:

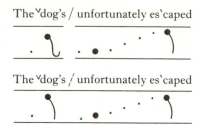

The second type of exception to the final lexical item rule typically involves final adverbials. The most common type of adverbial involved is one of time, e.g.

> I went to LONdon on Thursday
> I'm seeing JOHN this morning
> We had roast BEEF for dinner

Adverbials in this position in sentences with broad focus do not have to be without a nucleus but if they do have a nucleus then it has to be in addition to the one on what precedes it, e.g.

> I went to LONdon / on THURSday
> I'm seeing JOHN / this MORNing

In some sense such adverbials in final position, whether they receive a nucleus or not, represent minor additions to the preceding part of the sentence. If they receive no nucleus the importance of the addition is less than if they receive a nucleus. Often such adverbials represent after-thoughts; so it is not strange that many of the adverbials used in this way come from the class of 'sentence adverbials', e.g.

> He didn't know how to DO it fortunately
> I've found out her TELephone number incidentally
> She'll succEED probably
> cf. *He didn't know how to do it FORTunately
> *I've found out her telephone number inciDENtally
> *She'll succeed PRObably

Certain other types of expression which are very similar to adverbials are also commonly non-nuclear in final position, including vocatives and direct speech markers, e.g.

> That's my younger BROther Peter
> (cf. That's my younger brother PETer)
> You're a bloody IDiot he said

The third type of deviation from the final lexical item rule in broad focus sentences involves adjectival wh objects. This refers to wh questions where an adjectival wh word functions as the object of the verb, e.g.

> What SEEDS did you use?
> Which COURSE did you take?
> Whose ADVICE will you accept?

In these cases the nucleus falls on the object noun following the adjective. Notice that the nucleus does not fall on the object when this is a wh pronoun or when the verb has further complementation, e.g.

> What did you DO?
> Whose advice did you find most USEful?

A number of attempts have been made to explain nucleus placement in the apparent exceptions mentioned above. Explanations have basically been of two sorts: syntactic and semantic. One type of syntactic explanation is in terms of transformations and suggests that the exceptions to the rule of 'nucleus on last lexical item' are the result of movement transformations between deep and surface structure. So in:

> What SEEDS did you use?

what seeds is the object of *use* and as such has been moved from the post-verbal position and has taken its nucleus with it. Similarly in sentences (with broad focus) like:

> John has a DUty to perform

duty is again the object of the verb and similarly moved. This sort of structure is typically contrasted with the same string of words (still with broad focus) given the different nucleus placement in:

> John has a duty to perFORM

where *perform* is complementing the noun *duty* (or, by an alternative analysis, where *duty* and *perform* are in apposition to one another). The explanation in terms of a movement transformation seems very reasonable in these cases; it could even be made to account for non-nuclear final adverbials by saying they have been moved from initial or from post-verbal position, although this seems a rather counterintuitive explanation when such final adverbials are typically afterthoughts. But it certainly could not account for nucleus placement in event sentences (e.g. *Your TROUsers are smouldering*) in which the subject never was to the right of the verb, even in deep structure.

Opponents of the syntactic view of nucleus placement emphasise the semantic or informational aspects of accenting. Bolinger (1972a) puts forward the following contrasting examples (where ′ over a vowel indicates primary accent (= nucleus) and ‵ over a vowel indicates a secondary accent):

(a) The end of the chapter is reserved for various pròblems to compúterize.
(b) The end of the chapter is reserved for various próblems to solve.
(a) I have a pòint to émphasize.
(b) I have a póint to make.
(a) I can't finish in an hour – there are too many tòpics to elúcidate.
(b) I can't finish in an hour – there are simply too many tópics to cover.

Bolinger's argument is that the semantically richer verbs in the (a) sentences demand the extra accent. Several points can be made about these sentences. Firstly, all the (a) examples are, I think, capable of taking the nucleus on the noun rather than the verb. Secondly, notice that when the verb gets the nucleus the noun always gets an accent as well. The situation is in fact very similar to that mentioned for event sentences (if the verb gets a nucleus, the noun usually does too); and for some final adverbials (if the adverbial gets a nucleus, what precedes must also). Actually, one very likely pitch pattern is that already mentioned for event sentences adverbially modified, where intonational sandhi seems to merge two groups into one:

The ˅dog's ⁄ unfortunately es‵caped

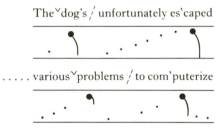

..... various ˅problems ⁄ to com‵puterize

Even if a type of analysis were made which did not permit intonational sandhi (and hence the above examples had to be regarded as each consisting of one intonation-group), what seems obligatory in all such cases is that we have a pitch accent on the earlier item (usually a noun); after that we may or may not have an accent on the later item (usually a verb). Additionally, the argument concerning semantic richness seems to be positively disproved by event sentences like *Your TROUsers are smouldering*, where *smouldering* is undoubtedly a semantically rich item. It may, as Bolinger suggests, be true that ultimately nucleus placement comes down to speaker choice, but there are too many regular correlations with syntax to say that it is totally irrelevant.

86

A more promising grammatical approach (and remember that we are still talking only of sentences with broad focus – clearly what is focussed on (and hence what governs nucleus placement) in sentences with narrow focus will depend in part on pragmatic contextual factors) looks for a hierarchy of accentability within syntactic classes. Lexical items are more likely to be accented than grammatical items but within the different classes of lexical items nouns are certainly more accentable than the other classes. This shows up in the three types of exception mentioned above. In event sentences the subject (and hence a noun) is more accentable than the verb. In those event sentences where the predicate contains a noun but still does not take the nucleus, such a noun is either part of an adverbial (e.g. *fire* in *Your HOUSE is on fire*) or else very closely semantically unified with the verb (e.g. *rails* in *The TRAIN ran off the rails*). In the case of many final adverbials, it is commonly the grammatical object before the adverbial which receives the accent. Noun preference also explains *DUTY to perform*, although it does not of course explain *duty to perFORM* (which may be explained either as a case of apposition demanding an accent, or as a 'double predicate'). Another type of example which suggests noun preference is:

> Dogs which chase CATS / are NORmal / dogs which CATS chase / are ABNormal

Here the last lexical item in the first group is a noun and is nuclear whereas the last lexical item in the third group is a verb and is non-nuclear. It is in fact no accident that, in nuclei counts, the majority are found to fall on nouns.

4.3.2 Narrow focus

Narrow focus works in essentially the same way as broad focus except that for various reasons some part of an intonation-group is considered to be out of focus (because, for example, it has just been mentioned in the preceding group). That part of the intonation-group which remains in focus will, like broad focus, most commonly have the nucleus on the final lexical item, e.g.

> (Have you had a good day?)
> I've had a bloody HORRible day

Here the adjectival group *bloody horrible* is focussed and the nucleus falls on the stressed syllable of the last lexical item, i.e. *horr-*. Similarly, in the following example the noun phrase *a golden handshake* is focussed and the nucleus falls on *hand-*:

> (What have they given Bill?)
> They've given him a golden HANDshake

It is important to realise that nucleus placement alone does not necessarily indicate the extent of the focus in the sentence. Consider alternative contexts for the two examples just given:

> (I suppose you've had a bloody lazy day?)
> I've had a bloody HORRible day

Here only *horrible* is in focus.

> (What've they done about Bill?)
> They've given him a golden HANDshake

Here *given* (*him*) *a golden handshake* (i.e. the whole of the predicate) is in focus rather than just the object *a golden handshake*. Or:

> (What's new at work?)
> The boss's given Bill a golden HANDshake

Here the whole sentence is in focus. What these examples demonstrate is that the nucleus does not in itself indicate the extent of the focus; more especially, it does not indicate how much of what precedes the nucleus is to be taken as in focus. Sometimes the beginning of the extent of focus is indicated by a pre-nuclear pitch accent; in the cases above this would probably involve a step-up to a higher pitch on the first stressed syllable within the focus, e.g. on *given* in the response to *What've they done about Bill?* But this is not obligatory, and this problem about ambiguities in the extent of the focus is really only a pseudo-problem since the context itself will usually make clear how much of what precedes the nucleus is actually in focus.

4.3.3 New and old information

Having given some indication of what is meant by the terms broad focus and narrow focus, it is now possible to investigate the conditions under which various focussings are used. Before this can be done, it is necessary to talk about the concepts of NEW and OLD information, because in many cases (though not all) the focal part of an intonation-group can be said to involve new information. It is in fact easier to start the discussion by considering what constitutes old information (the term 'given' information is also extensively used in the literature). Old information is basically that information which the speaker assumes to be already in some way in the consciousness of the listener and which is hence not in need of highlighting. The word 'information' is used in a very general sense to cover referents, actions and states, and even adverbial conditions on utterances. The speaker makes the assumption that certain information is in the forefront of the listener's mind (and therefore old) in a number of fairly predictable situations. In these situations the old information will then fall outside the focus and hence will not contain the nucleus (resulting in a narrow focus on some remaining part of the intonation-group). The most straightforward type of old information involves verbatim repetition, as in one of the examples above, which is repeated for convenience:

> (Did you have a good day?)
> I had a bloody HORRible day

Clearly at least 'day' is old information. A very similar situation is where what has been said before is repeated paraphrastically, e.g.

> Philip just couldn't make it work / but JOHN succeeded

In the second intonation-group *succeeded* is related paraphrastically to *make . . . work* (notice that to some extent here the speaker has a choice, because he could put the nucleus on *sucCEED*, even though it is old, if he wishes to highlight the contrast between not succeeding and succeeding). Another very similar situation is where some information follows as a logical assumption from what has been said before, e.g.

> Philip failed his exam / so JOHN got the job

The sorts of examples mentioned so far have involved **linguistically** old information; but old information often involves nothing but the physical situation. If, for example, I produce a snake from my bag to show an audience, I could well say *That's a POIsonous snake* (by the time I speak the snake is old information). Remember too that lack of a nuclear accent does not necessarily point to old information; when talking of broad focus above, attention was drawn to a number of instances where a linguistic item clearly constituted new information, yet did not get a nucleus even though it was the last lexical item, e.g. the predicate in event sentences, and some final adverbials.

4.3.3.1 **Contrastivity.** Old information will, then, regularly fall outside the scope of focus, and new information will generally constitute the scope of focus. But there are some occasions where we may wish to focus on a particular piece of information even though it is old. This applies particularly to cases of nucleus placement which have generally been described as 'contrastive'. 'Contrastive', like the terms 'lexical item' and 'grammatical item' mentioned above, is a term which most intonationists have to use but for which they find it difficult to give any precise definition. An informal definition of 'contrastive' would refer to it as involving comparison within a limited set. One problem concerns what constitutes a 'limited set'. The most clear-cut cases involve a binary set, often a pair of opposites, e.g.

> She found it very EASY to settle to married life / whereas he found it DIFFicult

As the above example illustrates, such comparisons sometimes involve two sets of pairs. In the above example *she* and *he* constitute the second pair (and they could both have additional pitch accents). A contrast will often more explicitly involve what is frequently referred to as a 'polarity contrast'. This can take two forms: either a subject is compared to two verbs, or two subjects are compared with respect to plus and minus values of one verb, e.g.

> She was able to WALK to the top / although she couldn't RUN
> She found it EASY / although he DIDn't

But many of the sets involved in contrastive comparison are not binary. Sometimes it is easy to see how they are nevertheless limited. *The lights were RED* is clearly contrastive when talking of traffic lights. Similarly *BLUE* is contrastive in *It turned out the getaway car was BLUE* (even though witnesses had said it was red or black). Notice that in these last two cases, the comparisons are implicit rather than explicit. But if we allow more than binary comparison as contrastive and we also allow something as 'contrast' even though it is only implicit, we then run into many difficult cases. What if I say *I've got a SILver car* (in a conversation about what colour cars people prefer)? The contrast would seem to be with all other potential colours of cars (or perhaps the contrast is with the mundane quality of all other colours of cars). Another, more difficult, example is:

> The TUC is launching a fifty thousand pound camPAIGN / to counter what IT calls / the Government's anti-union POLicy

It seems to be contrastive, but what exactly is the contrast with? ('the Government'? or 'many other organisations'?). I mention these difficult cases not because I have any special solution to the problems of defining 'contrastive', but simply to make clear that, like many other notions in intonation, we are dealing with elusive concepts which seem to exist in speakers' and listeners' minds but which defy stringent definition.

Information which is new and contrastive will automatically fall within the scope of focus. If such information involves a last lexical item within the focus, that item will receive the nucleus. In:

> Jane found it EASy to settle to married life / whereas John found it
> DIFFicult

easy and *difficult* are new and contrastive and final in the focus and hence receive the nucleus (*to settle to married life* being signalled as old information and hence out of focus). *Jane* and *John* are also new and contrastive and within the scope of focus but are not final lexical items within the scope of the foci and hence do not take the nuclei. The double contrast may, however, be highlighted by dividing the sentence into more intonation-groups:

> JANE / found it EASy to settle to married life / whereas JOHN / found
> it DIFFicult

In many cases (like the example just given) a contrast is highlighted in the speaker's mind when the first part of such a binary contrast is uttered but in other cases a contrast may not be highlighted until the second part of the contrast, e.g. if the above sentence was uttered as:

> Jane found it EASy to settle to married life / whereas JOHN / found
> it DIFFicult

Here *John* is clearly indicated as contrastive whereas *Jane* may not have been thought of as contrastive at the time of its utterance and hence not given a separate group (although it should be clear from the above discussion that the speaker can still be thinking of it as contrastive even though he does not give it a nucleus!).

This exploration of the concept 'contrastive' followed on from statements that old information will generally fall outside the scope of focus but that there are some occasions when we may wish to focus on a particular piece of information even though it is old. This applies particularly where information is old **and** contrastive, e.g.

> All three of them had a GO / Only the MOTHer / was sucCESSful

Mother is focused even though she has previously been referred to under 'all three'. Notice too that the second sentence could also be said with one intonation-group, when *mother* would not get a nucleus even though it might nevertheless remain within the scope of the focus suggested by the nucleus on *sucCESSful*.

We therefore have to modify our statement about old information falling outside the scope of focus by saying that old **and** contrastive information will frequently be separately focussed. There are two other types of old information which involve some kind of focussing. Whereas old and contrastive information typically involves single words (or sometimes phrases), these two other types typically involve whole sentences, and the sentences concerned – frequently elliptical – are (i) echoes and (ii) insists and counterpresuppositionals.

4.3.3.2 **Echoes.** ECHOES are most commonly questions which query the whole or some part of the previous utterance of another speaker, often with a note of incredulity, e.g.

> (I didn't go after all) You didn't GO?
> (Take two hours this morning to get that overseas order ready) Two HOURS?
> (What about going to Ascot tomorrow?) Go to ASCOT?

Echoes can be exclamatory rather than questioning, e.g.

> (He's got a distinction) A disTINCtion!
> (Get that bit of wood for me!) Get that bit of WOOD! Just who do you think you're talking to?

A difference is often made between echo question and echo exclamation by the choice of tone: echo questions commonly take high-rise; echo exclamations commonly take rise-fall. In both cases it is obvious that the nucleus is not falling on new information but on old information which has special importance for the speaker. Very similar to echoes are straight requests for repeats, e.g.

> (I caught a grass snake on the hill today) WHAT did you say?

Requests for repeats take high rise just like echo questions. Of course they usually result in the original speaker repeating his utterance verbatim and, what is more, with exactly the same intonation pattern. Any such repetition is clearly a further case of focus on old information. Yet another case of focus on old information, but one which is more difficult to explain, is where a wh query is attached to a preceding statement, e.g.

> (I went home pronto) Why did you go HOME?
> (We went into Manchester this morning) What did you go to MANchester for?
> (I don't smoke much at all these days) What do you SMOKE?

Notice that, in all three examples, the nucleus and hence focus falls on previously mentioned items (old information). It is possible to put the nucleus on the new item, the wh word, in such cases, but such a placement seems intuitively a less likely possibility. Such examples seem similar to echo questions, although they do not take the same tone: they most commonly take a high-fall. More generally, this short sub-section on echoes has provided a second area where focus does not align with new information but with various types of speaker-important old information.

4.3.3.3   **Insists.** The third common type of utterance which involves a focus on old information concerns counterpresuppositionals, which are the most common sub-category of a larger category of INSISTS. In counterpresuppositional utterances the speaker denies something which has been presupposed in the previous speaker's utterances. The presupposition is usually in the consciousness of the first speaker and indeed it is frequently present verbatim (hence we are dealing with old information). Counterpresuppositionals may assert something as true which the presupposition had assumed not to be true or *vice versa*. Nucleus placement in counterpresuppositionals (and indeed in the larger category of insists) is highly haecceitious. The nucleus is only rarely on a final noun, may fall on the main verb, but may also fall on classes of word not usually accented at all, in particular on auxiliary verbs, on a negator, and on a preposition immediately following copula 'be', e.g.

> (What sort of b.o. powder do you use?) I don't USE b.o. powder
> (Why didn't you see your supervisor?) But I DID see my supervisor
> (When was Catharine of Aragon executed?) She WASN'T executed
> (Why are we having meat for lunch?) We're NOT having meat for lunch
> (Did you meet the Ripper when you were in prison?) But I haven't been IN prison
> (He ought to be told about it) He's BEEN told about it

Some presuppositions are not present *verbatim*, e.g.

> (Here – have an aspirin) But I'm not ILL
> (Do you know of a good cure for herpes?) No, I don't, I've never HAD herpes

Such haecceitious nucleus placement may also be used for the more general category of insists and where no counterpresupposition is obviously present, e.g.

> I put my bag in your study because there was nowhere else TO put it
> (Why did you do that?) Because it's the only sensible thing TO do
> They're not very expert but there are lots OF them
> Please make sure you bring all your belongings WITH you

In the discussion of echoes and of insists I have so far avoided general consideration of whether broad focus or narrow focus is involved. In the case of echoes, there may be either broad focus or narrow focus and sometimes (as is commonly the case with other types of sentence) the nucleus marking is ambiguous between the two. In this example it seems to be broad focus which is involved:

(Get that bit of wood for me!) Get that bit of WOOD?

Whereas in the following it is clearly narrow focus which is being used:

(Take two hours off to get that overseas order ready)
TWO hours?

But if the reply in the above example had been *Two HOURS* we cannot be certain whether broad or narrow focus is involved. In the case of insists the problem is more difficult. In a counterpresuppositional like the following:

(What sort of b.o. powder do you use?) I don't USE b.o. powder

we seem to have narrow focus of a special sort (an insist focus which produces a special nucleus placement) superimposed on a sentence which is otherwise out of focus. It seems sensible to say that this sentence is out of focus (apart from the insist) because in some cases an insist focus can actually be associated with new information and hence can include lexical material within its scope, e.g.

I put my bag in your study / because there was nowhere else TO put it

In this example the scope of the insist focus is *because there was nowhere else to*, whereas the insist focus of *I don't use b.o. powder* was without scope. To conclude, foci which are insists involve special nucleus placements and may include some lexical material within their scope or may be completely without scope (as they are in the majority of counterpresuppositionals).

4.3.4 'Normal stress'

Two general restatements need to be made concerning this section 4.3:

(i)   nucleus placement is one way of indicating the focus within an intonation-group. Nucleus placement does not, however, always indicate the full scope of focus, which has partly to be inferred from the verbal and situational context.

(ii)   Focus indicates the highlighting chosen by the speaker for the utterance. Most commonly it is new information which falls within the scope of focus. However, in a certain limited number of conditions a speaker may wish to highlight old information.

At the beginning of section 4.3, when first introducing the notion of broad focus, I said that it was closely related to what had previously been called 'normal stress'. What seems to be meant by this phrase (although I myself would prefer to stick with broad focus) is that an utterance (more specifically, in my terms, an intonation-group) is regarded as 'all-new' or 'out-of-the-blue' or said in response to 'What happened?', if it is at all possible to imagine it said under these conditions. Under these conditions the nucleus will go on the last lexical item except in those cases which are exceptional (e.g. event sentences and where certain classes of adverbial are present in final position). But some sorts of sentence must involve partly old information, e.g. cleft sentences such as:

It was JOHN who gave it to me
It was John who GAVE it to me

Both sentences involve old information: in the first *gave it to me* is old information; in the second *John* is old information. Some sorts of sentence involve wholly old information, e.g. echo questions like:

Two HOURS?
TWO hours?

There is no principled way of saying what 'normal stress' is in these sorts of sentences where old information is involved. Of course it is possible to say what would be normal (or at least 'most likely') if any sentence is put into an appropriate context. But the usual idea behind 'normal stress' has been that it is some sort of decontextualised norm. Thus we are left with 'normal stress' meaning 'nucleus placement in all-new sentences'.

4.4 English nuclear tones

A large part of chapter 3 was concerned with deciding what sort of units of analysis to use for the description of the meanings of tunes. Section 3.3 in chapter 3 discussed levels v. contours; section 3.4 discussed PITCH ACCENTS and the concept of NUCLEUS; section 3.6 described the concept of NUCLEAR TONES; section 3.7 described a taxonomy of nuclear tones for English. In this section I shall discuss what sorts of meanings can be attached to nuclear tones (in some cases also taking into account additional variation produced by the use of particular pre-nuclear pitch accents). Different descriptions of intonation have emphasised grammatical meanings, attitudinal meanings, or discoursal meanings. Emphasising grammatical meanings suggests that there are typical tones associated with syntactic structures like declaratives, interrogatives and imperatives; and that the discoursal meanings usually associated with these structures, i.e. statements, questions, and commands, will also have typical tones even when they are not marked syntactically. This sort of viewpoint is not adopted in this chapter basically because it is not difficult to find examples, at least in English, of almost any nuclear tone combined with any syntactic type. For example, a *yes/no* question like:

Are you going OUT tonight?

can be said with any of the nuclear tones established for English in chapter 3, section 3.7 (with the possible exception of mid-level, which only rarely occurs on sentence-final intonation-groups). Either of the two falling tones (high-fall and low-fall) sounds more 'business-like' (with the low-fall also sounding 'bored'), the low-rise is more 'polite' and almost 'patronising', the high-rise is 'incredulous', the fall-rise is 'whining', and the rise-fall 'conspiratorial'. At this point I must remind the reader that I am in this chapter speaking principally of R.P., although it seems to me that the intonation of General American is not so very different (as regards the above discussion in particular, high-rise perhaps takes over from low-rise as the 'polite' tone and is hence not so 'incredulous'). However, the intonation patterns of many dialects of northern Britain are very different, particularly in the areas of large conurbations, and this is discussed in the next chapter. But to return to the real point of the discussion here: almost any nuclear tone can go with any syntactic type. Of course this does not entirely answer the grammatical approach to the analysis of nuclear tones: another viewpoint might be that one tone is 'unmarked' for each syntactic type, while all other tones are 'marked'. The 'unmarked' tone is then assumed to have the most neutral meaning. But the trouble with this approach is that it is not always easy to decide what the most neutral meaning is. It seems clear enough that either of the simple falling tones is more neutral than any of the other tones on declaratives. So, for example, *It's a very nice `garden* is clearly less marked than *It's a very nice ˇgarden*. But, returning to the earlier discussion of yes/no questions illustrated by *Are you going OUT tonight?*, it is not at all clear which tone should be taken as unmarked for yes/no questions. Usually books which take a grammatical approach assume that a simple rising tone is the 'unmarked' tone for such questions, low-rise in R.P. and high-rise in G.A. But why should the 'polite' tone be considered more unmarked than the 'business-like' tone? People who have actually counted the occurrence of rises and falls on yes/no questions in English have usually found that the occurrence of one or the other is heavily dependent on the type of situation involved; this is not surprising given the sorts of meanings they carry. The grammatical approach to the analysis of the meanings of English nuclear tones is therefore difficult to sustain, although it may be a necessary simplification in the teaching of English as a foreign language.

Other descriptions have emphasised the attitudinal aspects of meanings or the discoursal aspects of meanings, the attitudinal approach being the older, the discoursal approach being the more recent. Discoursal effects were of course very apparent in the last section, where whether information was new or old or contrastive was seen to be the most obvious factor in decisions about nucleus placement; discoursal effects will also be shown to be important in the notion of key, the use of which is discussed later in this chapter. A discoursal approach to the meaning of tones deals in concepts like the shared mutual knowledge of speaker and listener(s), the desire of a speaker to dominate listener(s), and the sort of expectations which a speaker has about a listener's reply. In practice it is not always easy to separate such a discoursal approach to tones from an attitudinal approach which involves labels like 'protesting', 'detached', 'interested', 'impressed' and 'encouraging' (notice that there are a number of emotions like joy, anger, fear, sorrow, which are not usually associated directly with tones, but may be indicated by a combination of factors like accent range, key, register, overall loudness, and tempo). For example, a common type of tag question in English is of the reversed polarity kind, i.e. if the preceding clause is positive, the tag is negative, and *vice versa*. These sorts of tag can typically take a tone which is high-falling or low-rising, e.g.

> He isn't `coming / `is he?
> He isn't `coming / ⁄is he?

The difference in meaning between the tags with the two intonations can be explained discoursally: while both expect the answer 'no', the falling intonation expects that answer much more strongly than the rising intonation. The fall only allows a slight possibility of 'yes' while the rise makes much more allowance for such a reply. But we could also, although in this case less satisfactorily, give attitudinal labels to the tones, the high-fall being 'demanding' and the low-rise 'doubtful'. In the description of the meanings of the nuclear tones of English later in this section, I shall make use of labels which sometimes seem somewhat more obviously discoursal, sometimes more obviously attitudinal; as far as the meanings of nuclear tones are concerned I see no great advantage in insisting that they are primarily one or the other.

Descriptions of the meanings of tones in English also vary in the extent to which they deal in LOCAL meanings or in ABSTRACT meanings. For instance, if we consider any one of the nuclear tones established for English in chapter 3, section 3.7, and describe what meanings that tone has when combined with each of the sentence-types declarative, yes/no interrogative, question-word interrogative, imperative, and exclamative, we may end up describing a number of local meanings like 'weighty', 'impatient', 'dispassionate', 'serious', and 'powerful', which are all meanings suggested by a low-fall (with a preceding pre-nuclear high pitch accent). But we may want to seek out the common factor in all the uses of a particular tone and say that they are all 'referring', or involve 'contrast with a given set', or make a selection from a contextual background which the speaker assumes he and the listener share (these are all general meanings ascribed to the fall-rise by different authors). The seven nuclear tones are generally reduced in number when abstract meanings are ascribed – this reduction being achieved by conflating some of the tones. Thus low-fall, high-fall and rise-fall are conflated as fall, differences between them being ascribed to accent range (in the case of low-fall and high-fall) which is said to involve only a gradient meaning (see sub-section 4.4.4.1 below) and to a specially emphatic onset rise in the case of rise-fall. Mid-level may be analysed as a variant of low-rise (they are frequently commutable with little semantic effect). Some analyses are thus left with four tones to which abstract meanings are ascribed (fall, low-rise, high-rise, fall-rise). Other analysts achieve reduction to three (by conflating low-rise and high-rise); and even to two (by conflating low-rise, high-rise and fall-rise). The more the number of tones is reduced, the more abstract the meanings become. In this chapter I shall first discuss and exemplify local meanings in sub-section 4.4.1 and then go on to discuss possible conditioning factors in sub-section 4.4.2 and abstract meanings in sub-section 4.4.3. Other features, like accent range (often referred to as pitch range) and 'stylisation', which involve phonetic modification of tones and to which independent meanings are sometimes attached, are discussed in sub-sections 4.4.4.1 and 4.4.4.3.

All the exposition in the preceding paragraphs has assumed that intonational meanings are systematic, that a particular tone always has a certain abstract meaning, and that, provided all the local conditioning factors are met (what all these local conditioning factors are is ill-understood at present, although one factor is clearly sentence-type), a particular tone will have a constant local meaning. But there are also INTONATIONAL IDIOMS, which involve the yoking of a particular lexical sequence to a particular pitch pattern. Such idioms involve pitch patterns which do not form part of the systematically exploited tones of the language. For example, a tune which almost all mothers use at some time or another to their children involves a sequence of a high-level pitch plus mid-level pitch on *all gone* (a similar, though not exactly equivalent, pattern is used for a 'stylised' tone mentioned in sub-section 4.4.4.3 below – see also chapter 6, sub-section 6.1.2 for more on intonational idioms). In other cases (which I do not wish to call idiomatic), although there is a yoking of tune and text, the tone used is one which is exploited systematically in the language, and the yoking arises simply because of the unique appropriateness of one tone to a very common lexical expression. So *Would you believe it!* almost always has a pattern with a low-fall on *-lieve-* with a preceding high pitch on *Would*, e.g.

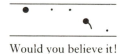

Would you believe it!

But this sequence of pre-nuclear high plus low-falling nuclear tone regularly has a local meaning of 'weighty', particularly when co-occurring with a sentence in the syntactic form of an interrogative, but functioning as an exclamation. So it is only intonational idioms 'proper', i.e. those involving unusual pitch sequences, which lie outside the central intonational system of the language.

4.4.1   Local meanings

I now turn my attention to the central intonational system, and exemplify some of the local meanings of the seven nuclear tones of English set up in chapter 3, section 3.7: high-fall, low-fall, rise-fall, low-rise, high-rise, fall-rise, mid-level.

4.4.1.1   **Falls.** The two simple falling tones, low-fall and high-fall, were treated as distinct nuclear tones in English in chapter 3, section 3.7 on the basis that a low-fall typically involves a step-down from any preceding pre-nuclear syllables and a high-fall typically involves a step-up. But this represented a bit of a simplification. A high-fall will certainly involve a step-up but not all steps-up can be regarded as high-falls: if, for example, the pre-nuclear syllables are on a very low pitch, the voice cannot help but go up in pitch if it is to accommodate a fall. So the distinction between low-fall and high-fall is only really clear-cut when preceding syllables are around the middle or high part of a speaker's range (see further discussion in sub-section 4.4.4.1 below). Because the distinction between high-fall and low-fall is not always clear-cut, many analysts conflate high-fall and low-fall simply as fall; and treat the difference in the height of falls as gradient and the meanings associated with them also as gradient. I shall return to this problem of gradience in sub-section 4.4.4.1 below. For the moment the distinction in meaning between high-fall and low-fall is based on the clear-cut cases involving steps-up and steps-down.

Both falling tones involve a sense of finality, of completeness, definiteness and separateness when used with declaratives; hence both tones are more common on sentence final intonation-groups than on sentence non-final intonation-groups. The low-fall is generally more uninterested, unexcited, and dispassionate whereas the high-fall is more interested, more excited, more involved, cf.

> He ˈstayed for three ˋhours
> He ˈstayed for three ˎhours

The presence of the high pitch accent (involving a step-up from *he* to *stayed* and marked ˈ) before the low fall makes the meaning more 'weighty'; whereas the absence of such a high accent makes the high fall more 'protesting', e.g.

> He stayed for three ˋhours

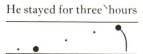

In their use with interrogatives and imperatives, the falling tones carry similar meanings to those they carry with declaratives, although the low-fall will often also be rather hostile. This is particularly the case with low-falls on tag response questions, e.g.

> (I've just started writing my new book) ˎHave you?

Clearly, in the context of the above example, interest is the expected attitude, and lack of interest is taken as hostility. As has already been mentioned in the preceding section, falling tones on reversed polarity tag questions generally indicate a high expectation of agreement (i.e. it is unlikely that there is any more to be said on the matter).

The rise-fall tone can be grouped semantically with the two simple falling tones just discussed; like them, the rise-fall involves a sense of finality, completeness, definiteness and separateness, particularly when used with declaratives. There are two rather different local meanings which are additionally characteristic of the rise-fall. The first is 'impressed', e.g.

(He got a first) ^Did he! / At ^Cambridge, / ^too!

With this sort of meaning, breathy voice is often also involved and the effect is one of 'gossip', e.g.

Have you heard about ^Jane? / She's ^pregnant!

(This meaning of rise-fall is also produced by humming it, i.e. [^mm].) As illustrated by the examples above, the 'impressed' meaning is often a local meaning of rise-fall in association with yes/no interrogatives as well as declaratives. Its particular use with yes/no interrogatives of the response tag sort seems to produce a sentence function of an exclamatory type; indeed the meaning is also common with exclamations grammatically marked as such, e.g.

I enjoyed the whole concert / but what a fi^nale!

The other local meaning commonly associated with rise-fall is 'challenging'. This may occur with clauses of any syntactic type (whereas the 'impressed' meaning does not seem to co-occur with wh interrogatives and imperatives), e.g.

(I don't like to keep reminding him) But you damn well ^ought to!
(They're emptying the dustbins) They ^always empty them on Fridays
(I couldn't find any adverbs) But there are ^lots of them in the text
(I need a nice long holiday) Don't we ^all!

On the face of it, the two meanings of rise-fall appear very different; even when a more general meaning has been ascribed to the rise-fall, such a general meaning has seemed to reflect only one or the other of these two local meanings. The meaning has been described as 'something sustained as overriding opposition' (Bolinger, 1947:136) which seems to be more akin to the 'challenging' meaning; and as 'besides, like fall, adding information to the common ground, also add[ing] to the speaker's own store of knowledge' (Brazil, Coulthard and Johns, 1980:56), which seems more akin to the 'impressed'. One of the reasons for giving abstract meanings to tones (discussed in the next section), as opposed to the local meanings now being discussed, should be to explain the diverse local meanings of tones. As will be seen, the pragmatic factors which govern local meanings are ill-understood, but in this case of the meaning of rise-fall, the explanation seems to lie in different speaker-listener relations. The 'challenging' as opposed to the 'impressed' meaning seems to arise where the speaker is disagreeing with the listener in some way; hence the examples of the 'challenging' meaning above are all responses, whereas the 'impressed' meaning may or may not be a response. Another local meaning sometimes ascribed to rise-fall is 'ironic' or 'sarcastic'; but these meanings arise in a rather different way. Like many types of humour, they depend on a mismatch, in this case between situation and linguistic expression. If you do something stupid and I say ^*Clever!* there is firstly a mismatch between the obvious stupidity of your action and my use of the word *clever*; but the sarcasm is made even more telling by my use of a tone which would normally indicate that I was 'impressed'.

4.4.1.2 **Rises (dependent).** So far I have discussed the three falling tones, low-fall, high-fall and rise-fall; I now turn my attention to the rising tones; low-rise, high-rise and fall-rise. In chapter 3, section 3.7, it was made clear that the distinction between low-rise and high-rise is established principally on the basis of their finishing point. Mid-level also has to be grouped with the rising tones because it is generally commutable with them in similar contexts and with similar meanings. The first point to be made about all four tones is that they are all very common on sentence non-final intonation-groups. This is not to say that falling tones are impossible in such positions but that they are altogether less common and also that they emphasise the separateness of the information in the intonation-groups rather than the dependency of one group (using a rising tone) on the other (using a falling tone). Sentence non-final intonation-groups are principally of three kinds (see above in section 4.2 of this chapter): noun-phrase subjects, adverbials, and subordinating and coordinating clauses. In all these cases the use of a rising tone signals dependency or non-finality. Noun-phrase subjects given a separate group frequently have a fall-rise, particularly when the contrastive nature of the subject is being emphasised, e.g.

> Private ᵛenterprise / is always efᵛficient / whereas public ˌownership / means ˋinefficiency

In this example the subject of the first clause has a fall-rise signalling non-finality **and** contrast whereas for the subject of the second clause the speaker chooses a simple low-rise, which means that he chooses not to repeat the contrastivity. The difference in usage between low-rise, high-rise, and mid-level in non-final positions is best characterised as one of style: the low-rise is the most oratorical and is also typical of a formal reading style, the high-rise is more casual, and the mid-level seems to carry no meaning other than that of non-finality, which is perhaps why it alone of these three tones occurs **only** in non-final position. Try reading the example above substituting firstly high-rise for the first three groups and then mid-level for the first three groups, i.e.

> Private ´enterprise / is always ef´ficient / whereas public ´ownership / means `inefficiency
> Private >enterprise / is always e>fficient / whereas public >ownership / means `inefficiency

The almost complete non-use of low-rise, and the increasing use of high-rise in non-final intonation-groups may be one feature distinguishing American English from British English; it also seems to be increasing in some types of Australian English (whereas fall-rise seems to be on the increase in these positions in British English).

The use of rising tones on adverbials is very similar to that on subjects, except that, in some cases, the fall-rise is not obviously contrastive but merely specially emphatic, cf.

> Unˇfortunately / their best player didn't turn `up
> Un´fortunately / their best player didn't turn `up
> Un´fortunately / their best player didn't turn `up
> Un>fortunately / their best player didn't turn `up

There are some adverbials which are exceptional in that they regularly take a falling tone in non-final position (and, for that matter, when given a separate group in other positions), and there are other adverbials which may take either a falling tone (i.e. low-fall, high-fall, or rise-fall) or a rising tone (i.e. low-rise, high-rise, fall-rise, or mid-level). This illustrates priorities in the ORIENTATION of the meaning of tones. Sometimes a tone may be oriented towards distinguishing non-final from final; at other times it is oriented towards the relationship between the information in the two groups, in this case between adverbial and main clause. Adverbials which limit the information in the main clause take a rise, while those that reinforce take a fall. Orientation towards the limiting/reinforcing dimension takes priority over orientation towards finality/non-finality. Hence reinforcing adverbials take a fall even in non-final position, e.g.

> `Literally / he banged his head against the `wall
> Of `course / if you do it ˇthat way / it won't `work
> Be`sides / he didn't get a high enough `mark
> cf. Preˇsumably / he thinks he `can
> ˇUsually / he comes on `Sundays
> Acciˇdentally / he got it `right

Some adverbials may take either a falling or a rising tone: it is as if they are only reinforcing enough to allow the speaker the **choice** of letting the reinforcement take priority, e.g.

> `Clearly / he's not as good as he `thinks he is
> ⌄Clearly / he's not as good as he `thinks he is
> Neverthe`less / I don't think I `shall
> Neverthe⌄less / I don't think I `shall

The rule of reinforcement priority also applies in reverse in sentence final position. Most adverbials take a rise in final position, because most adverbials are limiting, e.g.

> I went to `London / on ⁄Monday
> He didn't get a high enough `mark / un⁄fortunately

Only reinforcing adverbs allow a final falling tone, e.g.

> I do it `this way / `always
> He made a `mess of it / de`liberately

Some other types of expression can also take low-rise in final position: these include verbs of speaking like *answer* and *say* and epistemic verbs like *think*, e.g.

> You'll rue the day you `did that / he ⁄said
> He wants to see you de`flated / I i⁄magine

In the case of coordinate clauses, the first clause is most likely to have one of the rising tones (or mid-level), the choice between these tones again being made on similar grounds to those influencing the choice for noun-phrase subjects and for adverbials. In British English at least, low-rise and mid-level seem to be the most common, e.g.

> He took the ⁄car / and drove to `London
> He cleaned it >up / and sold it for two hundred `pounds

Use of a rise in the first of two coordinate clauses followed by a fall in the second involves two (successive) aspects of a single action, whereas use of a fall in each clause involves two distinct (and often parallel) actions, cf.

> She's twenty-eight years `old / and lives in East `Grinstead
> She's twenty-eight years ⁄old / and thinking of starting a `family

In the case of subordinate clauses, the situation is more complex. In almost all cases, one of the two clauses (i.e. subordinate clause or main clause) will take a falling tone while the other takes a rising tone (i.e. only very rarely will both take a fall or both take a rise). The rising tone will indicate non-finality and/or informational dependence, while the falling tone will indicate finality and/or informational ascendency. In the typical case non-finality, dependence, and syntactic subordination co-occur, e.g.

Because I hadn't had any ᵛaspirins / I felt a bit ˋbetter

Also very common is the case in which the subordinate clause is in second position and in which it still takes the rise, informational dependence taking priority over finality in the choice of tone, e.g.

I feel a bit ˋbetter / when I don't take any ˊaspirins

It is also possible for informational dependency/ascendency to clash with subordination, e.g.

I felt a bit ᵛbetter / because I hadn't taken any ˋaspirins

The one combination which seems unlikely is where informational dependency clashes with both syntactic subordination and non-finality, e.g.

*Because I don't take ˋaspirins / I feel a bit ᵛbetter

It should by now also be apparent that the type of rising tone involved in sequences of subordinate clause plus main clause, or main clause plus subordinate clause, is most likely to be fall-rise in non-final position or low-rise in final position (the same applies to adverbials given a separate intonation-group), e.g.

When you think how much is inᵛvolved / it's not altogether ˋeasy
It's not altogether ˋeasy / when you think how much is inˊvolved
Last ᵛspring / we managed to get away to ˋParis
We managed to get away to ˋParis / last ˊspring

There is no convincing explanation for the preference for fall-rise in one position and low-rise in the other. In fact such a preference raises one of the most difficult problems of intonational meaning: how far are tones meaningful and how far habitual? Is it due to mere habit that different types of rise are preferred in different positions? Or again, if one particular speaker consistently prefers a high-rise on coordinate clauses in non-final positions as opposed to the more common low-rise of other speakers of his dialect, is this to be considered as indicating that he is a 'casual' person or is it just his habit? There is no easy answer to this question; indeed it is a question which can apply in many areas of linguistics (e.g. how far does the habitual use of a certain construction like the passive rob that construction of its impact?).

4.4.1.3 **Rises (independent).** We now have to consider the uses of low-rise, high-rise, and fall-rise in those cases where their meanings do not

depend so obviously on their relationship with the tone of another intonation-group; principally, this means independent clauses. The low-rise is
probably the most difficult of the nuclear tones to which to attach typical
local meanings; part of this difficulty exists because with this tone the
presence or absence of an additional high pitch accent before it often makes
a considerable difference to the meaning. On declaratives, the tone always
involves an element of uncertainty. With no preceding high pitch accent,
an additional meaning of 'non-committal' or even 'grumbling' is conveyed,
e.g.

> It's ⁄ not
> He didn't help ⁄ me

This use of the tone seems to have something in common with low-fall,
a feeling of 'distance' or 'non-involvement' (and this common factor is
one argument for a feature analysis of English tones, i.e. that the
feature [+low] has a consistent meaning). With a preceding high pitch
accent, however, the additional meaning is best described as 'soothing',
'reassuring' or even 'patronising' (it is a tone frequently used by adults
to very young children), e.g.

> You must ˈlet me ⁄ help you
> All you'll feel is ˈone little ⁄ prick
> I'll be ˈback next ⁄ week

What seems to have happened here is that the uncertainty is felt by the
speaker to be in the mind of the listener (i.e. the tone is listener-oriented).

The meanings which the low-rise has with declaratives are reflected
in their use with other sentence-types. Here are some examples of the
'non-committal' usage (i.e. without a preceding high accent):

> Why ⁄ should I?
> What's it got to do with ⁄ her?
> ⁄ Really!

This type of use is uncommon with imperatives and with yes/no interrogatives. It is, however, very common with tag interrogatives where the
element of uncertainty is very much more apparent with low-rises than
with a falling tone, cf.

> He's ˋpassed / ˋhasn't he?
> He's ˋpassed / ⁄ hasn't he?

It is also used with constant polarity tag interrogatives, often with a
'menacing' overtone. With such tags falls are impossible, cf.

> You're ˋgoing / ⁄ are you?
> *You're ˋgoing / ˋare you?

Part of the reason for the non-occurrence of falling tones here may be that this sort of tag is frequently used in situations where the relevant information has already been overtly presented, or at least implied, by a previous speaker (who is now usually the listener); a falling tone would demand agreement from the listener, but demanding agreement when the listener has already himself presented the information is pragmatically inappropriate. An alternative explanation for the impossibility of falls on constant polarity tags (and absolute impossibility is a rare thing in intonation) analyses them as always non-prominent and only occurring as tails to nuclear tones begun on the main clause. By this analysis *You're ˅going ˊare you?* is not to be taken as two groups but as a single unified fall-rise nuclear tone beginning on *going*. Support for this analysis comes from:

(i)   the fact that a pause is not usual between main clause and tag whereas a pause is common in the case of reversed polarity tags

(ii)   the 'menacing' meaning present in many constant polarity tags comes very close to one of the common meanings of fall-rise, that of 'warning' (see below, this sub-section)

(iii)   constant polarity tags also occur on the tail to a simple rise beginning on the main clause, e.g.

You're going are you?

This pattern is very common on sentences where the subject is elided, e.g. *Watch a lot of ˊtelevision do you?* Together the three arguments suggest that the fall-rise solution to constant polarity tags is the correct one.

Here are some examples of low-rise with a preceding high pitch accent on sentence-types other than declaratives:

ˈWhy don't you do it ˊthis way?
ˈCan you ˊhelp me?
ˈDon't let him ˊbully you

The 'reassuring' meaning is generally clearly present with wh interrogatives and imperatives, but is generally less apparent with yes/no interrogatives, where the meaning seems to be something like 'politely interested' as compared with the more 'brusque' use of a fall, cf.

Are you coming to the ˊmeeting tonight?
Are you coming to the ˅meeting tonight?

I have already mentioned that this is an area where there are differences (not yet fully studied) between R.P. and G.A. English. The use of low-rise on yes/no interrogatives may indeed sound 'patronising', or 'ingratiating' to Americans, who are more likely to use high-rise.

While the low-rise has a group of local meanings which are particularly difficult to summarise, the high-rise, on the other hand, involves a fairly consistent meaning across all sentence-types. This meaning is basically that of 'echo or repeat question' (see this chapter, sub-section 4.3.3.2 above), sometimes also called 'contingent queries' or 'pardon questions'. Here are some examples on various sentence-types:

> (I'm taking up taxidermy this autumn) Taking up ╱what?
> (She passed her driving test last week) She ╱passed?
> (When are you going to do it?) When am I going to ╱do it?
> (Are you going to let him get away with it?) Am I going to let him get a╱way with it? / Of ╲course I'm not
> (Make sure you get there at ten) At ╱ten?

Some of these responses clearly add a note of incredulity as well as being questioning. This note is also present where high-rise is used on simple repetition requests, e.g.

> ╱Pardon? ╱Uh? ╱What?

High-rise can also be used on yes/no interrogatives which are not responses. This use of high-rise as compared with low-rise produces a more casual air in R.P., e.g.

> Are you ╱going?
> cf. Are you ╱going?

However, high-rise seems to be the more common pattern in many types of American English and also in some varieties of British English (e.g. Norfolk).

Fall-rises have been mentioned three times before in this book. In chapter 3, sub-section 3.2.4, I discussed sequences of two pitch accents involving a fall and a rise which were best analysed as involving two intonation-groups with intonational sandhi operating to delete the boundary marking between the two groups. In chapter 3, section 3.7, I noted that (even leaving aside the cases where the best analysis is into two groups) there appear to be two very different meanings associated with fall-rise tones. This is very clear when we consider examples of divided fall-rises which involve a sequence of two pitch accents, where the first accent (the fall) is nuclear because the second accent (the rise) is downgraded (see chapter 3, section 3.4 above), e.g.

(A)   I ╲thought she was ╱married (but I did not know so, and it turned out she wasn't)

(B)   I ╲thought she was ╱married (and so she was!)

Of these two examples, (B) has the meaning which listeners are more likely to ascribe to the sentence when said in isolation. The meaning involved has an element of 'I told you so' and is 'self-justificatory' and/or 'appealing'. Here are some more examples with similar meanings on different sentence-types:

> I \knew she wouldn't ⁄ do it
> I'm \longing to see your new ⁄ coat
> Do you \have to be so ⁄ stubborn?
> \When will you learn to keep your ⁄ mouth shut?
> \Please sit ⁄ down

From 'appeal' it is but a short step in meaning to 'warning' which is a very common meaning of fall-rise on both declaratives and imperatives, e.g.

> You won't ᵛ like it
> Be careful you don't ᵛfall

However, it is the meaning of the (A) sentence above which probably represents the group of meanings most typical of fall-rise. This group of meanings can be summed up in the word 'reservations' and includes what might be called 'emphatic contrast' and 'contradiction'. It is limited to declaratives; here are some examples:

> (When will we be seeing you?) Well ⁄ I could come on ᵛSaturday
> I like his ᵛwife (although I can't stand him)
> (Is that part of the coast very crowded at weekends?) Well ᵛHastings
>   will be
> (That was quite a good hotel really) It wasn't what you'd call ᵛclean
> (She's twenty-two, isn't she?) Twenty ᵛnine

A special use of fall-rise (although, as we shall see, not necessarily a special meaning) concerns its interaction with negatives. The word on which the nucleus falls is always included in the scope of negation but the fall-rise limits the scope of negation so that it does not apply to the main verb (unless the main verb itself takes the fall-rise). In the following examples the scope of negation is indicated by the use of italics:

> I'm *not going to perform* \anywhere
> I'm *not* going to perform ᵛ*anywhere* (= 'I'm going to perform but
>   not in any place')
> Cheap tickets are *not available to* \anyone
> Cheap tickets are *not* available *to* ᵛ*anyone* (= 'Cheap tickets are avail-
>   able but not to any person')
> They *don't accept* \any sort of CSE results

They do*n't* accept ˅*any sort of CSE results* (= 'They accept CSE results but not any sort of CSE results')

She *didn't go to the conference because she needed a* ˋ*holiday*

She did*n't* go to the conference *because she needed a* ˅*holiday* (= 'She went to the conference but not because she needed a holiday')

He *wouldn't have done it if you'd* ˋ*hit him* (= 'He didn't do it nor would he have done it even if you had hit him')

He would*n't* have done it *if you'd* ˅*hit him* (= 'He did it but he wouldn't have done it if he had been hit')

ˋ*All of them didn't pass the exam* (= 'None of them passed')

˅*All of them* did*n't* pass the exam (= 'Some of them passed the exam but not all')

He *didn't get* ˋ*one credit* (= 'He got none')

He did*n't* get ˅*one credit* (= 'He didn't get only one but lots')

Notice that the meaning of the example with the fall-rise can always be glossed with a 'but . . . . .' In this way these examples are not so very different from the use of the fall-rise in a positive sentence, e.g.

I like ˅John ('but . . . . .')

In both negative and positive sentences this meaning of fall-rise can be glossed as 'reservations'. This meaning indicates that the statement is true under certain conditions but not under others. In the case of the *any* sentences this results in a different meaning of *any*. Some grammarians have actually argued that there are two lexical items any_1 (= 'absolutely *any* . . . . .') and any_2 (= 'any . . . . . chosen at random'). If we adopt this analysis, by a process of semantic harmony, the use of a fall will always call up any_1, while the use of a fall-rise will always call up any_2.

I have so far talked about two groups of meanings associated with the fall-rise: the (A) meanings ('reservations', 'contrast', 'contradiction') and the (B) meanings ('self-justification', 'appeal', 'warning'). Although the detailed pitch patterns associated with the two meanings are commonly identical, some speakers will realise the two meanings differently when two pitch accents are involved. Let us return to the examples which opened the discussion of fall-rise, i.e.

(A)   I ˋthought she was ⁄ married (but I did not know so and it turned out she wasn't)

(B)   I ˋthought she was ⁄ married (and so she was!)

Both meanings may involve the following pitch pattern:

I thought she was married

But only the (A) meaning may alternatively be realised as:

I thought she was married

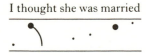

In this realisation there is no second pitch accent (although *marr-* may carry a tertiary stress dependent on length and loudness). Hence many analysts regard the (A) meanings as involving a 'genuine' fall-rise and the (B) meanings as involving a 'fall plus rise'. Whatever we call them we are certainly justified, on grounds of both meaning and form, in enlarging our inventory of English nuclear tones to differentiate fall-rise (A) from fall-rise (B).

One last type of fall-rise is worth mentioning: a 'whining' variant of high-rise in echoes and tag responses, e.g.

(I didn't go after all) You ˅didn't? (or: ˅Didn't you?)

This type of fall-rise appears to involve a different contour from those used in the preceding examples, cf.

(He didn't go away) He ˅didn't?
(He went away) He ˅didn't.

The main factor which distinguishes the two seems to be the depth of the trough. This piece of evidence could be used to argue for the setting up of a further distinction of low fall-rise versus high fall-rise (although I pursue the matter no further because the occurrence of this 'echo fall-rise' is very restricted, both in its contexts of use, and as regards the speakers who use it, at least within R.P.).

This section has illustrated some of the typical local meanings of the nuclear tones of R.P. and most of these meanings will also apply to American English. Many other dialects of English, particularly some urban dialects of north Britain, operate with a very different set of nuclear tones, but the tones and meanings just described will in most cases be at least receptively familiar. The tones and local meanings exemplified in this section will hopefully give the reader some (albeit slight) body of concrete data which will form the basis of the more theoretical discussions in later sections of this chapter.

4.4.1.4   **Tonal sequences.** It is worth surveying the preceding sections on local meanings of tones and summarising the most common tonal sequences in sentences. The most common sequence is undoubtedly that of a rising tone on a non-final group followed by a falling tone on a final group. The rising tone may be low-rise, high-rise, fall-rise, or mid-level, and it typically occurs on an adverbial, or a noun-phrase subject, or on a subordinate or coordinate clause, e.g.

> Sur>prisingly / it all worked out O. ˋK.
> If I were ˇyou / I'd get a ˋmove on
> The ˊspeakers / were John and Mary ˎSmith
> He joined the ˊArmy / and spent all his time in ˋAldershot

The second tone of this sort of sequence may be varied where the sentence itself is not a straightforward statement (it may, for instance, be a question or an appeal):

> If I ˇhelped you / would you try aˊgain?
> Of >course / he could have got a much better reˇsult

A second very common sequence involves a falling tone on the first group followed by a low-rise on the second group. The low-rise typically occurs on an adverbial, or on a tag question of the reversed polarity kind where the listener is given considerable latitude to disagree, e.g.

> But I play ˋsquash / on Monday ˊ evenings
> You'd like to hear what ˋI think // ˊwouldn't you?

The second tone in this type of sequence may be fall-rise when the adverbial involves a particularly emphatic restriction, e.g.

> I do it ˋthat way / ˇusually

A third common type of sequence consists of a falling tone on the first group and a falling tone on the second group. This is frequent on structures involving reversed polarity tags where the speaker is demanding agreement, or on structures involving adverbials of the reinforcing type, e.g.

> Ann said she'd help as much as sheˋcould / ˋnaturally
> It's a bit too good to be ˋtrue / ˋisn't it?

These three types of sequence are the most frequent in English. This is not to say that other sequences do not occur. Indeed if we examine enough data, we will find almost all sequences occurring at least occasionally.

4.4.2 Conditioning factors

The preceding section 4.4.1 has surveyed various common local meanings associated with nuclear tones in English. The meanings of any one nuclear tone clearly vary at least slightly in different contexts; in some cases such variation is considerable rather than slight. We must now face

the question of what actually brings about this slight or considerable variation in meaning. This is a very ill-understood area of intonational and
pragmatic study. All I am able to do in the present state of knowledge
is to summarise the factors which seem to be relevant and recapitulate
some examples of each factor at work.

The most obvious contextual factor is syntactic type. There have been
numerous examples in the preceding sections of different meanings
attached to a particular nuclear tone according to its use with various
syntactic types. For example, the meanings associated with the various
rising tones when they are used in sentence non-final intonation-groups
clearly do not carry many of the attitudinal implications which such tones
carry in final intonation-groups; rather, a meaning of 'non-finality' is
apparent in them all, together with a variation in the degree of formality
associated with each tone. In sentence final intonation-groups there is often
variation in meaning which depends on whether the tone is combined
with declarative, or yes/no interrogative, or question word interrogative,
or imperative, or exclamative. For example, the use of a low-rise nuclear
tone (preceded by a high pitch accent) is frequently patronising with declaratives but less obviously so with yes/no interrogatives, for which it
seems in many ways to be the more neutral tone, cf.

> You ˈmustn't let him ⁄hassle you
> Do you ˈthink it would ⁄work O.K.?

It seems likely that tense also affects the interpretation of a nuclear
tone. One group of meanings associated with fall-rise was described as
'self-justificatory' or appealing or warning. It seems to be the case that
the 'self-justificatory' meaning is associated with a past tense whereas the
other meanings are associated with present or future tense (in the main
clause), cf.

> I knew you wouldn't be able to ˇdo it
> I know you won't be able to ˇdo it

Where differences of meaning associated with declaratives compared
with yes/no or question word interrogatives are concerned, it is obvious
that different speaker/listener relationships are involved. Such differences
in speaker/listener relationships may, however, show up in other intonational ways. The meaning of a nuclear tone may turn out differently according to whether the speaker is agreeing or disagreeing with the previous
speaker (who is now the listener). For example, the 'impressed' meaning
of the rise-fall seems to arise where the speaker is agreeing with the listener

whereas the 'challenging' meaning arises where he is disagreeing; it is as if the 'challenging' meaning is 'negative-impressed', cf.

> (He got a distinction!) ^Did he!
>
> (I don't like to keep reminding him) Well, you damn well ^ought to!

Speaker-listener relationships are also involved in the degree to which a speaker matches his tone to that of a previous speaker. If a speaker uses a fall of the low variety (which shows a lack of involvement) in response to a high-fall (which shows involvement), the listener will interpret the tone as 'bored' and possibly 'hostile', e.g.

> (I've decided to apply for the `Aston job) \ Have you?

More general contextual effects may be at work in the interpretation of tonal meaning. By these I mean the context set by the preceding utterances and by the co-occurring physical situation. A mismatch between tone and context may reinforce an ironical effect already present in the co-occurring grammar and lexis, e.g.

> (How do you know he's reliable?) He's my `brother / /isn't he?

Here the situation was such that the first speaker certainly knew that the person referred to and the listener were brothers, and the second speaker certainly knew that the first speaker knew. The words themselves were therefore ironic; but notice that the speaker uses a low-rise on the tag, a tone which is more obviously questioning than a fall. The use of a questioning tone where nothing is in question strengthens the irony. A tone frequently used to reinforce irony is the rise-fall; adjectives like *brilliant, clever, splendid* are frequently used with a rise-fall to comment on a situation which is actually a disaster in the speaker's view. The fact that tones are sometimes deliberately used in contexts where they would be inappropriate if they were not interpreted ironically clearly implies its opposite: that some tones are very appropriate to some contexts. This is apparent in the fact that 'limiting' adverbs like *usually* and *accidentally* take rises whereas 'reinforcing' adverbs like *frequently* and *deliberately* take falls.

A number of potential context effects have been identified in this section: non-final v. final; declarative v. yes/no interrogative v. wh interrogative v. imperative v. exclamative; tense; agreement v. disagreement; relationship to preceding tone; and general context, including preceding utterances and physical situation. Lurking behind many of these particular factors is the more general one of speaker/listener relationship. A good part of the variation in local meanings associated with nuclear tones may be attribu-

table to such contextual factors and, in particular, to speaker/listener relationships. It is, on the other hand, also possible that some of the variation
may be ascribable to tonetic variation which has not been as yet adequately
described. For example, the 'menacing' overtone which frequently accrues
to the low-rise used on constant polarity tags may result from a slight
tonetic variation in the actual tone; it might, for instance, involve a very
narrow rise (this applies regardless of whether we analyse it as a separate
low-rise nuclear tone, or as the rising part of a fall-rise beginning in the
preceding main clause). We still have much to learn about the influence
both of context and of relatively fine-grained tonetic changes.

4.4.3   Abstract meanings

At the beginning of this section it was suggested that nuclear
tones have fairly abstract basic meanings which as a result of conditioning
factors turn up with a variety of local meanings. In sub-section 4.4.1 some
typical local meanings were described. In sub-section 4.4.2 some potential
conditioning factors were described. When we now come to look at abstract
meanings, the problems of description are further multiplied. Firstly, no
analyst has systematically related abstract to local meanings; rather, some
have concerned themselves principally with the description of local meanings and some with the characterisation of abstract meanings. Therefore,
when we come to look at the abstract systems proposed, we will find
no easy way of relating them to the local meanings described in sub-section
4.4.1. Secondly, the inventory of seven nuclear tones which I have used
to describe the local meanings is generally reduced in number by collapsing
a number of nuclear tones under one heading. Typically, we end up with
either a simple distinction between falls and rises, or else we are presented
with a three-fold distinction between falls, rises and fall-rises. In both
cases other distinctions are seen as involving more delicate divisions within
these primary categories. I propose to look briefly at one representative
of each of these two types of analysis: unless otherwise indicated, page
references in the following two sections are to Brazil (1975) and to Gussenhoven (1983a).

4.4.3.1   **A two-tone approach.** The basic tonal distinction in Brazil's
system is between fall and fall-rise. The distinction is seen as principally
discoursal: the falling tone is 'proclaiming' while the fall-rise is 'referring'.
'Fall-rise tone marks the matter of the tone-group as part of the shared,
already negotiated, common ground occupied by the participants at a par-

ticular moment in an on-going relationship. Choice of falling tone, by contrast, marks the matter as new' (p. 6). Intensified versions of the fall-rise and the fall are the simple rise (= a rise ending high) and the rise-fall respectively. Intensification indicates 'an extra measure of involvement on the part of the speaker' (p. 7). There is also a 'neutral' tone which may either be level or low-rising. With this tone 'the speaker avoids making the tone-group either proclaiming or referring . . . . . . The common factor . . . . . seems to be a kind of withholding or withdrawal from the interactive situation' (p. 8). However, this tone appears only rarely in his transcriptions, and I think we are justified in regarding Brazil's approach as essentially two-toned. The semantic distinction between 'pro-claiming' and 'referring' is obviously related to the distinction between given and new information (see this chapter, sub-section 4.3.3 above). Brazil explains the difference in a way which makes the rise of the 'referring' tone a sort of half-way house between the completely new information of the falling tone and the completely given information of stretches of utterance which have no pitch prominence, e.g.

/ p *John* / r painted the *shed* / (p. 22)

(/ = tone-group boundary; p = proclaiming tone; r = referring tone; italic indicates tonic (= nucleus).)

This example might occur as the response to 'Who painted the shed?' Such a reply is said by Brazil to be 'helpful' because it takes 'account of the respondent's assessment of the state of convergence' (p. 23). The additional term 'termination' is used to refer to the pitch level of the turning-point of the tonic (i.e. in the terms I have used, it describes varia-tions in accent range); for example, this takes care of variations between a fall starting at a high pitch, at a mid pitch, and at a low pitch. A mid termination is said to anticipate passive agreement, a high termination to invite an active response, and a low termination to close matters. This system of termination interacts closely with the system of key (which prin-cipally concerns the pitch of the first prominent syllable) which I shall discuss in section 4.5 below.

The basic problem with this sort of labelling of tones is that it appears to become very much *post hoc*. Consider the following examples:

/ r I've come to *see* you / p with the *rash* / r I've got on my *chin* / p and under*neath* / r which has de*vel*oped / p in the past three *days* / r well it's *irri*tating / r and at *work* / r with the *dust* / r us being a *cloth*ing factory / r well I find it's *irri*tating / p makes me want to *scratch* it / (p. 7)

Brazil does say that 'the decision as to what parts of what he says can be marked as referring rests, of course, with the speaker' (p. 7) but even so it is difficult to see any reason why some tonics (nuclei) should be called 'referring' and others 'proclaiming' other than that the use of rises and falls requires these labels. Part of the problem is that **any** labels for abstract meanings are likely to appear *post hoc* in the absence of a detailed working out of their relationship to local meanings. Another part of the problem lies in Brazil's choice of the labels 'proclaiming' and 'referring' which are heavily discourse-oriented, when, as we have seen, at least some part of the local meanings of almost all tones is attitudinal. This can clearly be seen if we return to the first example quoted:

/*p John*/*r* painted the *shed*/ (p. 22)

The *p* (fall) on *John* 'proclaims' him as new, whereas the 'referring' *r* (fall-rise) on *shed* indicates 'the respondent's assessment of the state of convergence'. But the fall-rise actually conveys much more than this here. It says: 'As to who painted the shed, it was John. But in my view there is something else which has happened, which is of more importance, and which I would have expected you to ask about.' It carries one of the typical local meanings of fall-rise, i.e. 'reservations'. It could of course be argued that all the attitudinal meanings arise from conditioning factors, but without a systematic illustration of this position, less theoretically biased labels for abstract meanings would be more appropriate.

4.4.3.2   **A three-tone approach.** Gussenhoven (page references following are to (1983a)) has a basic threefold distinction of tone: fall, fall-rise, and rise (note that this is not so very different from Brazil who, in addition to the proclaiming fall and the referring fall-rise, has, in theory if not much in practice, a 'neutral' tone (level or low-rise)). The linguistic material which is placed in focus (and thus indicated by one of the tones) is seen as 'the speaker's declared contribution to the conversation', while that which is out of focus 'constitutes his cognitive starting-point' (p. 383). In-focus material is termed the 'variable' and out-of-focus material is termed the 'background'. Choice of nuclear tone is seen as the choice of a different 'manipulation' of the variable with respect to the background. Thus Gussenhoven, like Brazil, also sees the meanings of the tones as mainly discoursal; nevertheless, he uses a less loaded set of labels. A fall is said to involve 'V-addition'. Its meaning is paraphrased as: 'I want you to know that from now on I consider [this material] to be part of our Background' (p. 384). A fall-rise involves 'V-selection' and can be paraphrased as: 'I want you to take note of the fact that this material is part of our Background' (p. 384). A rise involves 'V-relevance testing' and can be paraphrased as: 'I will leave it up to you to determine whether we should establish this Variable as being part of the Background' (p. 384). Gussenhoven illustrates the meanings of the three tones by reference to the following examples:

> The ˋhouse is on fire
> The ˅house is on fire
> The ˊhouse is on fire?

Variation in the height and complexity of tones is produced by pitch range (= accent range), which operates in gradient fashion (see sub-section 4.4.4.1 below); and by a feature of 'delay', which operates on the three tones to produce rise-fall, rise-fall-rise, and delayed rise (see Gussenhoven, 1983b and further discussion in 4.4.4.2 below). Tones can also be either 'speaker-serving' or 'hearer-serving' and this produces considerable variations in local meanings, cf.

> Of ˋcourse / he's an ˋexpert (I remember now)
> ˊSee / he's an ˋexpert (Now you must believe me)

It is still difficult to see how certain uses of the tones fit into the system. For example, how exactly do we deal with the requirement of a fall on *always* but a rise or a fall-rise on *usually*? In what sense is *always* an addition but *usually* a selection?

This sort of difficulty applies to any characterisation of the abstract meanings of intonation. One way of dealing with such problems is to regard tones as having differences of ORIENTATION. The application of tones to *always* and *usually* may be regarded as a lexical orientation, whereby the fall involves an absolute modifier but fall-rise a selective modifier. This does not of course explain the potential alternative of simple rise on *usually* (I cannot see how 'V-relevance testing' is involved). Other orientations (and these are discussed by Gussenhoven himself in 1983b) may apply to:

(i)   sentence non-final intonation-groups (remember how the local meanings of tones were very different in non-final groups as compared with final and independent groups)

(ii)   conversation initiators. Compare the following initiations:

> ˅Mary (the speaker reactivates the conversation)
> ˋMary (the speaker demands a conversation)
> ˊMary (the speaker wonders if a conversation can begin)

(iii)   interrogative structures. Here the orientation of the tones is transferred to the potential answer of the hearer. A fall invites the listener to add a variable to the background, whereas a fall-rise invites the listener to recall something from the background, cf.

What did you do ˋlast year?
What did you do ˇlast year?

This last example raises an altogether different problem which must at least be mentioned before finishing this discussion of abstract meanings. On both question word interrogatives like the one above and on yes/no interrogatives, some dialects of English (for example, the North-West Midlands accent of Staffordshire, West Derbyshire, Cheshire, and South Manchester) use fall-rises on interrogatives very frequently, while R.P. uses them relatively infrequently. What does this tell us about the abstract meanings (and their different orientations) when compared across different dialects? It is highly unlikely that speakers from one area recall material from the background more frequently than those from another dialect. It is too easy to answer simply by saying that dialects have different 'systems'. The North-West Midlands area referred to uses a set of nuclear tones which is not substantially different from that of R.P.; the difference between the two is principally that certain tones are used consistently more frequently in certain contexts. The local uses and meanings of tones are not only a product of abstract meaning plus orientation (and any further conditioning factors not covered by orientation) but also seem to involve some purely habitual influences. It becomes a habit, for example, to use a fall-rise on interrogatives, and when this happens some of the meaning of the fall-rise is lost. This sort of process must in some way be involved in intonational change. To some extent it calls into doubt the hypothesis that abstract meaning plus orientation plus additional contextual factors can account for **all** intonational usage and meaning. Of course the problem should not only face the intonationist but also the grammarian, as I have already suggested in sub-section 4.4.1.2 above (does the formality of the English passive disappear if the construction is used excessively?). The question of dialectal variation is returned to in chapter 5, section 5.3.

4.4.4   Tonal features

In the previous section we saw that the number of tones is severely reduced when systems of abstract meanings are set up. In order to achieve this reduction, some tones are seen as basic, while other tones are seen as variants of these basic tones. Such variants can be related to the basic tones by means of TONAL FEATURES. Approaches to tonal features are of two types. The first type merely decomposes and cross-classifies, and can be illustrated from Vanderslice and Ladefoged (1972). Their features apply to syllables and a rough gloss on the features is as follows:

[+accent], referring to the presence of a pitch accent
[+intonation], referring to the presence of a nuclear accent
[+cadence], referring to the presence of a falling tone
[+endglide], referring to the presence of a rising tone
[+emphasis], referring to the presence of a widened pitch range

The validity of this type of feature analysis obviously stands or falls by the degree to which it covers a pre-established set of tones. In this case the features [+cadence] [+endglide] jointly define a fall-rise, but the authors admit that the features do not cover rise-fall (although one could define it [−cadence] [−endglide]). This type of intonational feature analysis is clearly similar to distinctive feature analysis in segmental phonology; the features are meaningless in themselves, and only a particular combination of features (or a particular sequence of combinations of features) has meaning. It is a relatively straightforward affair to devise such a set of features to cross-classify tones. But there is another type of approach to tonal features which is more difficult and more important: this seeks to identify features which have a relatively constant meaning or which contribute a relatively constant meaningful part of nuclear tones. Features of this type have been proposed to account for variation in four major areas: (i) accent range (often just referred to as pitch range); (ii) the relationship of the so-called 'complex' tones like fall-rise and rise-fall to simple tones like rise and fall; (iii) the occurrence of 'stylised' tones involving sequences of levels; and (iv) the occurrence of 'downstep' whereby a series of high pitched accents is successively lowered. I deal with these four areas in the next four sub-sections.

4.4.4.1 **Accent range**. ACCENT RANGE refers to the width and height of a nuclear tone. In the case of falling tones in English, it principally involves variations in the height of the starting-point above the baseline, e.g. ⟋ compared with ⟍ ; in the case of rising tones in English, it principally involves variations in the height of the finishing-point above the baseline, e.g. ⟋ on the one hand, compared with ⟋ and ⟋ on the other. Many analysts have argued that the difference in meaning between the higher falls and rises on the one hand, and the lower falls and rises on the other, is of a gradient kind, i.e. any height of fall or rise may occur from the highest to the lowest, and, moreover, the presence or absence of some factor of meaning is directly proportional to the height of the tone. This factor of meaning may be loosely glossed as 'involvement', the higher starts of the falls and the higher ends of the rises being more involved, cf.

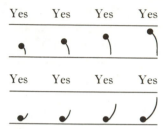

When various heights of falls and rises are presented on isolated words like this, it is difficult to quarrel with this approach. Nevertheless, many systematic expositions of English intonation have typically made distinctions between high-fall and low-fall and between high-rise and low-rise (some have even added a third type of fall or rise, while others have made distinctions among falls but not among rises). The reasons for this are twofold: firstly, it is difficult to incorporate gradient distinctions into linguistic analysis, which has traditionally couched its descriptions in terms of contrasts; secondly, an 'all-or-none' contrast (which is the term generally used as the opposite of gradient) seems to be present when a typical pre-nuclear onset of mid-high syllables is present, cf.

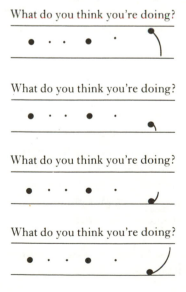

The all-or-none contrast depends on whether the starting-point of the fall, or the finishing-point of the rise, is higher or lower than the preceding syllables, i.e. the apparent contrast arises from the relationship of the nuclear tone to what precedes. But despite the fact that I introduced distinctions between high-fall and low-fall and between high-rise and low-rise when discussing the local meanings of nuclear tones in section 4.1 above, I think these contrasts are indeed more apparent than real and are principally a pedagogic way of dealing with difficult-to-handle gradient differences. One piece of evidence supporting this view comes from the fact that the starting-point of a fall and the finishing-point of a rise can be at the same level as the preceding syllables, and it is impossible in such cases to say whether such a fall or such a rise is nearer the lower or the higher variety. Compare the following examples with the preceding set:

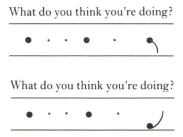

Thus, theoretically, differences of accent range appear to operate in a gradient fashion (even though for practical descriptive purposes it may be convenient to divide up the range to produce apparently discontinuous differences like those between high-fall and low-fall and between low-rise and high-rise).

4.4.4.2 **Complexity.** In the discussion of some of the proposed systems of abstract meanings for tones in sub-section 4.4.3 above, one approach mentioned was that of Gussenhoven (1983a and 1983b) which sets up a basic three-fold distinction between fall, fall-rise, and rise. A tonal feature of 'delay' is then said to produce rise-fall, rise-fall-rise, and delayed rise. So the beginning-point of the major movement of the tone is delayed, producing variations on the basic tones in the following way: ⟍ → ⟋⟍ ; ⟍⟍ → ⟋⟍ ; and ⟋ → ⟍ . The meaning of the modification 'delay' is glossed by Gussenhoven as: 'This manipulation is very non-routine, very significant.' Certainly the 'impressed' meaning of rise-fall discussed in sub-section 4.4.1.1 can be seen in this way when compared with the simple sense of completeness carried by a non-delayed falling tone. A rise-fall-rise (which has not previously been discussed as an independent tone) also seems clearly to be a variant of fall-rise; in fact it seems to add the meaning of rise-fall to that of fall-rise, cf.

> I can do it toˇmorrow
> I can do it toˆmorrow

Here the sense of contrast presented by the fall-rise is added to by some such meaning as: 'and you ought to be impressed by this fact' (i.e. something like a listener-serving use of the rise-fall). The relationship between fall-rise and rise-fall-rise could therefore also be regarded as a 'non-routine, very significant' modification. A delayed rise, also, has not been discussed before, nor does it appear in any of the better-known descriptions of English intonation, but cf.

> Have you received any ∕ letters today?
> Have you received any ‿letters today?

Whatever the exact meaning associated with the second example, it certainly does not appear to me to be 'non-routine, very significant'; if anything, it sounds 'bored' because the range of the delayed rise is usually low and narrow. Hence the argument for a consistent meaning ascribable to the feature 'delay' is weakened.

Brazil (1975) has a basic division between the 'proclaiming' fall and the 'referring' fall-rise (in theory he does, like Gussenhoven, have a third tone, low-rise, which is said to be neutral between the two, but this is only briefly discussed and appears very rarely in his texts; indeed the rises which he terms low-rises must be very narrow rises if they appear as rarely as they do in his transcriptions). Brazil has 'intensified' variants of his two basic tones: rise-fall and rise (the latter must of course exclude the low-rise just discussed). Intensification is said to indicate 'an extra measure of involvement on the part of the speaker' (1975:7). In the case of the basic fall-rise and its 'intensified' variant simple rise, fall-rise is said to refer to vividly present background material while the rise refers 'to matter which, while deemed to be present in the area of convergence, has need of reactivation' (1978:48); rise is also said to be sometimes used to achieve social dominance. Without going into local comparisons in the use of these tones, it can be seen from the table that Brazil's grouping of tones is somewhat different from Gussenhoven's. While falls and rise-falls are grouped similarly in both analyses, rises and fall-rises are grouped differently, being basically treated as part of the same group of tones by Brazil but not by Gussenhoven. Here we are faced of course with the sort of problem which has arisen many times before: intonational meanings are so nebulous that it is not easy to prove purely on the basis of meaning that one sort of grouping is better than another. Notice also that the tonetic modifications involved in Brazil's two intensified tones are not the same (indeed they are exactly opposite: FR → R but F → RF) and hence the advantage of describing a semantic modification as associated with a consistent pitch feature is lost.

	Brazil (1975, 1978)		Gussenhoven (1983a, 1983b)	
	Basic	Intensified	Basic	[+delay]
1.	fall	rise-fall	fall	rise-fall
2.	fall-rise	rise	fall-rise	rise-fall-rise
3.	(low rise)[1]		rise	delayed rise

[1] Strictly speaking, this is regarded by Brazil as 'no tone' rather than a third tone.

An alternative way of grouping tones together, so as to be able to ascribe abstract meanings to such groups and then add semantic modifications by way of intonational features, is to consider the commutation possibilities of the tones. While it is generally a truism that **almost** any tone can be used in any context, there are nevertheless occasional contexts where there are limitations. One such context already mentioned is that where sentence adverbials and adverbials of time and place are given separate intonation-groups. The majority of such adverbials used in this way take some sort of rising tone, but a small group of heavily reinforcing adverbials take some sort of fall. The evidence from such adverbials suggests that all tones with a final falling movement be placed in one group and those with a final rising movement in another. A simple fall or a rise-fall can be used on the final adverbial in the first example below, while a simple rise or a fall-rise or a rise-fall-rise can be used on the final adverbial in the second:

> When I'm in ˅London / I visit my ˎmother / ˎalways
> When I'm in ˅London / I visit my ˎmother / ˏusually

Within the two groups, of falls on the one hand and rises on the other, there is as yet no principled way of saying that one tone is semantically more basic than the others in the same group. Indeed, there is as much reason for saying that the tonetically complex tones rise-fall and fall-rise (and rise-fall-rise as well) are intensified versions of fall and rise (and hence keeping a consistent functional **and** formal tonetic feature of COM-PLEXITY) as for Brazil's system involving opposite tonetic modifications. All systems seem to agree that rise-fall is indeed a complex version of fall; and, considering the second example above, a fall-rise on *usually*

certainly seems more emphatic than the simple rise. So, in the present
state of knowledge, I prefer to keep a two-fold division between falls and
rises and to regard rise-falls and fall-rises (and rise-fall-rises) as COMPLEX.
This analysis comes close to Brazil's although, as already mentioned in
4.4.3.1 above, the labels which he uses, 'proclaiming' fall and 'referring'
rise, seem if anything too concrete as abstract meaning labels, more vague
labels like CLOSED and OPEN being more appropriate to cover the range
of local meanings described for falls and rises in sub-section 4.4.1 above.
But it must be reiterated that the study of the relationship between local
and abstract meanings (and hence also feature relationships like those
within rises and falls) has only recently begun and nothing approaching
a definitive exposition can be made.

4.4.4.3   Stylisation. The third tonal feature to be discussed in this section
is that of STYLISATION (the term derives from Ladd (1978) although so-
called 'call contours' were discussed in the literature long before that).
Stylisation involves the use of levels rather than glides and Ladd
(1978:520) glosses the meaning as 'What is signalled . . . . . is the implication that the message is in some sense predictable, part of a stereotyped
exchange or announcement. "Nothing you couldn't have anticipated" it
says.' The levels involved in the stylisation of tones are either a sequence
of pitches corresponding to the two ends of the related gliding tone or
else a simple level corresponding only to the end pitch of the related gliding
tone. The best-known example of stylisation involves a sequence of two
levels with the second lower than the first by approximately the musical
interval of a minor third. These two pitches correspond approximately
to the beginning and endpoint of a fall-rise, and both the sequence of
levels and the fall-rise are commonly used as 'call contours'; hence this
sequence is said to be a stylised version of fall-rise. Here are some examples:

> Good ⁻mor-ning
> ⁻Ma-ry
> Anyone ⁻the –ere?
> Come and ⁻get –it!

This stylised tone does not necessarily have to be a call however: it can
often be 'teasing', e.g.

> You've got a hole in your ⁻ti–ights!
> I don't think it's going to ⁻wo–ork

One of the seven nuclear tones discussed in the sub-section on local meanings in 4.4.1 was mid-level, and it was also noted there that mid-level

and low-rise were often commutable in sentence non-final intonation-groups. Ladd (1978) suggests that the relationship between the two is one of stylisation and also suggests a similar relationship between high-rise and high-level. Compare the following examples:

> As I was passing the ⟋jewellers / the aˋlarm bell went off
> As I was passing the ⟩jewellers / the aˋlarm bell went off (mid-level)
> Where are you ⟋going?
> Where are you ⟩going? (mid-level)
> Is that ac⟋ceptable?
> Is that ac⟩ceptable? (high-level)

However, the relationships of stylisation between low-rise and mid-level and between high-rise and high-level are very much less easy to support semantically than that between fall-rise and the sequences of two levels discussed above. For example, the high-rise on a declarative form has the effect of turning statement into question, whereas high-level does not have such an effect, cf.

> He ⟋didn't?
> He ⟩didn't (high-level)

Nevertheless, level tones do, at least in English, generally seem to have some common element of meaning that makes the concept of stylisation a useful one.

4.4.4.4 **Declination and downstep.** In chapter 3, section 3.9 the formal model of Pierrehumbert (1980) was described. One of the concepts involved in this model was DECLINATION. So far this is the only mention I have made of this concept, yet it is one which has been much discussed in the literature, particularly in the literature based in experimental phonetics. Declination refers to the fact that the pitch of the voice is most commonly lower at the end of a sentence than it is at the beginning. It has often been suggested that declination operates at both ends of the pitch range. The evidence for baseline declination derives principally from the fact that unaccented syllables at the beginning of a sentence are often at a higher level than unaccented syllables at the end of a sentence; other than this, the evidence is only indirect, i.e. that the best computation of 'top line declination' is based on the assumption of an also declining baseline. 'Top line declination' refers to the fact that a series of high peaks which are judged by listeners to be of equal prominence are actually found by experiment to decline in absolute pitch. Some analysts judge declination to be a feature of sentences; others judge it to be a feature of intonation-groups. There seems to be some truth in both positions:

certainly the baseline is 'reset' at the beginning of each intonation-group (remember this was one of the criteria for an intonation-group boundary in chapter 3, sub-section 3.2.2), yet it is also true that final unaccented syllables are commonly even lower in a sentence final intonation-group than in a sentence non-final intonation-group. Furthermore, the peaks of a sentence final intonation-group are often on average lower than those of a preceding sentence non-final intonation-group (there is further discussion of this under KEY in the next section). So declination seems to be operating at two levels; within intonation-groups but, at a higher level, across intonation-groups which are within the same sentence. There is in addition some suggestion that it may be operating at an even higher level to produce 'paratones' in speech (particularly in read speech) akin to paragraphs in written language.

The concept of declination (or 'downdrift' as it is sometimes called) has been criticised as being purely an artefact of the specially wooden style in which informants tend to read sentences when asked to do so in decontextualised experimental conditions. Acoustic measurements of peaks in naturalistic, particularly conversational, speech have found little evidence for declination. However, this sort of argument, that declination only occurs in fairly 'mechanical' reading styles, is in one way an argument for the usefulness of the concept. If we do speak in a way giving equal weight to each part of an intonation-group (and hence sounding mechanical), then declination will occur. This mechanical style is therefore a useful reference-point for comparison with all those non-mechanical styles where textual and situational effects intrude.

There remains a difficult theoretical and empirical problem concerning declination in English. There are clearly two typical types of sequences of high-pitched accents in English, one in which all the accents are on the same pitch and another in which the accents form a descending series, e.g.

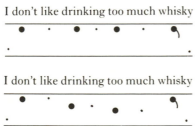

I don't like drinking too much whisky

I don't like drinking too much whisky

It is not clear whether the first example above, which often occurs with **slight** downdrift of the successive accents, is to be taken as the 'unmarked' form with declination, with the second example representing a descent beyond normal declination; or whether the second example is in fact itself the pattern representing normal declination (with the first example representing a special case of maintained high level). In other words, are declination (or downdrift) and something often called DOWNSTEP to be taken as two different phenomena in English? The semantics of the two examples above suggests that the second example is in fact more emphatic. This is generally the case with this pattern; hence it is better taken as a 'marked' pattern than as a pattern involving simple declination.

The conclusion of the last paragraph suggests that we should in English have a further tonal feature of DOWNSTEP, which may apply to any series of high-pitched accents (strictly speaking, to the peaks of high-pitched accents, since it may apply to rise-falls as well). In the second example above, it applied only to the series of pre-nuclear accents, but it may also apply to a nuclear accent following such a series, e.g.

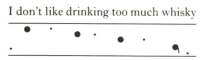

The series of high-pitched accents with downstep may be level, as in the previous examples, or they may be falling (particularly before a fall-rise nuclear tone), e.g.

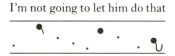

A series of low-pitched accents in English may, conversely, be subject to a feature of UPSTEP. Sequences of this sort are less common than the descending series; probably the most frequent type is one where the top-ends of a series of rises are upstepped, e.g.

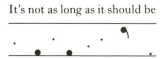

The general concept of declination is one which has been investigated in many languages and is returned to in chapter 5, sub-section 5.5.1. Although less well documented, the features downstep and upstep seem likely to be relevant to the description of series of accents in many languages (the feature downstep was actually first used to describe a contrast between a high tone and a downstepped high tone in African tone languages).

4.5 Key and register

In chapter 3, section 3.5 the concepts of KEY and REGISTER were introduced. Key was said to involve the width of the pitch range over whole intonation-groups. This variation in pitch range width is produced principally by varying the overall height of a series of high-pitched syllables (i.e. raising of the 'top line'); in other words, extra width for key variation is obtained by upward stretching rather than by any change in low-pitched syllables. Of course, in very short intonation-groups (in particular those with only one pitch accent) it is in theory not always clear whether we are dealing with variation in accent range (as in 4.4.4.1 above) or in key (moreover both involve gradient features). In practice, however, short intonation-groups of this sort are most common in response utterances, whereas key is particularly used to link together in various ways successive intonation-groups from the same speaker. When there is more than one pitch accent present in an intonation-group, key is typically set by the height of the first high accent (sometimes referred to as the 'onset'). The most consistently remarked use of key is to indicate the beginning and end of a topic: high key indicates the beginning of a new topic and low key indicates the end of a topic. One example is where someone is giving reasons for a course of action, e.g.

> It would ˈnot be easy to ˋfind such people / ˈnor would it be easy to inˋstruct them correctly / and moreover their sucˈcess rate would be ˋlow

(Here ˈ indicates high level syllables, i.e. high 'onsets', and the level of these high syllables is slightly lower in each successive group.) Key is commonly used in this way in reading and unscripted commentaries (e.g. by radio newsreaders and commentators) and the sections which correspond to topics, and which are delimited by high key and low key, are sometimes referred to as 'paratones'. Another very common use of low key is for parentheticals, e.g.

> Well I saw ˋJim the other ⁄ day // inciˋdentally / he's just got ˋmarried again // and ˅he said . . . . .

(Here double slashes indicate the boundaries of the parenthetic remark.)

REGISTER differences, as opposed to key differences, involve a raising of the baseline; in other words, the range itself within which a speaker is operating is raised. Because speakers normally use only the bottom third of their potential pitch range in speech, there is not much scope for lowering the register we use. Hence the 'normal' register used by speakers is low, and high registers are generally marked in some way. Raising our intonational register involves an overall increase in fundamental frequency, and because one physical factor involved in such an increase is additional tension in the vocal cords, it is often suggested that a high register is used under any condition of emotional tension or stress. There may be some truth in this as a general tendency but, nevertheless, use of high register does appear to become conventionalised in some cultures. In English and in many other languages it seems that use of a high register is in some way associated with social or emotional deference. It has been suggested, for example, that some women put on a 'little girl voice' if they wish to indicate a subservient or 'helpless' role. Brown and Levinson (1978) report deferential uses of high register from Tamil and Tzeltal: it is used when social politeness is called for, when sons speak to fathers, and when those of low caste speak to those of high caste.

Key and register difference have been the subjects of many instrumental studies concerned with the communication of emotional states. However, the way in which the two dimensions of variation have generally been measured has not kept them clearly apart. Certainly, key has been measured by computing the interval between some sort of average of high-pitched syllables and a similar average for low-pitched ones, but register has generally been measured by taking an average overall fundamental frequency (many studies actually refer in fact only to 'pitch range' and 'pitch level'). Since a wide key usually involves stretching at the top end of the pitch range, this will itself produce a higher average fundamental frequency, even though the baseline remains unaltered. It is hardly surprising, therefore, that studies of vocal indicators of emotional states tend to report wide key and high register as co-occurring; and narrow key and low register as co-occurring. Among those emotions reported as having wide key and high register are joy, anger, fear, and surprise; among those reported as having narrow key and low register are boredom and sorrow. From what I have argued above about such studies it seems that these differences are principally ascribable to key rather than to register.

4.6 Summary

At the end of the previous chapter I recapitulated the theoretical constructs which had been established. It is now worth reviewing these, noting where they have been refined and what sorts of functions have been associated with the constructs, particularly in English. We have seen how INTONATION-GROUPS generally correlate with major syntactic constituents, although a good deal of choice is available to speakers concerning **which** constituents intonation-groups should correspond with. Hence we cannot say that syntactic constituency completely predicts intonation-group boundaries: it merely indicates probabilistic tendencies within the choices available. NUCLEUS PLACEMENT indicates the scope of the FOCUS within an intonation-group, though not unambiguously; it merely constrains the range of possibilities. The scope of focus itself is governed by considerations of NEW and OLD information, and contrastivity; while a special type of focus applies to ECHOES and INSISTS.

LOCAL meanings of NUCLEAR TONES in English have been outlined, as have common sequences of nuclear tones: some of the conditioning factors which account for the variation in local meanings were discussed. Approaches to the setting up of ABSTRACT meanings for nuclear tones were illustrated. Some TONAL FEATURES which might be extracted from all nuclear tones and given a meaning component of their own were presented: these features were ACCENT RANGE, COMPLEXITY, STYLISATION, and DOWN-STEP (this last being discussed with reference to the related DECLINATION tendency). Finally KEY and REGISTER, which are overall features of intonation-groups, were discussed.

Virtually all this chapter has involved a detailed discussion of theoretical issues with reference to English only; in the case of local meanings, a considerable amount of descriptive detail of English was presented. This concentration on English reflects our present state of knowledge; descriptions and theoretical discussions of intonation in other languages have much less weight of analysis and scholarship behind them. Nevertheless, in the next chapter, I shall attempt to widen the discussion to include intonational variation in English dialects, the intonation of languages other than English, intonational acquisition and change, and possible intonation universals.

Sources and further reading

For intonational phrasing, see Halliday (1967) and Crystal (1975).

For statistics on correlations between intonation-groups, nucleus placement, and syntax, see Quirk *et al.* (1964).

For the intonation of adverbials, see Allerton and Cruttenden (1974, 1976, 1978).

For the intonation of *too* and *either*, see Thompson (1981).

For broad focus v. narrow focus, see Ladd (1979a) and Gussenhoven (1983a).

For the distinction between lexical items and grammatical items, see Crystal (1975).

For event sentences, see Guéron (1980), Allerton and Cruttenden (1979), Fuchs (1980) and Gussenhoven (1983a).

For final adverbials, see Allerton and Cruttenden (1976, 1978).

For expressions in final position, see Bing (1979b).

For the intonation of wh objects, see Ladd (1979a).

For discussion of syntactic v. semantic views of nucleus placement see Bresnan

(1971), Lakoff (1972), Berman and Szamosi (1972), Bolinger (1972a) and Schmerling (1974, 1976).

For discussion of nucleus placement in structures of the *duty to perform* type, see Newman (1946) and Stockwell (1972); and the six items in the previous set of references.

For nouns as more accentable than verbs, see Ladd (1979a) and Bing (1979a); for noun v. verb accenting in relative clauses, see Garro and Parker (1982). For statistics on correlations between nuclei and grammatical classes, see Quirk *et al.* (1964).

For new and old (or 'given') information, see Halliday (1967), Chafe (1974), Halliday and Hasan (1976), Huckin (1977), Lehman (1977), Firbas (1980), Prince (1981), Nooteboom and Terken (1982), Brown (1983), Brown and Yule (1983), and Gussenhoven (1985) (reprinted in Gussenhoven, 1984).

For a discussion of 'contrastive', see Chafe (1976) and Taglicht (1982).

For a classification of echoes, see Quirk *et al.* (1972: section 7.80).

For discussion of counterpresuppositionals, see Dik (1980), Taglicht (1982), Gussenhoven (1983a), and Bolinger (1985).

For a discussion of 'normal stress', see Schmerling (1974, 1976).

For the use of unmarked tones defined in grammatical terms, see Halliday (1967) and Crystal (1975).

For the discoursal approach to the meanings of tones, see Brazil (1975, 1978), Brazil, Coulthard and Johns (1980), and Sinclair and Brazil (1982).

For the attitudinal approach to the meanings of tones, see Kingdon (1958a), Schubiger (1958), and O'Connor and Arnold (1961, 1973).

For emotional markers, see Fónagy (1978).

For the frequency of various tones with yes/no questions, see Fries (1964) and Lee (1980).

The local meanings suggested by a low-fall are from O'Connor and Arnold (1973). The abstract meanings suggested for fall-rise are from Brazil (1975), Ladd (1977) and Gussenhoven (1983b).

For intonational idioms and other yoked expressions, see Bolinger (forthcoming) chapter 2.

For reduced sets of nuclear tones, see Ladd (1980) (four), Gussenhoven (1983b) (three) and Brazil (1975, 1978) (two).

For local meanings, see in particular O'Connor and Arnold (1961, 1973). See also Kingdon (1958a), Schubiger (1958), and Halliday (1967). For American English see in particular Pike (1945) although Pike's meanings vary considerably in their degree of abstraction, nor does he use a notion of nucleus; instead, all pitch accents, final or non-final, are said to initiate certain patterns, to which fairly general meanings are attached.

For the intonation of adverbials, see Allerton and Cruttenden (1974, 1976, 1978) and Cruttenden (1981a). For other expressions taking low-rise in final position, see Bing (1979b). For the treatment of the low-rise of constant polarity tags as a tail to an overall fall-rise, see Gussenhoven (1985) (reprinted in Gussenhoven, 1984).

For high-rise in Australian English, see McGregor (1980), Allan (1984) and Guy and Vonwiller (1984).

For the interaction between intonation and negatives, see Palmer (1922), Lee (1956), Halliday (1967), Jackendoff (1972), Liberman and Sag (1974), Ladd (1977), Bing (1980), and Cruttenden (1984). For various approaches to the analysis of *any* (including the two-*any* approach) see Taglicht (1984).

For the use of fall-rise on sentences of the *I thought* . . . . . type, see Nash and Mulac (1980), and Oakeshott-Taylor (1984).

For sequences of tones in sentences, see Trim (1959), O'Connor and Arnold (1973), and Fox (1973).

For discussion of conditioning factors, see Crystal (1975).

Brazil's system of tones is expounded in Brazil (1975, 1978), in Brazil, Coulthard and Johns (1980), and in Sinclair and Brazil (1982).

Gussenhoven's system of tones is expounded in Gussenhoven (1983b) and, more briefly, in Gussenhoven (1983a).

Gussenhoven's use of the term 'variable' is taken from its use in generative studies of focus in which the main presupposition of an utterance is said to be derived by placing the focus on a variable. (See Chomsky (1971), Jackendoff (1972), Akmajian (1979), Wilson and Sperber (1979) and Smith and Wilson (1979).)

For another approach to the relationship between local and abstract meanings, see Pakosz (1982).

For gradient meanings in intonation, see Bolinger (1958) and (1961), Trim (1970), and Bailey (1978).

For a description of a 'narrow' rise which seems to be equivalent to Gussenhoven's 'delayed' rise, see Lewis (1977).

For a case for a simple division into falls and rises, see Cruttenden (1981b).

For an overall feature approach to intonation, but one which is closely tied to syntax, see Hirst (1977).

For a general feature approach to tones, see Ladd (1983).

For stylisation, see Pike (1945 : 71), who referred to a 'spoken chant [whose] meaning is of a CALL, often with WARNING by or to children', Fox (1969, 1970), Crystal (1969b), Lewis (1970), Gibbon (1976), who reports the more extensive use of 'call contours' in German, Ladd (1978), and Gussenhoven (1983b).

For declination in English, see Cooper and Sorensen (1977), Pierrehumbert (1979), Sorensen and Cooper (1980), and Liberman and Pierrehumbert (1982). For a criticism of declination as an experimental artefact, see Umeda (1982).

For downstep in African tone language, see Fromkin (1972) and Welmers (1973).

For the discoursal functions of key, see Brazil (1975, 1978) and Brown, Currie and Kenworthy (1980). For high register as social deference, see Brown and Levinson (1978). For vocal indicators of emotional states, see Fairbanks and Pronovost (1939), Williams and Stevens (1972), Fónagy (1978) and Scherer (1981).

5
Comparative intonation

5.1 Introduction

In this chapter I shall consider various aspects of intonational variation, namely, aspects of sociolinguistic (including dialectal) variation, cross-linguistic differences and similarities in intonation, and intonation acquisition and change. Regrettably, however, in many of the areas covered, our knowledge of basic descriptive facts is either minimal or disputed.

5.2 Style, class, and sex

It seems probable that all languages and dialects involve at least some intonational variation in all three areas (style, class, and sex), although the amount of published systematic and reliable information is small. Clearly, in all languages there will be varying styles of intonation appropriate to different situations. In the description of the local meanings of nuclear tones in chapter 4, sub-section 4.4.1 above, occasional reference was made to such stylistic variation. For example, it was noted that, of the four tones which are most typical of sentence non-final intonation-groups in English (low-rise, high-rise, fall-rise, and mid-level), two (low-rise and fall-rise) were more typical of formal styles. Of the two informal styles, high-rise is the particularly 'casual' one: it is, for example, typical of a number of teenage groups, particularly in Australia and America, for whom casualness is the 'in thing'. Mid-level, while being a common non-final tone in conversation, is also common in the speeches of politicians who pride themselves on possessing the common touch, e.g. Harold Wilson. The two more formal sentence non-final tones, low-rise and fall-rise, are particularly common in reading. Indeed the intonation of reading, as might be expected, exhibits other features of a formal style, e.g. intonation-groups are more clearly delineated (partly because there are fewer false starts and hesitations), and intonation-groups are generally longer. Conversation, on the other hand, is the archetypal informal style, which, besides using the informal non-final tones, will involve a very high proportion of short intonation-groups and, moreover, a high proportion of cases of one intonation-group per (short) sentence (many such short sentences are of course response utterances). So sentence non-final intonation-groups constitute only a small proportion of the total number of intonation-groups. Hence it is not surprising that there are a high number of falling tones in conversation, since falls are the most common and attitudinally most neutral tones of independent clauses. So far I have mentioned variation in intonation-groupings and in choice of tone, but variations in nucleus placement may also be characteristic of the difference between two styles. Contrastive focus early in an intonation-group seems to be more common in conversation than in reading, probably because the latter makes more use of grammatical variations involving changes of word-order and constructions like clefting to achieve similar effects. Another type of variation across different styles is in the use made of accent range. For example, sports commentators use accent range to link long passages together, usually ending with a very wide fall. Listen, for example, to any radio commentary on a horse race or a soccer game (in, for example, the U.K., or the U.S., Italy, or Argentina).

Although there has in recent years been an ever-growing number of studies of the relationship between language and social class, intonation has not figured in this growth, and any studies which have been made of it have remained buried in research reports or in working papers which have not had a wide circulation. But it is undoubtedly a field which will prove fertile for those who can handle it. I will briefly illustrate the potential of the field from the excellent study made by McGregor (1980). He examined the increasing use of high-rise in Australian English, particularly in Sydney. Remember that high-rise, as described in chapter 4, sub-section 4.4.1 on local meanings, is particularly 'casual' when used on sentence non-final groups. In its use with independent or sentence final intonation-groups it is typically an echo question when used on declarative or elliptical sentences. It is also the typical tone used with yes/no questions in a number of English dialects – although not in R.P. So if we had to sum up what has already been said about its meaning it would be that it is used to indicate casualness and to indicate a 'check'. But I also mentioned in the preceding paragraph that it was being increasingly used by teenagers, particularly in Australia and America. McGregor's study was of this increasing use in Sydney. He studied its use in final intonation-groups in non-question forms in adolescent and adult samples. Among adolescents it was more common in state schools than in independent schools; more common when parents were of lower occupational status; more common when children were of below average intelligence; and more common when a broad dialect was used. Among adults high-rise was generally used less than among adolescents. It was also particularly associated with zones of Sydney which had residents of lower occupational status and was used less by those over the age of twenty-five than by those under that age. This may of course indicate one or both of two things: either high-rise is purely a signal of youth of a certain sort and will remain limited in use principally to this age-group, or it may in addition be an intonational change being initiated by youth, in which case we would expect present youth to keep this tone as it ages. One interesting further finding from this study was that there was a slight tendency for females rather than males to use high-rise. A number of other studies have shown more generally a greater use of rises among females; but studies have also shown that females have a stronger tendency to avoid stigmatised broad dialectal forms. It appears that use of high-rise in Sydney is not yet sufficiently stigmatised to have this latter effect. On the other hand, if it does become thus stigmatised, this might actually prevent its further spread as an intonational change. The development of easy recording facilities in the latter half of this century has made it possible to study potential intonational changes of this sort, although no one has yet done so in any detail (but see section 5.6 below).

The last paragraph mentioned the slight tendency in Sydney for females to use more high-rises than males. Greater use of rises among American females is reported by Brend (1975), who also reports their use of wider key. Girls are often said to use a more 'expressive' intonation than boys, who 'play it cool'; 'expressive' intonation refers to the two factors of more rises and wider key. The fundamental frequency of women's voices is, of course, physiologically conditioned to be higher than men's (its progression through life also seems to be different: the fundamental frequency of females generally continues to lower with age, whereas the fundamental frequency of males generally lowers until approximately the age of 60 and then rises again). But there are a number of pieces of evidence which suggest that the differences between the mean fundamental frequency of groups of females and that of groups of males is often greater than would be predicted simply by comparison of the size and length of the larynx and the vocal cords. Among many groups there may thus be a tendency for females to exaggerate their femininity and/or males to exaggerate their masculinity. But some people may actually take a decision to reverse this tendency: many American women consciously adopt low-pitched voices.

It is also true that stereotyped ideas about the differences between men and women can lead to a general overestimation of those differences. One study by Edelsky (1979) had interviewers ask men and women a number of simple questions like 'what is your favourite colour?' and found very few intonational differences between the men and women; but when replies were played back to listeners, rises, whether used by men or by women, were commonly judged more feminine.

5.3 Dialectal variation

There is no book or article which includes any detailed comparison of the intonation of various English dialects: all that is available at present is a number of sketchy articles, and paragraphs in books and articles which are only suggestive. The brief survey which follows can therefore only be regarded as programmatic. Only salient features of the intonation of some dialects are pointed out: no attempt is made, given the present state of knowledge, to make a systematic point-by-point comparison. The difficulties involved in making such a comparison are immense. In comparing the consonants and vowels of two dialects, we have one stable criterion: are two sounds in contrast in a particular dialect (i.e. do they make a difference of meaning, or at least hold the potential of doing so)? This gives us an inventory of phonemes in each dialect, from which all types of comparison follow: is the inventory of phonemes the same in one dialect as in another, is their distribution in words the same, and how does the phonetic quality of each phoneme compare? But we have no such stable criterion in any comparison of intonation across dialects; it is merely a glib remark to say that we must start by asking the same question as in segmental comparisons (i.e. what intonations are in contrast within one dialect?), since, as should be very apparent by now, intonational meanings are nebulous things involving all sorts of fairly arbitrary decisions like 'is the difference of meaning of the "all-or-none" or of the "gradient" kind?' (see chapter 4, sub-section 4.4.4.1 above). Ideally, a comparison would compare the basic tones of each dialect together with their abstract meanings (see chapter 4, sub-section 4.4.3) and would also compare the use and meanings of various tonal features like downstep, accent range, stylisation, and so on (see chapter 4, sub-section 4.4.4). The comparison would go on to compare variations in the local meanings produced in each dialect. But since most of these concepts are still at a formative stage even in the description of standard dialects, it is impossible to use them systematically in dialectal comparison.

In chapter 4, sub-section 4.4.1, I discussed the difficulty of sustaining a grammatical approach to the description of the nuclear tones of English: almost any tone can occur with any sentence-type or construction and in addition it is not always clear which tone should be taken as neutral or 'unmarked' for each sentence-type (e.g. why has the 'polite' low-rise or high-rise usually been taken as unmarked for yes/no questions rather than the 'business-like' high-fall?). However, we are forced to settle for a somewhat unsatisfactory grammatical approach of this kind when we compare dialects, for two reasons:

(a)   a grammatical framework is the only agreed framework in which to anchor our comparison (i.e. analysts do generally agree on what constitutes a declarative, a yes/no interrogative, a question word interrogative, an imperative, a noun-phrase subject, and so on)

(b)   almost all the limited number of dialectal descriptions available have used this sort of framework.

So in the dialectal comparison which follows I shall talk about the typical tones associated with declaratives, sentence non-final intonation-groups, and so on. In other words, we are keeping our dialectal comparison at the level of the local meanings of tones, using one of the strong conditioning factors (see chapter 4, sub-section 4.4.2), that of co-occurring grammatical type, as the framework.

The presumption of this section so far has been that the most important variable involved in intonation across dialects is that of nuclear tone. Typical patterns of pre-nuclear accents are also likely to vary (although these are even less well documented). Variations of intonation-groupings and nucleus placements conditioned by dialect are apparently minimal (but see the discussion of Caribbean English below) whereas differences of key (= pitch range width) are much more common. There are many other potential prosodic differences between dialects which await further study: for instance, how far does length supplement the pitch prominence of the nucleus (e.g. the vowel of the nuclear syllable is even more elongated in Glaswegian English than it is in other dialects)? How far does loudness supplement the nucleus and at precisely what point in the nuclear syllable is the peak of loudness reached? Do some dialects prefer a glide on the nuclear syllable while others prefer a jump between the nuclear syllable and the syllable following it if there is one? (E.g. it is sometimes said that British English prefers glides while American English prefers jumps, although I know of no experimental support for this.)

5.3.1   British English

Undoubtedly the most noticeable variation within British English is the more extensive use of rising tones in many northern cities.

This phenomenon is reported for Birmingham, Liverpool, Glasgow, Belfast, and Tyneside, and something very similar is reported for Welsh English. It is not reported for rural areas of England or Scotland, nor does it occur in Edinburgh. It must surely be no accident that in most of the areas involved there is a strong Celtic influence. This influence is a direct linguistic influence in the case of Welsh English, where many speakers also speak Welsh; an indirect influence in the case of Belfast, where a majority of speakers of Irish English do not speak a Celtic language; and an even more indirect influence in other cases like Liverpool and Tyneside, where the influence is dependent on an influx of people from Ireland or Scotland, who again usually do not actually speak a Celtic language. I referred above to the basic phenomenon as the more extensive use of rising tones; this is an oversimplification because in fact four varieties of tone are involved:

(i)   a rising glide on the nuclear syllable or a jump-up between the nuclear syllable and the following unaccented syllable ('rise')

(ii)   a jump-up on the unaccented syllable following the nucleus and the maintenance of this level on succeeding unaccented syllables ('rise-plateau')

(iii)   a jump-up on the unaccented syllable following the nucleus and the maintenance of this level on succeeding unaccented syllables, except that the last one or two syllables may decline slightly ('rise-plateau-slump')

(iv)   a rise-fall in which the voice reaches the baseline and which is accomplished without any plateau between rise and fall ('rise-fall')

Generally there is an increase in the occurrence of all such varieties in the dialects mentioned, although each dialect has a preference for one variety. Glasgow appears to prefer type (i), the 'rise' (with considerable lengthening of the nuclear syllable); whereas Welsh English prefers type (iv), the rise-fall. However, types (ii) and (iii) appear to predominate in Belfast, Liverpool, Tyneside, and Birmingham (I am of course speaking principally of 'broad' dialect speakers in the areas concerned; there will be many speakers in those areas who use Received Intonation or some form of hybrid or who are bi-intonational). In Belfast, for example, rise-plateau and rise-plateau-slump are the two most common tones on declarative sentences, e.g.

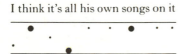
I think it's all his own songs on it

It's a double album

Rise-fall occurs less frequently and seems to function as a more emphatic tone, often involving narrow focus, e.g.

I was disappointed the Halle didn't do any more

The tones used in sentence non-final intonation-groups in Belfast English are not so obviously different from final intonation-groups as they are in R.P., while both yes/no and question word interrogatives involve a higher pitch but usually no difference of tone. Simple falling tones are almost entirely limited to exclamations. The intonation of Liverpool (reported in detail in Knowles (1974) and more briefly in Knowles (1978)) is in many ways similar to that of Belfast. Rise-plateau, rise-plateau-slump, and rise-fall all occur, e.g.

Everton used to be the best team

He's got some animals

They're usually everywhere

Another tone, so far undiscussed, is also common in Liverpool. It involves a high peak on the nucleus followed by a jump-down and then a spreading at the lower level, either by the elongation of a syllable or by the maintenance of the same pitch on succeeding unaccented syllables ('fall-plateau'), e.g.

When we got to the ground

Is it usually so easy?

Did you go to the new supermarket?

This tone is common on non-final groups (which also commonly have mid-level) and on yes/no interrogatives (which may also take a high-level, which is rather like the high-rise of R.P. without the final upward kick – see chapter 3, section 3.7; and which, as another alternative, may take a high fall-rise as discussed in chapter 4 at the very end of sub-section 4.4.1.3). Knowles (1974) argues, I think convincingly, that such fall-plateaus are to be viewed as narrow fall-rises, and ultimately as rising tones; while rise-plateaus and rise-plateau-slumps are to be viewed as narrow rise-falls, and ultimately as falling tones. Certainly this is the way speakers of other dialects interpret the tones (although often attributing to them a variety of attitudinal implications) and certainly the distribution of the tones according to sentence-type suggests this solution. Rise-plateaus and rise-plateau-slumps occur on unmarked declaratives and on question word interrogatives in Liverpool, where R.P. commonly has a simple falling tone; fall-plateaus, on the other hand, occur on non-final groups and on yes/no interrogatives, where fall-rises or simple rises are common in R.P. So, although at the beginning of this section I suggested that rises were generally heard as more common in many areas of northern Britain, it now becomes apparent that such rises are really in some sense falls! With increased knowledge of dialectal intonation we may be able to write generative rules to explain this sort of variation by the use of features like delayed peak (= rise-fall), peak spreading (= rise-plateau), and valley spreading (= fall-plateau). Rules of this sort have already been used to explain dialectal variation in the patterns associated with the lexical tones of Swedish, whereby the same basic tone (functionally defined as occurring in the same set of words) occurs in tonetically very different forms.

The use of rise-falls, rise-plateaus and related patterns is then a feature of areas of Celtic influence in the north and west of the British Isles. In other areas at least the tonal inventory seems similar to R.P. Thus the few studies done on the intonation of rural dialects of England report little difference from R.P. apart from the isolated report of an occasional different tonal usage (e.g. a high-rise – involving a step-up in pitch to the nucleus – is preferred to low-rise for yes/no interrogatives in Norfolk), and there are isolated reports that some dialects use a narrower pitch range (involving both accent range and key) than R.P., e.g. Liverpool, Yorkshire, and Lincolnshire. For Scotland, apart from Glasgow, a typical sentence, either declarative or interrogative, will involve a sequence of falling tones, e.g.

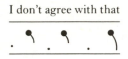

I don't agree with that

Variations in the height of the peak may arise when a new topic is introduced, raising the first peak; or when there is a narrow focus, often for contrast, on one of the words containing an accented syllable; or when the last peak is raised to indicate a question. Rises of any sort are rare (although they do sometimes occur on tentative questions and on echo questions) and fall-rises non-existent. The outstanding feature of this type of intonation is that the basic intonation pattern is subject to very little change due to grammatical, attitudinal, or discoursal reasons; there appears, for example, to be only slight downgrading of peaks because of the occurrence of old information. This sort of intonational system is reported for areas as far apart as Edinburgh, Thurso, Ayr, and Paisley.

5.3.2 Variation in English dialects outside Britain

Once again, detailed information concerning intonational variation in dialects outside Britain is slight, but what information there is suggests that variation within the U.S. and Canada is much less than it is within Britain; that differences between the intonation of American English on the one hand and that of R.P. on the other are themselves less than variation within Britain; and that the position as regards Australia and New Zealand is much the same. What this means is that nowhere is the difference in tonal inventory as great as that between R.P. and Belfast or Liverpool, and that intonational differences which do exist concern principally differences in the use of similar tones. The collection of considerable amounts of data will be necessary before such differences are clearly apparent and it is not therefore surprising that little information is available. General American clearly makes more use of high-rise rather than of low-rise in yes/no questions; and the use of high-rise seems to be increasing, on declaratives, as a marker of casualness, particularly among adolescents and teenagers, and particularly in narrative monologues, e.g.

> So we stand there for a long ′time / and then wander into ′class
> / about five minutes ′late / We're just standing outside the ′door
> / and the whole class is kind of ′talking / . . . . .

In addition to the more common use of high-rise, Americans also appear to use a high fall-rise more commonly than R.P. speakers, and, at least to British ears, this also contributes to the effect of casualness. The tone is often used with the same sort of 'casual continuation' effect as that of the high-rise in the above example, but is also frequently used in answers to questions:

A.   Did he pass the exam?
B.   He certainly ˅did

It is often said that the intonation of Black American English is very different from that of General American, but once again reports which substantiate this are almost non-existent: it is nevertheless reported that it uses more rises, a wider key, and a higher register (including much use of falsetto).

Section 5.2 above reported an increasing use of high-rises among the youth of Sydney, Australia; this usage seems to represent the image of casualness much as it does for some American youth. McGregor (1980 : 1) suggests that it 'can also be heard in other regions of Australia and it may be that this intonation contour will in time be recognised as a characteristic marker of Australian English'. McGregor goes on to note that it is not reported in earlier studies of Australian intonation or of the speech of Australian adolescents. Indeed the image of Australians among other English speakers is often one of aggression, and my own informal observations of middle-aged and older Australians lead me to believe that this is, at least in part, due to a greater use of falls than in other dialects, particularly on sentence non-final intonation-groups. So Australian English intonation may indeed be in a state of flux.

Finally, some brief discussion is needed of Caribbean English and of Indian English. Although the status of the language is somewhat different in each case (Caribbean English is usually an L1 while Indian English is an L2), the problems in analysing the intonation of the two areas are very similar. In both cases, speakers use a rhythm which is considerably different from other types of English, because it makes very much less use of reduced syllables; in both cases speakers have many words which differ from other dialects in their stress patterns; in both cases it is said that nucleus placement is not as moveable as it is in other dialects, that it is generally fixed on the last stress, and that hence, like Edinburgh English mentioned above, there is no de-accenting for old information; and that contrast is indicated by pitch height rather than by using a different nucleus placement or a different nuclear tone. Furthermore it is reported for both areas that the most common nuclear tone is a rise-fall (and hence

Indian English is often reported as sounding like Welsh English). Wells (1982) reports on the difficulty of deciding whether Jamaican Creole is using a different stress pattern or whether it just gives the impression of a different word-stress because of the use of a rise-fall. The example he gives is of *I was going into the kitchen*, where /kɪ-/ has a mid pitch and /-tʃɪn/ a fall from high to low. Wells' conclusion is that rise-fall rather than changed word-stress is the correct solution in this case, but others have reported new lexical contrasts based on word-stress arising in Caribbean English, e.g. *bróther* (sibling) v. *brothér* (monk). Like Black American English, West Indian English is also reported as using a wide key.

This brief exploration of dialectal variation in intonation has been almost entirely limited to English. Such variation is even less documented for other languages than it is for English (although there has been some study of dialectal variation in the tones of tone languages and considerable study of the variation in word-tones in those languages which make only a limited use of tone, like Swedish and Norwegian). But a number of the variables which have been mentioned in dialectal variation, like differences of key, restrictions on nucleus movement, differences in tonal inventory versus differences in the use of tones, will reappear in the following sections, which go on to discuss intonational differences and similarities across languages.

5.4 Cross-linguistic comparisons

In this section I attempt to identify some of the dimensions of variation in intonation between languages; in the next section I attempt the converse and discuss some possible universals of intonation. As usual (I tire of saying it and no doubt the reader tires of reading it, but it has to be said) there are many difficulties – many more, for example, than there are in making segmental comparisons. There are indeed many mentions of intonation in written grammars of languages; but these are, on the vast majority of occasions, superficial, often simply saying for example, that statements have a falling tune and questions a rising tune. Description of a tune as rising can hide a multitude of possible variations within the tune, e.g. where does it rise, at the beginning, at the end, from beginning to end, or in some other way? Thus, for example, in Atayal, a language of Taiwan, it is said that: 'Towards the end of a sentence there are two relevant intonation patterns, one containing a high pitch element which expresses question '?' or emotion '!', and one which does not contain such a relevant high pitch element. If the last syllable of the sentence is a final particle, the high pitch is usually on the syllable preceding the particle' (Egerod, 1966 : 130). But what presents even more difficulty is that there is no agreed theoretical framework within which descriptions are couched. The majority see intonation as directly governed by grammar: they talk of the intonation of sentences, not intonation-groups; they talk of the tunes of declaratives and yes/no interrogatives; and the relationships between intonation and accent are rarely stated in any detail. Even where detailed models have been set up, as is the case for some European languages (e.g. for Swedish and Dutch), the models are often very different from the nuclear tone approach which has been the cornerstone of this book (see sub-section 5.4.3 below for comparisons); and hence even in these cases comparisons are often difficult. Nevertheless, some attempt must be made to look at variation across languages, and in the following sub-sections I shall consider variation in intonation-groupings, variations in nucleus placement (these two very briefly) and variations in tone (this in rather more detail). At the beginning of the consideration of tone, I shall digress for one sub-section to show what two highly-regarded alternative models of intonation look like. The variations discussed by no means cover all potential variation. For example, I have no comparative data with which to discuss in any detail variations in key and register. It is occasionally suggested that some languages use a narrow key (e.g. Danish) or that they use a high register (e.g. many varieties of Chinese) or that variation in key and register according to sex and style is greater in some languages than in others (e.g. it has been suggested that the difference in register between Japanese men and women is greater than it is in English). But most such suggestions are not much more than anecdotal. A further difficulty with studying comparative intonation across languages is that a non-native speaker of a particular language, even one with phonetic training and a good ear for pitch, is almost always unaware of many of the nuances of meaning, and often even of the correctness, of intonation patterns. Therefore we are almost entirely dependent on native speakers for our descriptive data on intonation.

5.4.1   Comparative intonation-groupings

Information on intonation-groupings is entirely limited to European languages and almost entirely to Indo-European languages. Hence information is also limited to languages of similar grammatical structure. In this sort of limited comparison it is, nevertheless, immediately striking how much similarity is reported across languages. The most frequent correspondence of intonation-groups is undoubtedly with clauses, but similar correspondences with grammatical structures smaller than the clause are regularly reported. Four such structures in particular can be identified where many European languages are similar to English and to each other:

(i)   Non-pronominal subjects:
         French: Pour les Anglais / le sens de l'humour / ça les aide à . . . . .
         Italian: Il primo uomo sulla luna / era Neil Armstrong
         Hungarian: A barátom fia / megnősült (Varga, 1984 : 136)
         Portuguese: O homem da gabardine branca / é o líder da manif

(ii)   Recapitulated subjects:
         German: Sie kam heute an / die Brigitte
         Portuguese: Ela comeu / a galinha
         French: Où est ce qu'il est supposé habiter à Paris / Wayne?

(iii)   Initial and final adverbials:
         Portuguese: Ele não respondeu / claramente
         German: In Köln / gibt es eine schöne Kathedrale
         French: Tandis qu'en France / c'est très rare

(iv)   Non-defining structures in medial position:
         French: L'homme / désolé / a parlé à la foule
         French: Le général / Jacques Massu / a écrit un livre
         Portuguese: O meu irmão / em Lisboa / tem um novo emprego

Another typical usage in many European languages is that of a low level pitch for 'parentheticals' in final position (such 'parentheticals' are often separated from what precedes by a pause but whether such sequences are to be analysed as separate intonation-groups or not is problematic – see chapter 3, sub-section 3.2.4). One structure which commonly has this low level pitch in European languages is the reporting clause:

         Hungarian: 'És ha nem?' / kérdezte (Varga, 1984 : 133)
         French: 'Qui est là?' / demande-t-elle
         English: 'Where are you going?' / he said
         Portuguese: 'Vou-me embora' / disse ele

Many of the examples above have concerned French, and although in French and English potential intonation-groupings are apparently much the same, studies of French actually show that the number of words in intonation-groups in French is on average smaller than in English, i.e. French intonation-groups are shorter than in English. This suggests that while the options open to speakers of two languages may be the same, the actual use made of the options may be different. French appears to make more use of the options involving short intonation-groups than does

English. This is related to the fact that French does not have the mobile nucleus characteristic of English (see following sub-section) nor the same potential for pre-nuclear accents, and hence is forced to introduce extra intonation-groups for the purpose of highlighting. So the following example is not untypical (where the nucleus is on the final syllable in each group, the non-final groups ending on a mid or high level, the final group ending with a fall):

> Il est parti / hier soir / avec sa famille / dans le train / de Manchester / à Londres

5.4.2 **Comparative nucleus placement**

Nucleus placement is only one means whereby languages put syntactic constituents into focus. Morphosyntactic means include word-order, clefting, and emphatic or topic markers in the form of words or bound morphemes. Sometimes nucleus placement operates in conjunction with one or more of the morphosyntactic means, and in such cases it is not always easy to decide which is primary. Usually word-order change and the use of clefting are taken to be primary because they are more widely used. A full typology of focus would therefore be based at least as much on considerations of word-order and clefting as on nucleus placement. This is not the place for such a full typology, but clearly such considerations cannot be completely excluded. In particular, word-order will have to be brought into all discussions of nucleus movement.

Nucleus placement involving broad focus on declarative sentences in SVO languages appears regularly to fall on the object, producing the same sort of ambiguity between broad focus and narrow focus on the object as in English. There are sometimes reports that broad focus will involve nucleus placement on the subject in SVO languages but there are always doubts about the interpretation of such reports. One such language is Finnish where one report categorically states that neutral intonation has 'stress' on the leftmost constituent (Heringer and Wolontis, 1972) but this is contradicted by another report which says that the prominent syllable in non-contrastive utterances comes at the end (Iivonen, 1978). In this particular case one misleading factor may be that many Finnish intonation patterns have their highest pitch at the beginning of the intonation-group and moreover word-stress falls on the first syllable. Broad focus involving the nucleus on the subject in SVO languages remains doubtful. In SOV languages, broad focus seems to fall most usually on the object again, as in Turkish, e.g.

> Dün sokakta AhmeD'igördüm
> 'Yesterday in the street Ahmed I saw'
> Erkekten kahve yi aldı
> 'From the boy coffee he bought'

But things are not quite what they appear to be at first sight. It would be more correct to say that the nucleus falls on a pre-verbal nominal, e.g.

> Elmaları bir çocuǒA verdik
> 'The apples to a child we gave'

A similar situation is often said to apply in Hungarian, although there are further qualifications. If the pre-verbal nominal is actually a pronominal the nucleus may go on the verb (although of course in this case it could be said that broad focus is not involved because the pronominal refers to old information). Moreover, the sorts of locationals which we saw occurring in various positions before the verb in the Turkish examples above may occur in post-verbal position in Hungarian and are then likely to take the nucleus when verb and locational are in focus, e.g.

> (Mit csinálnak a gyerekek?
> 'What are doing the children?')
> A gyerekek játszanak a KERtben
> 'The children are playing in the garden' (Varga, 1984 : 139)

All that can be stated with certainty regarding nucleus placement in broad focus sentences is that there is undoubtedly a tendency to prefer nouns to verbs as locations for the nucleus. Notice the following examples from German (and compare chapter 4, sub-section 4.3.1 above):

> Wach AUF! Das HAUS brennt
> Es war ihm SCHLECHT / weil er zuviel BIER getrunken hatte

There is probably also a tendency to prefer the nucleus on the **final** noun. Strictly speaking, one should say noun-phrase, since the nucleus may usually fall on the adjective in languages where adjectives regularly follow the nouns they modify (e.g. French). It should also be made clear that the preceding statements apply only to broad focus declaratives. In many languages the nucleus may fall on the verb in questions (e.g. Roumanian).

When we come to consider narrow focus we find that many languages are like English in allowing the nucleus to move up and down an intonation-group according to the demands of contrast and of new and old information. For example, nucleus placement in German and Russian seems to respond to the demands of contrastivity and of new and old information in a way almost identical to English. In these languages an early nucleus placement results in the downgrading of later accents to dependence on length and/or loudness alone. (This does not apply in languages like Swedish which make a limited use of lexical tone, and where prominences produced by these tones occur even in post-focus positions.) As mentioned above, such languages will, like English, have a potential ambiguity related to nucleus placement on the final noun, which may indicate narrow focus on the noun or broad focus on the whole intonation-group. The ambiguity is usually resolved by giving extra height to a nuclear tone to signal narrow focus on a final noun. But at least one SVO language uses another device to signal narrow focus on a final noun: Polish may move the nuclear tone from the usually stressed syllable of the noun, the penultimate, to the first syllable of the noun, cf.

> Ważność komunikacji samochoDOwej
> 'The importance of travelling by car'

(Nucleus on the penultimate in this example is ambiguous between broad and narrow focus.)

> Ważność komunikacji sAmochodowej (Dogil, 1980 : 225)

(Nucleus on the initial syllable of the last word indicates narrow focus on that word.)

Other languages do not necessarily have the potential for nucleus movement that English does. In those languages where the nucleus has a fixed position in intonation-groups (and by fixed position is usually meant the last stressed syllable of the last noun), early prominences in the sentence may be achieved by breaking the sentence into a series of short intonation-groups. This was exemplified for French at the end of the preceding sections; it also applies to Portuguese, cf.

> He SPOKE to Madalena
> Eu faLEI / com a MadaLEna

The only exceptions to the rule of final nucleus placement in both French and Portuguese involve the sort of adverbials and 'parentheticals' mentioned in the preceding section, e.g. reporting clauses, vocatives, and adverbials of time and place. These adverbials and 'parentheticals' do not take the nucleus when in final position, e.g.

> Je vais à PaRIs le lundi

However, French and Portuguese differ from each other in that Portuguese uses word-order variation much more than French as an alternative to nucleus movement, cf.

> eu prefiro que ela vEnha
> eu prefiro que venha Ela

Word-order variation is the most common alternative to nucleus movement used in languages. Indeed, as already stated at the beginning of this section, it may be regarded as the more basic device, certainly on grounds of frequency: additionally, it is almost always the case that languages which use nucleus movement also use word-order variation, even if only infrequently (like English), whereas the reverse is not true. Italian and Spanish are two languages which rely on simple word-order variation and, to a lesser extent, on clefting for narrow focus, cf.

John arrives on Monday	Giovanni arriverà lunedì
JOHN arrives on Monday	Lunedì arriverà Giovanni
Charles knows Robert	Carlos conoce a Roberto
CHARLES knows Robert	Es Carlos quien conoce a Roberto
Charles KNOWS Robert	Carlos le conoce de verdad a Roberto
Charles knows ROBERT	Es a Roberto a quien conoce Carlos

Other languages use word-order variation as their main device for narrow focus but still use nucleus placement as a secondary device. Such a language is Finnish. The least marked word-order is SVO and the nucleus falls on the object under broad focus conditions. If narrow focus is required on the verb or the object, it is moved to sentence-initial position, e.g.

Otto LOVES Karen	Löi Otto Kaarinaa
Otto loves KAREN	Kaarinaa Otto löi
	(Heringer and Wolontis, 1972 : 153)

If narrow focus is required on the subject, then the nucleus is moved to the subject (compare the clefting of Spanish and Italian above), e.g.

OTTO loves Karen   OTTO löi Kaarinaa

(It will be remembered from earlier in this section that there is some dispute about nucleus placement under broad focus in Finnish. Those who regard the subject as taking the nucleus under broad focus go on to say that it takes 'heavy stress' under narrow focus conditions.)

5.4.3   Comparative tone: alternative models

The model of intonation within which most of the information in this book has been presented has involved the concepts of intonation-group, nucleus, and nuclear tones. Historically there have been two alternative approaches to the analysis of English intonation: the older British 'whole tune' approach, which describes the overall tunes associated with sentences or in some cases with clauses within sentences (and which does not therefore have a concept of nucleus and nuclear tone); and the (post-1945) American approach involving pitch levels and terminal junctures (see discussion in chapter 3, section 3.3 above). In fact the pitch levels approach is not as different from the one that I have been using as might at first glance appear; sequences of levels are fairly easily translatable into contours or *vice versa* (see earlier discussion in chapter 3, section 3.8) and the nucleus is indicated by the accompanying marking of primary stress. In this section I want briefly to look at two recent models of intonation developed specifically for European languages, one for Swedish and one for Dutch. The model developed for Swedish is closer to a 'whole tune' approach, whereas that developed for Dutch involves sequences of tonal elements but does not identify anything like a nuclear tone.

The model developed for Swedish is principally associated with Gårding and has been reported in a number of articles (e.g. Gårding, 1983). It is solidly based on acoustic analysis and synthesis. Four lines are used to generate the overall pitch pattern of a sentence: the two outermost lines representing the floor and the ceiling of a speaker's normal pitch range and the two innermost lines representing the basic tune of the sentence, e.g.

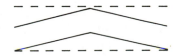

Onto this grid are projected Highs and Lows associated with word accents, phrase accents, sentence accents, and boundaries. In Swedish, phrase and sentence accents are High-Low, word accents are High (differences in the two lexical tones being represented by a difference in the timing of the High), and boundaries are Low (Swedish has a Low phrase-boundary even in sentence-medial position). All Highs and Lows are on the inner lines except the sentence accent (the nearest approach to nucleus) which is on the ceiling (= the outer top line). Here is an example from Gårding (1983 : 18):

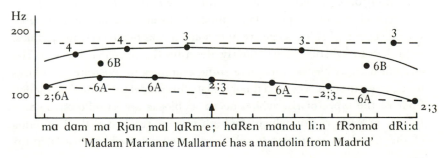

'Madam Marianne Mallarmé has a mandolin from Madrid'

(In this example 2 = phrase and sentence boundaries; 3 = phrase and sentence accents; 4 = word accents; 6A and 6B = contextual modifications involving a preparatory Low before a High and the assimilatory raising of a Low between two Highs.) In this system, modifications for intonational meaning include contrastive accent, which involves widening the range between the outer lines; and changing the tune represented by the inner lines, cf.

Statement   Question without inversion

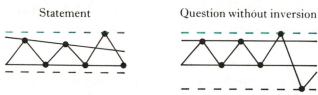

Notice that the second example also involves the optional use of a final rise. Rules like those given here have been used to synthesise natural-sounding Swedish sentences. The main problem associated with this model is that, when analysing sentences with varying discoursal and attitudinal effects, there seems to be no principled way of limiting the number of different grids necessary to model all the sentences. As usual with instrumental research in intonation, the phonetic details are very explicit and workable on 'neutral' declarative (and possibly interrogative) sentences, but there is no systematic study of relationships between forms and meanings in 'non-neutral' sentences. The basic difference between this sort of model and the nuclear tone model is that here accents supposedly ride on a previously allocated whole tune or 'grid', whereas in a nuclear tone model the accents themselves actually build the overall tune. I remain sceptical that systematic meaning differences can be more easily plotted against overall tunes than against nuclear tones together with pre-nuclear modifications.

The model developed for Dutch (see in particular Collier and 't Hart, 1981) involves an inventory of building 'blocks' which are put together in a variety of sequences to form the tunes of sentences. Each block consists of a type of rise or a type of fall; some blocks are obligatorily associated with accented syllables, some are not; some blocks begin early in syllables, some late in syllables. I will firstly describe the principal types of rise and fall used as blocks; then give some examples to illustrate the blocks in sequence in sentences; and finally relate this model to the nuclear model. Four of the types of rise which occur as blocks are as follows. Type 1 Rise is an 'early rise' in which the high pitch is reached at the beginning of the vowel; it is similar to what has been referred to as a 'step-up' in chapter 3, section 3.4, above. Type 2 Rise is a 'late rise' in which the rise does not begin until late in the syllable; it is similar to what has been referred to in this book as a low-rise or a full-rise. Type 4 Rise (the numbering is as in Collier and 't Hart (1981), Type 3 Rise not being described here) is simply the transitional rise between two falls, i.e. ⌐⌐⌐ . Type A Fall is a rapid fall from high to low, similar to what I have previously called a high-fall. Type B Fall is the same as A except that it is inaudible, i.e. it is only inferable from what precedes and follows (see, for instance, the first example below). Type D Fall is the transition between two rises, i.e. ⌐⌐⌐ . Type E Fall is a fall which does not reach the baseline. All these types of rises and falls can be seen in the following examples from Collier and 't Hart (1981):

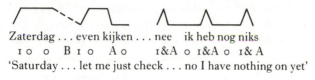

Zaterdag . . . even kijken . . . nee   ik heb nog niks
  1 o o   B 1 o   A o   1&A o 1&A o 1& A
'Saturday . . . let me just check . . . no I have nothing on yet'

Ik eet vrijwel altijd in de mensa
1   o   o   oEo   o   o A o
'I almost always eat in the cafeteria'

Kook jij eigenlijk vaak zelf?
  o   1 D D D D   2
'Do you actually often cook yourself?'

O   zo   kan ik het ook
1&A 1&A 4   4   4 5&A
'Oh I can also manage that myself'

Notice that a Type 5 Rise is used in the last example: this seems to occur almost always between a Type 4 Rise and a Type A Fall; Ladd (1983) suggests that it represents a 'raised peak'. Notice also that where syllables have no pitch movement they are marked with a o.

Like the Gårding model developed for Swedish, this model developed for Dutch is based on acoustic analysis and synthesis and is capable of synthesising natural-sounding Dutch intonations; it is, in other words, phonetically explicit. The authors themselves claim that phonetic explicitness is of more importance than the functional aspect of intonation; it is not surprising therefore that criticisms of the model all concern the functional aspect. A Type B Fall (the inaudible one) seems to cry out for an analysis into intonation-groups; as regards meaning, this Type B Fall seems to have nothing in common with a Type A Fall, yet regarding them both as types of Fall might suggest so. Similarly Type 1 Rise (early in the syllable) and Type 2 Rise (late in the syllable) seem to be from the point of view of function very different: indeed Type 1 Rise seems more similar to a fall functionally (see chapter 3, sub-section 3.8.1 above). Collier and 't Hart also say that a sequence of two 1 & A's, as in the second example above, can, by a sandhi phenomenon, become a single occurrence of 1A with a plateau in between, i.e. ∧＿∧ → ⌐‾\, which suggests that the two accents (1 and A) are somehow similar). More-over there is no way of identifying sequences of blocks which function similarly, e.g. 1EA and 1A4A are both typical of relatively neutral declarative sentences, but by giving equal importance to all the blocks (and not saying, for example, that the movement on the last accented syllable is semantically most prominent), these two sequences are claimed to be no more similar than, for example, all those which end with an A.

Both the models mentioned here (i.e. those developed for Swedish and for Dutch) involve ascribing differences of tune to differences of 'phasing' or 'timing' of highs and lows relative to accented syllables. This sort of explanation of tonal differences stems originally from studies of lexical tone in Norwegian and Swedish. It is being increasingly used in the description of intonation; besides the models here, a difference of phase occurs as [+ delay] in Gussenhoven's system for English (see chapter 4, sub-section 4.4.4.2 above) and as [+ delayed peak] in Ladd (1983). In both these cases, it is used to explain a rise-fall as compared with a rise. It is also used for German by Isačenko and Schädlich (1966) who use the terms 'pre-ictic' and 'post-ictic' to explain differences within rises and within falls thus:

	Rises	Falls
Pre-ictic	die ⌐Kinder	die ⌐Kinder
Post-ictic	die Kin⌐der	die Kin⌐der

The use of any device in intonational description, including 'phase', is justified if it leads to simpler functional generalisations. In the case of the model for Dutch above, it does not seem to me that it does. In the case of the Isačenko and Schädlich model, on the other hand, it seems to be the case that functional generalisations are at least maintained: a pre-ictic rise is 'progredient' (i.e. indicating more to come), while a post-ictic rise is 'interrogative' (i.e. indicating more to come, but from a different speaker); whereas both types of fall are terminal. Whether such a treatment is in any way superior to a description in terms of high-rise versus low-rise and high-fall v. low-fall has, however, not been shown.

5.4.4 Comparative tone: basic typology

The two alternative models discussed in the previous sub-section involved two descriptive procedures which have not been used in the basic theoretical exposition in this book: that of whole tunes, as in Gårding's grids, and that of 'phase', as in Collier and 't Hart's various types of falls and rises, and in the way Gårding's lexical tones ride on the sentence 'grids'. In the sections which follow the comparisons will nevertheless remain within the nuclear tone approach. There are basically two reasons for this. One is pragmatic: it is difficult enough finding sufficiently detailed data to compare pitch movements following just the last pitch accent, let alone basing a comparison on the patterns of pitch movement borne on a sequence of pitch accents. The other is theoretical: I remain convinced that the final pitch movement following the nucleus **is** the most important pitch movement in an intonation-group and, moreover, that on this basis one may make wider and more valuable functional generalisations, as discussed concerning the Dutch model in the previous sub-section. Such considerations certainly support a nuclear tone rather than a whole tune approach. The question of 'phase' is a little more difficult to dismiss. It may turn out that some of the differences in nuclear tone types can be ascribed to differences of 'phase' (e.g. that rise-fall is really a delayed fall); it certainly seems that this method can lead to greater generalisation in certain areas (e.g. rise-fall has semantic similarities with simple fall) and a good case for this approach has been made in Ladd (1983). However, I shall not make use of phase features in the comparative typological sections which follow because I view the breaking down of tones into phase features as rather like the breaking down of phonological segments into distinctive features. Distinctive feature comparisons across languages could not really have been carried out without previous typological comparisons of the phonological segments of languages. The typological comparison of tones which follows is on speculative enough ground without carrying speculation one stage further – into intonational features.

Ideally, comparison of tones would be divided up along lines similar to those followed for the comparison of segments across dialects and across languages. It would be nice to be able to divide our comparison into inventory, realisation, and usage. Inventory would involve the number and type of tones in each language; realisation would involve the exact contour associated with each tone (e.g. does a rise-fall start lower/higher or finish lower/higher in one language than in another?) and usage would compare the different (or same) meanings associated with similar tones across languages. This sort of framework does lie behind the descriptions in the following sections but it is a framework which is difficult to sustain in any precise way, because all sorts of, at present unanswerable, problems are raised. For instance, it is difficult to decide when we are dealing with two different tones and when with two different realisations of the same tone (i.e. when is a difference of inventory as opposed to a difference of realisation involved?). One answer might be that only different (sequences of) pitch directions count as different tones with respect to the inventory; by such a criterion only rise, fall, fall-rise, rise-fall, rise-fall-rise, fall-rise-fall, count as different tones, the remaining differences being differences of realisation. This is certainly the most obvious workable criterion but considerable problems still remain, e.g. how do we equate level tones across languages? And can we really equate tones of the same contour but very different beginnings or endpoints, e.g. two rise-falls like ∧ and ∧ (it may be that in this case we should treat these two tones as different for the purposes of inventory comparison, because one ends on the baseline and one does not). I have at the moment no precise solutions to these problems. Indeed, as the reader will discover in the next section, there is as yet no developed procedure in intonational typology.

Regarding the comparison of uses of tones in various languages, I can only repeat what was said at the beginning of section 5.3 above (on dialectal variation). An ideal comparison would compare the abstract meanings associated with each tone, but, for practical reasons, we are forced to anchor our comparisons in grammatical sentence-types. Most individual descriptions of the intonation of particular languages talk of the typical tones associated with declaratives, yes/no interrogatives, and so on. One of the questions one would always like to have asked the writer is 'how typical?' i.e. how much variation does the word 'typical' conceal? This raises a further question regarding the comparison between English (where much detailed work has been done) and other languages; is the amount of potential tonal variation in English (conditioned by discoursal and attitudinal factors) typical or not of languages in general? Or, putting the question the other way round, are tones much more conditioned by syntax in other languages than they are in English? One does not really know the answer to these questions: one does not really know whether the lack of apparent and reported variation in many languages is due to the analyst or to the languages concerned.

With all these various 'hedges' in mind, we can now go ahead and compare the intonations associated with various sentence-types across languages. I take a 'sentence-type' to involve a pairing of a typical use with a typical syntactic form in a language. So, for example, in English a yes/no question is typically associated with inversion of subject and verb. The five main sentence-types of similar use which can be identified across languages are: statement, yes/no question, question word question, command, and exclamation. The syntactic form associated with each sentence-type I call declarative, yes/no interrogative, question word interrogative, imperative, and exclamative. Of course a pairing may not be maintained on all occasions, e.g. a sentence in the syntactic form of a yes/no interrogative in English will sometimes function as an exclamation, e.g. *Am I mad!* Intonation may play a part in indicating a non-basic use of a particular syntactic form, e.g. *Am I mad!* is limited intonationally if it is to be taken as an exclamation. Another common change brought about by intonation involves the syntactic form of a declarative being turned into a yes/no question by the use of a particular tone (usually high-rise in English); indeed in some languages syntactic marking of yes/no questions may be absent and intonation is the only formal way of marking a yes/no question (of course to some extent interpretation of an utterance as a question is always dependent on context as well). A similar change which is very common in languages involves the softening of an imperative to a request by the use of some sort of rising tone. I shall now compare the intonation of the major sentence-types in detail.

5.4.4.1 **Declaratives.** Bolinger (1978) is the only existing survey of intonation across languages. In a consideration of 57 non-tone languages he finds 38 to have a 'terminal fall' at the end of a declarative, with the implication in most cases that the terminal fall begins on the last pitch accent. The list includes such widely diverse languages as Polish, Kunimaipa, Maya, Tamil, and Yurok. Moreover, of the remaining 19 it is not the case that they are reported as necessarily having a terminal rise or the absence of a fall; simply that the reports on the languages concerned are not altogether clear. A few languages are reported as not having a fall at the end of a sentence but a fall at the end of a 'discourse' or 'turn'. In Chamorro (Topping, 1969 : 71) 'most terminal contours (except discourse-final) are marked by rising pitch'. Reports of this sort which suggest a rise as the unmarked tone for declaratives are rare. Something of the sort has been reported for some British urban dialects in sub-section 5.3.1 of this chapter (although the evidence now being surveyed suggests even more strongly that such rise-plateaus should be analysed as 'deep' falls). I know of only one report in which it is suggested that the semantics of fall and rise are reversed: Swadesh (1946:317) states: 'Chitimacha contrasts with English and other European languages in using a rising intonation for statement and a falling one for interrogation.' Since the population of the tribe was only sixty or so in 1946, and since only **one** person was reported as speaking the language, we should not pin too much theoretical significance on this statement! It is undoubtedly true that it is a nearly absolute linguistic universal that unmarked declaratives have a final falling pitch. What is more, this final falling pitch will reach the speaker's baseline or, putting it another way, will at least reach the bottom end of his normal pitch range; additionally, the final falling pitch is often reported as reaching the level of creaky voice (e.g. in Castilian Spanish).

Of course there remains considerable variation in the type of fall involved. Some languages may have a preference for a step-up followed by wide fall while others may prefer a step-down followed by a narrow fall; still others may allow both with approximately equal likelihood. English falls into the latter category, cf.

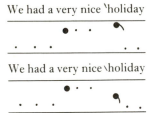

In chapter 3, section 3.7, this was described as the difference between high-fall and low-fall. Bolinger's (1978) survey suggests that the following prefer high-fall (or in his terms an Accent A): Cayuvava, Chuave, Cora, French, Hawaiian, Papago, Russian, Seri, Tamil, Waltmanjari, and Yurok, although this list must not be taken too seriously; in French, for example, the step-down and low-fall is probably at least as frequent as the high-fall. Indeed a number of Romance languages seem to prefer the low-fall, for instance Spanish (particularly the Castilian variety), Italian, and Portuguese, e.g.

No habla espa\ñol   'I don't speak Spanish'

Credo che sia il \mio   'I believe that it's mine'

Ela casou com o \João   'She married John'

In some other languages the typical type of fall seems to be a rise-fall, e.g. in Welsh, Hindi, and Copenhagen Danish.

While a terminal fall is reported as the unmarked pattern for declarative sentences in most languages, there are often remarks in individual descriptions to the effect that 'statements with implications' may produce different tones on a declarative sentence. On an uncertain statement like *Je ne sais pas* a French speaker may use a rise; Kunimaipa has a rise for 'politeness', Thai a rise for 'surprise' or 'doubt', and in Western Desert a rise 'reveals the speaker's recognition of the person addressed'. Von Essen (1956) reports the use of a *Höflichkeitsmelodie* involving a rise on declaratives in German, e.g.

Ich möchte zehn Liter Benzin   'I want ten litres of petrol'

One of the most frequent tones used in English to convey 'implications' is the fall-rise and this seems almost idiosyncratic to English in that, although simple rises are frequently reported in other languages as being used for implicational meanings on declaratives, fall-rise is rarely reported. Implications conveyed by the use of fall-rise and indeed by other tones in English may be conveyed by the use of special particles or by variations in word-order in other languages, cf. English and German:

She's very ᵛpretty (but . . . . .)
Sie ist zwar schön (aber . . . . .)

You ˈmustn't be aˌfraid
Sie dürfen sich doch nicht fürchten

You're very ^lucky
Du hast ja Glück gehabt

and English and Spanish:

It's not ᵛmy book
Ese libro no es mío

All the preceding examples in this section have discussed sentence final falls on declaratives but, of course, many sentences are divided up into more than one intonation-group, a non-final intonation-group corresponding with a non-final clause or with syntactic constituents such as subject, displaced object, sentence adverbial (see this chapter, sub-section 5.4.1 above) or with the non-final items in lists. English generally has some sort of level or rising nuclear tone in such groups (rising, of course, includes falling-rising). Other languages seem to prefer one of these two possibilities or a third possibility of a non-low fall (i.e. a fall which does not reach the baseline). A level tone is one possibility in Venetian and in Tagalog, e.g.

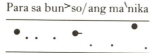

Para sa bun⁊so/ang maˋnika   'The doll is for the baby'
['For the baby / the doll']
(Bowen, 1969:45)

A rise is one possibility in German and Dutch. The most common type of rise used in non-final positions in languages is a high-rise, but notice in the following example from Dutch a fall-rise is used:

Naˇtuurlijk/maar het is niet erg netjes

'Naturally, but it's not altogether clear'

(Collier and 't Hart, 1981:76)

A non-low fall is reported to occur in Persian, in Swahili, and in Italian, e.g.

Delle arancie/delle mele /e delle banane

'Some oranges, some apples, and some bananas'

Although a non-low level, a rise, or a non-low fall (all really various types of non-low) are generally reported for non-final groups, there is the occasional reference (e.g. in Swahili) to the optional possibility of a fall to low in non-final groups. This is of course a possibility in English, although unusual except on reinforcing adverbs like *literally* (see chapter 4, sub-section 4.4.1.2), and it seems likely that most languages have the possibility of using a 'final-sounding' tone in sentence non-final positions to emphasise the 'separateness' of each component intonation-group, much as in English we can, exceptionally, give a falling tone to each item in a list.

In many languages a non-final intonation-group may involve an adverbial phrase; in English an adverbial phrase may also occur with a separate intonation-group in final position, usually involving a rising tone (as in non-final positions there are certain exceptions to this involving strongly reinforcing adverbs, which take a fall), e.g.

> I went to `London / on ⁄ Sunday

But this sort of occurrence, involving a 'minor' rise at the end of a sentence following an earlier fall does not appear to be a common one in languages. For some languages it is actually reported as virtually impossible, e.g. German:

> *Ich ging nach `London / am ⁄ Sonntag

A rise does not occur on adverbials in this position in German; an adverbial must either occur as the 'tail' to the preceding fall, or else it must take an independent fall of its own, e.g.

> Ich ging nach `London am Sonntag
> Ich ging nach `London / am `Sonntag

(A final rise of this sort **is** reported as possible in some German dialects when the time adverbial precedes the place adverbial, e.g.

> Ich ging am `Sonntag / nach ⁄ London.)

5.4.4.2 **Yes/no interrogatives.** Interrogatives fall basically into two major classes: yes/no interrogatives and question word interrogatives. Question word interrogatives ask for information in a more general way whereas yes/no interrogatives ask for an opinion about the truth of a proposition. Yes/no interrogatives may be grammatically marked in languages in various ways: by the use of a special particle or enclitic (as in Russian and Latin), by the use of a special verb morphology (as in Greenlandic), or by the use of a special word-order (as in English). In addition most languages are reported as having some sort of intonational marking of interrogatives. In some languages the **only** way of formally differentiating yes/no questions from statements is by intonation (e.g. in Portuguese, Jacaltec and modern Greek); a convenient label for a question marked as such in this way only is to call it a 'declarative question', since the morphology and syntax are basically unchanged from the form of the declarative. While the declarative question is the only way of marking yes/no questions in some languages, it is frequently an alternative option even in those languages which do mark yes/no questions by morphology or syntax. In some of these languages it appears to be a real alternative option, i.e. the declarative question can be used on unmarked yes/no questions (e.g. in Russian), while in other languages (e.g. Hungarian, German, Finnish, and English) it is most commonly used only for echo questions, e.g.

(A. He passed his exam)	B. He passed his e′xam?
(A. Sie ist tot)	B. Sie ist ′tot?

In fact this type of echoic intonation, usually high-rise, can typically be superimposed on any sentence-type, e.g.

(A. Where are you going?)	B. Where am I ′going?
(A. Are you happy?)	B. Am I ′happy?
(A. Mekkora?)	B. ^Mekkora?
	'How big is it?' (Hungarian)

The intonation of yes/no questions, whether co-occurring with morphological/syntactical marking or not, is almost invariably reported as having either a 'terminal rise' or in some way a higher pitch than the corresponding statement pattern. Bolinger (1978) surveyed a sample of 36 non-tone languages and reported all except 4 as having a rise or a higher pitch for questions. Ultan (1978), in a sample of 53 languages, found 71% reported as having a terminal rise, 34% reported as having a higher pitch somewhere, 5.7% as having a fall or rise, and 5.7% as having a fall only. 5.7% in absolute terms meant three languages: Fanti, Grebo, and Chitimacha, of which the first two are tone languages, leaving the last as the only clear exception. This reference to Chitimacha has already been mentioned in the last section on declaratives; it is in Swadesh (1946), is very brief, and may not tell the whole story.

Even in tone languages a terminal rise is usual in yes/no questions (although it is not of course associated with a 'nucleus'). For example, Miller and Tench (1981) report for Hausa that, whereas a statement will have a falling glide added to a terminal high tone, a yes/no question will have a final jump to an extra high level, whether the terminal tone is high or low. But there are some apparent exceptions to this (reported in Williamson, 1979) where a final low tone is added as a marker of yes/no questions. Such a low tone seems usually to arise where historically yes/no questions were marked by a segmental particle which was itself low-toned; subsequently the particle was lost but the tone of the particle remained. This is the case, for example, in Degema, which has lost its question particle but adds a final low tone, whereas Engenni, a language closely related to Degema, retains a question particle *a* having low tone.

Although a very large number of intonation languages (i.e. non-tone languages) are reported as having a final rise for yes/no questions, what remains uncertain is just how many of these languages have a fall as an alternative, since descriptions very rarely mention alternative intonations for a particular sentence-type. From many of the brief descriptions of English in pedagogic textbooks, it might be imagined that only a rising tone occurred on yes/no questions, whereas this is clearly not the case.

Some languages have a preference for a low-rise on yes/no questions (i.e. where the rise does not go higher than approximately mid pitch) while others prefer a high-rise (i.e. where the rise ends at the upper limit of the speaker's pitch). The low-rise typically involves a step-down with the end pitch of the rise not reaching the level of any preceding syllables, e.g. ——— whereas the high-rise may or may not involve a step-down but will certainly end higher than any preceding syllables, e.g. ——— or ———. Among those which prefer a low-rise are Chrau and Tagalog, whereas among those which prefer a high-rise are Portuguese, Sa'ban, and Azerbaijani.

In the surveys of Bolinger (1978) and Ultan (1978) mentioned above, the alternative to a final rise on yes/no questions was reported to be a 'higher pitch somewhere'. This phrase sometimes means the 'suspension of declination'. Declination was briefly mentioned in chapter 3, section 3.9, when discussing Pierrehumbert's model, and considered in somewhat more detail for English in chapter 4, sub-section 4.4.4.4; it is further discussed as a possible universal in sub-section 5.5.1 below. For the moment all that has to be remembered is that there is at least a tendency for high-peaked accents of equal perceptual prominence to decline in real terms within one intonation-group (and possibly a similar phenomenon across intonation-groups). Thus the declination effect shows up in one way as: . Declination is reported as typical of declarative sentences in many languages. But it is also frequently reported that declination may be suspended in yes/no interrogatives, e.g. in Danish and Swedish. In Copenhagen Danish the typical pitch accent is rising-falling: Thorsen (1983) shows how in a statement the beginning-points of a series of accents will typically decline, e.g.

whereas in a yes/no question which is unmarked syntactically (i.e. a 'declarative question') declination will not occur, e.g.

In those cases where a yes/no question **is** marked syntactically by inversion or interrogative particle, declination is shown to be present but not to the same degree as in declaratives.

Another type of pitch pattern which represents a 'higher pitch some-where' involves giving extra height to the nucleus of yes/no questions. In many East European languages this extra height goes together with a rising-falling nuclear tone. Some variety of rise-fall for yes/no questions occurs in Russian, Czech, Serbo-Croat, Hungarian, and Roumanian. The rise-fall is commonly reduced to a simple high-rise if the nucleus occurs on the last syllable of the intonation-group. In the case of Russian and Czech a high-rise is said to be an alternative (related to age or dialect) in **all** cases. In Russian neither of the two possibilities for yes/no questions (rise-fall or high-rise) is commonly used if the interrogative particle *li* is present, but they must occur if *li* is not present (i.e. when we are dealing with a declarative question), e.g.

ee zovut Nataša?

её зовут Наташа?

'her call-they Natasha?' = 'Is she called Natasha?'

Igor' poet?

Игорь поёт?

'Igor sings?' = 'Is *Igor* singing?'

ego zovut Boris?

его зовут Борис?

'him call-they Boris?' = 'Is he called Boris?'

Notice that the first two examples have rise-fall because the nucleus is on a non-final syllable, whereas the last example has a high-rise because the nucleus falls on the last syllable.

A special type of yes/no question is the biased question, i.e. the yes/no-question which is biased towards the expectation of either a *yes* or a *no* question. This type of question is often indicated by some sort of tag at the end of a sentence. The tag may be of a fixed type involving a negative particle like French *n'est-ce pas* or Portuguese *não é*, a positive particle like Rotuman *ne* or an interjection like Hausa *ko*; or the tag may be sensitive to the syntax of the preceding main clause as in English (although this is relatively rare in languages). For both types of tag, some sort of rising tone or higher pitch is favourite, just as it is for yes/no questions generally. Ultan (1978) reports 25 out of 29 languages in his sample as having a rising tone or higher pitch on their tags. English, of course, has a distinction between a falling toned tag (demanding confirmation) and a rising toned tag (which, while still biased, leaves the matter somewhat more open to disagreement). This sort of distinction is not to my knowledge reported for any other language, although some languages, e.g. Portuguese and German, seem to convey a similar difference by the use of high-rise (more demanding) versus low-rise (more open).

5.4.4.3 **Question word interrogatives.** The number of question words available varies from language to language (but the equivalent of *who* and *what* seem to be always present). The question word is most frequently in initial position although in a few languages it is in the normal position for a constituent of the type it represents; sometimes inversion and/or a special morphology is involved. Ultan (1978), in a sample of 53 languages, found a preference for falls in 52.1% and a preference for a rise or a higher pitch in 47.9% of them. (He gives no information on how a fall starting higher than in declaratives was classified, i.e. there is a potential problem about deciding what precisely is meant by the distinction between fall and higher pitch.) Languages preferring a fall include Portuguese, French, and Tagalog; languages preferring a rise include Diola and Telugu. Bolinger (1978) says that of 17 reports on the intonation of question word interrogatives in different languages, all but 3 were said to have the same tune as declaratives. What is clear from both surveys is that falls are the dominant pattern for question word interrogatives in contrast to the rises associated with yes/no questions. Those languages which have a fall on question word interrogatives frequently have the same tune as for declaratives except that the initial question word is very often given a specially high pitch. This applies to Russian, Chrau, and Azerbaijani.

Although falls may be the dominant pattern for question word interrogatives, another feature of this sentence-type is that there are far more languages reported to have both fall and rise available for it than is the case for yes/no interrogatives. In his sample, Ultan (1978) found falls also available in 62% of those languages which had a rise as the dominant type; and, although he gives no information on the converse, it is undoubtedly true that languages preferring a fall do often have a rise available as an alternative, e.g. Norwegian, German, and Venetian. The meaning of the alternative employing the rise is frequently glossed in a similar way to that suggested for Norwegian: 'show[ing] interest, sympathy, kindness, patience, or liveliness' (Vanvik, 1966).

5.4.4.4 **Imperatives and exclamatives.** Imperatives may be marked in languages by the use of sentential or verbal particles or clitics; in addition an affixless verb stem is often used, commonly without a subject. Exclamatives may sometimes be marked by an exclamatory particle but are often identical in syntactic form to declaratives or interrogatives (e.g. *You're so per`suasive!* and *Am I `pleased!*). In fact an exclamatory function is easier to identify than an exclamative form: basically, exclamations are expressive while statements are informative.

There are no surveys available concerning the intonation of these two sentence-types; there is generally some mention of the intonation of imperatives in individual language descriptions but there are only occasional mentions of exclamatives. In all the language descriptions I have checked, the preferred tune for imperatives is said to be equivalent or very similar to that used on declaratives; this of course means that a falling tone is the regularly reported pattern, e.g. in German, French, Italian, Norwegian, Russian, and Tagalog. But in almost all the descriptions of the intonation of imperatives, it is also reported that the command function of the imperative can be softened to a request by changing the intonation (sometimes along with the use of a softening particle), which usually means changing to the typical intonation of yes/no questions, i.e. changing from a fall to a rise. Some sort of rise for requests as opposed to fall for strong commands is reported, for example, for Norwegian, Russian, and Tagalog. Finally, reports on the intonation of exclamatives are rare but those reports which I have been able to find (e.g. French and Italian) suggest that the tune used is regularly the same as that used for declaratives.

5.4.4.5 **Pre-nuclear accents.** This is likely to be an area of variation between languages which is one of the key factors which contribute to the unique 'sound' of a particular language. But unfortunately again it is one of those areas where we have very few descriptions available. It seems that the basic division is between those languages which typically use a series of high-peaked accents and those which typically use a series of low-peaked accents. Among those preferring high-peaked accents are north German and Hungarian; among those preferring low-peaked accents are south German, Norwegian, and Welsh. There is, of course, considerable scope for variation within each type; for example, the high-peaked type may involve a series of simple falls, or it may involve a series of rise-falls as in Danish, or it may involve a series of high levels, each succeeding level being slightly lower than the preceding one, as is frequently the case in R.P.

5.5   Intonational universals

A number of universals suggest themselves concerning the use of pitch in intonation languages: intonation-groupings as a marker of major syntactic constituents (see sub-section 5.4.1 above); nucleus placement as a form of focussing attention (although there are considerable restrictions on this in some languages – see sub-section 5.4.2 above); and the use of variation in key for discourse-linking and the use of high register for deference. However, the evidence for these universals is slight: the very limited amount of evidence available does support such putative universals, and at the same time there is no negative evidence. But there are two areas in which there is more substantial evidence for universals: declination and tone.

5.5.1   Declination

Earlier discussion of declination occurred in chapter 4, subsection 4.4.4.4 above. Declination is the phenomenon whereby pitch (strictly speaking, fundamental frequency) is on average lower at the end of an intonation-group than at the beginning. Remember that most of the evidence comes from sentences which are said specially for the purposes of experiments and which have been subjected to precise acoustic measurement. Such conditions are of course unnatural and may lead to particularly 'wooden' intonation patterns. However, as was pointed out in 4.4.4.4 above, this may actually be an asset, since they may represent neutral intonation patterns from which more expressive intonations in natural conversation may deviate. The declination which occurs in such neutral sentences is represented by a slightly declining baseline and a more steeply declining top line, thus producing a narrowing of pitch range as the intonation-group progresses. The baseline and the top line are then 'reset' at the beginning of the next group; the top line may not, however, be reset to the same level as at the beginning of the previous group because intonation-groups may themselves be linked together by key. Declination within intonation-groups has been reported for many languages, including

Danish, Italian and Japanese. Moreover, suspension of declination in yes/no questions is reported for some languages, including Danish and Russian; but this is a weak universal, i.e. if suspension of declination does occur, it will be used to mark yes/no questions, but there are some languages in which such suspension does not seem to occur, e.g. English.

The explanation for declination has often been related to the decline in transglottal pressure as the speaker uses up the breath in his lungs. A more recent explanation suggests that an upward change of pitch involves a physical adjustment which is more difficult than a downward change of pitch, the evidence being that a rise takes longer to achieve than a fall of a similar interval in fundamental frequency. It has also been shown that listeners actually perceive a declining series of peaks as being of the same height. None of these explanations seems incompatible with any of the others.

5.5.2 **Tonal universals**

The tonal usages described in sub-sections 5.4.4.1 to 5.4.4.4 above clearly exhibit near-universal differences between the use of falling tones on the one hand and the use of rising tones on the other:

Falling	*Rising*
Neutral statement	Implicational or tentative statement
	Yes/no question
Sentence final	Sentence non-final
Neutral question word question	Sympathetic question word question
Command	Request

Two more differences can be added from English: reinforcing adverbs (like *frequently*) take a fall, whereas limiting adverbs (like *usually*) take a rise; question tags demanding agreement take a fall whereas tags which are more open to disagreement take a rise. Neither of these divisions is confirmed from other languages but neither are they disconfirmed. The group of meanings associated with falls on the one hand clearly has something in common which is not shared by the group of meanings associated with rises on the other; there appear to be metaphorical links between the meanings of each group. But it is not easy to put a cover label on each group of meanings. The meanings associated with falling intonations are generally assertive and non-continuative; I suggest the label CLOSED as a cover term for such meanings. Similarly, the meanings associated with rising intonations are in general non-assertive and continuative and the cover term OPEN is suggested.

Closed falls and open rises represent, of course, no more than a strong universal tendency in languages and, as we have seen in several areas of cross-linguistic comparison, the distinction between fall and rise is sometimes replaced by the distinction between low and high. A fall to low for sentence final groups is sometimes opposed to a fall to mid for sentence non-final groups; a simple fall for statements is sometimes opposed to a rise-fall for yes/no questions, where the rise-fall involves a higher pitch than the simple fall.

Although we may say that there are near-universal links between closed meanings and falls (or lower tones), and between open meanings and rises (or higher tones), this is of course in no sense to say that there are no differences in tones across intonation languages. Clearly languages can differ very considerably in the types of rises or the types of falls that they use. Moreover, there will be preferences for tones in certain positions in one language which are not even allowed in another language: English, for example, allows a rise in subsidiary intonation-groups in final position (consisting of adverbials, comment clauses, vocatives, and the like) which is clearly not usually permissible in German and probably not in most other languages. There are certain areas which are particularly susceptible to idiosyncratic uses of tones. Greetings, farewells, and social formulas are one such area: the conventional way of intoning the equivalent of *Good morning* will vary from language to language; moreover variation within one language in such areas will be sensitive to very subtle social conventions.

But the undeniable links between open meanings and rises, and between closed meanings and falls, remain. Although intonational changes may take place (see next section), changes never continue far enough to make intonation as arbitrary as segmental morphemes. Bolinger (1978 : 510–11) summarises the position thus: '. . . . . we can think of an intonational core, an innate pattern . . . . ., from which speakers and cultures may depart, but to which some force is always pushing them back. [There is] some kind of regeneration from below, a tendency perhaps for an inherent drive to reassert itself whenever dialect mixture or any other iconoclastic force opens the way.'

5.6 **Intonational change**

Because of the availability of audio-recording machines, it has recently become possible for work to begin in this area, and it is likely to be a fascinating area of research. Two potential areas of intonational change can be identified: (a) linguistic interference and (b) de-attituding.

Linguistic interference applies here as it does on other levels of language. The rise-plateau (-slither) pattern which was described as typical of many northern British cities (sub-section 5.3.1 above) must surely be related to Celtic in some way since its incidence corresponds almost entirely to areas of Irish settlement. The characteristics of Mexican Spanish intonation are often reported to be of Amerindian origin, and are often called the 'Indian whine'; its most noticeable pattern is described by Kingdon (1958a) as featuring an early high-fall followed by a final high level, e.g.

This sort of intonation is not uncommon on non-final groups in English, e.g.

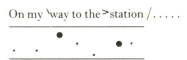

It looks on the face of it as if a level nucleus, which generally belongs in languages with the rises as a tone conveying open meanings, has here become the norm on unmarked declaratives. I return to this problem below.

The second type of intonational change is de-attituding. Basically, what happens with this sort of change is that a particular intonation which is attitudinally marked becomes very frequent (at first in the speech of certain groups) and as its frequency increases (and as it spreads to other groups) it loses its attitudinal connotation. Fónagy (1979) describes how the interrogative intonation in Hungarian (this is one of the eastern European languages which has rise-fall) began to be used with imperatives about fifty years ago. At first it was used by particular groups, in particular tram drivers and shop assistants, and it was evidently used as a polite imperative. Next its use began to become fashionable among some groups of young people; the older use of fall for the imperative is now considered excessively aggressive. In section 2 above, I referred in some detail to the work of McGregor (1980) on the increasing use of high-rises in Sydney on sentence final intonation-groups; this tone was said to be particularly prevalent among adolescents and among lower social classes. Remembering that a very typical use of high-rise in other dialects of English involves a 'casual' attitude on non-final groups, we can see how high-rise is being used by young people in Sydney as an indicator of informality. If the change continues, at some stage (perhaps even now) high-rise will have lost its connotation of casualness.

The two types of change or change-in-progress mentioned in the last paragraph both involved the spreading of a rising or rising-falling tone normally associated with open meanings to a use normally associated with closed meanings and hence with a falling tone. This sort of change seems the most common. The reverse, i.e. the occurrence of falls in uses normally associated with rises, is not documented, although it is not difficult to imagine situations in which it might arise. In English, for example, certain situations regularly involve a fall on yes/no questions; Fries (1964) remarked upon its regular use in a TV game in which contestants were only allowed to answer *yes* or *no* and in which the interviewer was trying to hustle the contestants into quick answers. Such a situation might easily start a fashion where falls predominate in many or most uses of yes/no questions.

What predictably will not occur are changes which lead to the complete interchange of falls and rises. This is where the theme of 'regeneration from below' applies (which was mentioned in the last section). There seems to be some sort of physiological force at work which maintains falling tones as basic for closed meanings and rising tones as basic for open meanings. What exactly this physiological force is, is not clear; one explanation is that an increase in tension (and hence in pitch) is always involved if in some way 'more is expected' whereas a decrease in tension (and hence a lowering of pitch) signifies that we are in some way 'through' or 'finished'.

5.7   Intonation acquisition

Four periods are identifiable in the early vocal development of infants. The crying period lasts from birth until approximately three months; during this period most vocal output consists of crying although there are some labial and glottal sounds connected with bodily functions, principally sucking and straining. The babbling period lasts from approximately three months to one year; during this period a child begins to play with sounds purely for pleasure and there occurs an increasing range of sounds and sequences of sounds. The one-word period lasts from approximately one year up to one year nine months; during this period a child has for some months only a small number of words but in the last months the number of single words increases substantially. Around one year nine months a child begins to use two-word sentences and the two-word period lasts for approximately three months. There is of course some overlap of the principal features associated with each period: crying continues in the babbling period; babbling continues alongside first words; and single word utterances continue into the two-word period.

During the babbling period children often show considerable mimicry of adult pitch patterns. Imitation of this sort is reported as early as eight months. A commonly imitated intonation of English is the pattern used by mothers on *all gone* involving a sequence of high-level and mid-level, e.g. ●━ ●━ . An imitation like this may be performed on any sequence of segments which is typical of the child's babbling at the time. Late in the babbling period and continuing into the residual babbling in the one-word period a child may actually produce whole sentence intonations, e.g.

ga gi ba ba ba la li

This is sometimes called 'jargon intonation'. Other children show a special use of pitch during the early one-word period, each word being yoked to a particular pitch pattern. Halliday (1975) reports on such a child, who, for instance, had the following three words (among many others) at the age of one year:

[nā]	(with mid-fall)	'Give me that.'
[a:]	(with high rise-fall)	'Yes, I want what you have just offered.'
[gwɣi]	(with low-fall)	'I'm sleepy.'

Using pitch patterns in this way a child seems to be hypothesising that English is a tone language.

The uses of pitch in mimicry, in jargon intonation, and as if learning a tone language, do not, however, appear to be the genesis of intonation. The genesis of intonation lies in the ability to contrast a fall and a rise on one syllable or spread at most over two syllables. Some reports have suggested that this contrast is sometimes present in the babbling period. For many children (although again not necessarily all) it is certainly present during the one-word period. The meanings ascribed to the two tones are almost always said to be falls for deictics and rises for requests. In fact the falling tone is usually the more frequent tone and some children even in the one-word period use only falls. It is commonly the case that the residual babbling of the one-word period will display a wider variety of pitch patterns than the first words.

The detailed order of acquisition of tones and the order of acquisition of the local meanings associated with each tone have yet to be plotted in detail (if indeed there is any fixed order – there are probably just strong tendencies, as in the order of acquisition of segmental phonemes). Some of the meanings reported for rises during the one-word and two-word periods are counting, echoing, listing, questioning, attention-getting, and various formulas learnt from parents, e.g. *thank you*, *bye-bye* and *there you are*. The distinction between high and low varieties of falls and rises will follow fairly rapidly once a body of such local meanings is established: for example, high-rise may be used for echoes and attention-getting, while low-rise continues for the other meanings mentioned above, and high-fall will be distinguished from low-fall as the more emphatic tone carrying meanings like surprise and insistence. At the two-word stage there may be some uses of fall-rise, possibly for warning or contrast, e.g. *That not ˇyours*. In this section I have so far talked about the acquisition of English tones but there is no reason to believe that the acquisition of intonation in other languages is substantially different. Differences do of course have to be acquired: the detailed realisations of falls and rises peculiar to one language may show up very early in a child's speech (and even in babbling, where their presence may be a prime factor in the recognition of a particular child's linguistic background); additionally, there will later be different local meanings to be acquired in every language.

Once a child has developed two-word sentences, he can then vary the nucleus placement. Early in the two-word stage nucleus placement is often linked to sentence-type. So possessives will regularly have the nucleus on the possessor, e.g. *DADdy garden*, while locatives will regularly have the nucleus on the locative, e.g. *Daddy GARden*. By the time a child is producing three- and four-word sentences, he is also stringing sentences together, and at the very beginning of doing this, he seems, like adults, to be able to vary the nucleus to take account of old information.

Although some uses of intonation develop early, it should be clear by now that claims that children learn the intonation of their language before they learn any words are overstatements. Indeed studies of intonation comprehension show clearly that children at the age of ten are not able to use intonational meaning in the way that adults do. For example, in reading football results, the intonation of B.B.C. newsreaders gives some clues to the second score before it actually occurs, e.g.

Liverpool ˇtwo / Manchester U ˋnited . . . . .

where a score of two for Manchester United also is a certainty because the nucleus has been moved on to the team, suggesting that the score will be old information, i.e. the same as for the first team. Adult English speakers are able to guess the second score in such cases almost without fail; whereas ten-year-olds still find the task more difficult than adults do, although easier than seven-year-olds find it. Two other examples of intonations where ten-year-olds show a lesser degree of comprehension than adults are illustrated on the following:

> She dressed and fed the ˋbaby. (One intonation-group indicating that the baby was dressed as opposed to two intonation-groups which would indicate that the verb was intransitive)
> It's a very nice ˅garden (but . . . . .)

So certainty of judgement about the local meanings associated with intonation patterns is still being developed at least at the age of ten.

Finally in this section let us return to the early stages of intonation acquisition and ask a question which has often been asked: how much of intonation is innate? Falls seem to predominate at the one-word stage while rises are learnt for special meanings; this, together with the evidence from tonal universals in sub-section 5.5.2 above, suggests that there is undoubtedly an innate substratum to intonation: falls for closed meanings and rises for open meanings. But of course a child still has to learn the fine details of the types of fall and rise involved in a particular language. Moreover he has also to learn the conventional overlay involved in a lot of local meanings and the conventional use of tones indicating certain attitudes, e.g. a certain culture may find it appropriate to be tentative in certain circumstances, whereas another might find such a usage hypocritical (for example, speakers of Scottish English say they find low rise on imperatives hypocritical). So the answer to the question at the beginning of this paragraph is that the foundations of intonation are innate, but many of the details are conventional.

5.8 Summary

In this chapter I first surveyed what we know about social and dialectal variation in intonation. Although the majority of English dialects share a very similar intonational system, the intonation associated with some of the larger cities of northern Britain (and that of Indian and Caribbean English) was shown to be very different from that of R.P. and G.A.

Language-universal tendencies are apparent in intonation-groupings and in nucleus placement, and in the tones used with various sentence-types. Indeed the evidence suggests that all aspects of intonational meaning are based on a universal and innate foundation. Finally some facts of intonation acquisition and change were presented, and related to the innate foundation.

Sources and further reading

For intonation and style, see Crystal and Davy (1969).

For intonation and class, see McGregor (1980) on Australian English; see also Pellowe and Jones (1978) on Tyneside English.

For intonation and sex, see Key (1972), Brend (1975), and McConnell-Ginet (1978).

For the relationship between fundamental frequency and age, see Oates and Dacakis (1983).

For the relationship between larynx size and fundamental frequency in men and women, see Sachs, Lieberman, and Erickson (1973).

For intonational stereotyping, see Edelsky (1979).

For intonation in British dialects, see Jarman and Cruttenden (1976) for Belfast; Knowles (1974, 1978) for Liverpool; Pellowe and Jones (1978) for Tyneside; Wilde (1938) for Birmingham; Haldenby (1959) for Lincolnshire; Brown, Currie and Kenworthy (1980) for Edinburgh, Glasgow, and Thurso; Jones (1956) for Welsh English; Bilton (1982) for Hull; McClure (1980) for Ayr, Paisley, and West Kilbride; and Rohrer (1952) for six rural English dialects.

For dialectal variation in the realisation of the Swedish word accents, see Gårding (1977a); and for Norwegian see Fintoft, Mjaavatn, Møllergård, and Ulseth (1978).

For the intonation of American English, see Pike (1945); for Black American English, see Tarone (1976); for Australian English, see McGregor (1980).

For the intonation of men and women in Japanese, see Loveday (1981).

For comparative intonation-groupings and comparative focus, see Agard and di Pietro (1965) and Nespor and Vogel (1983) for Italian; Fox (1982, 1984) and Fuchs (1984) for German; Varga (1984) for Hungarian; Cunningham (1983) for Spanish; Heringer and Wolontis (1972) and Iivonen (1978) for Finnish; Dogil (1980) for Polish; and Kenning (1979) for French.

For the history of studies in English intonation, see Crystal (1969a) and Cruttenden (1981a). The nuclear approach began with Palmer (1922); the 'whole tune' approach dates back to Jones (1909, 1918) and Armstrong and Ward (1926); and the pitch levels approach was expounded in Pike (1945), Wells (1945), and Trager and Smith (1951).

For the model of intonation developed in Sweden, see Gårding (1979, 1981, 1983).

For the model of intonation developed in the Netherlands, see 't Hart and Cohen (1973) and 't Hart and Collier (1975, 1978) and Collier and 't Hart (1981).

For a detailed survey of sentence-type across languages, see Sadock and Zwicky (1985).

For comparative tone in intonation languages, see Bolinger (1978).

For comparison between intonation and model particles in English and German, see Schubiger (1965, 1980).

For the intonation of interrogatives, see Ultan (1978).

For the intonation of particular languages, see Topping (1969) for Chamorro; Swadesh (1946) for Chitimacha; Stockwell and Bowen (1965) for Spanish; Moulton (1962), von Essen (1956), Trim (1964), Bierwisch (1966), Pheby (1975), Kohler (1977), and Fox (1982, 1984) for German; Bowen (1969) for Tagalog; Canepari (1977) for Venetian; Collier and 't Hart (1981) for Dutch; Maw and Kelly (1975) for Swahili; Chapallaz (1979) for Italian; Obolensky, Panah, and Nouri (1963) for Persian; Thomas (1975) for Chrau; Clayre (1973) for Sa'ban; Householder (1965) for Azerbaijani; Miller and Tench (1981) for Hausa; Williamson (1979) for various Nigerian languages, including Degema; Thorsen (1978, 1983) for Danish; Boyanus (1955), van Schooneveld (1961), Jones and Ward (1969), and Svetozarova (1975) for Russian; Romportl (1973) for Czech; Leed (1968) for Serbo-Croat; Ladd (1981) and Varga (1984) for Hungarian; Ladd (1981) for Roumanian; Coustenoble and Armstrong (1934), Delattre (1972), Martin (1978), and Kenning (1979) for French.

For declination, see in particular Vaissière (1983). For particular languages, see Cohen and 't Hart (1967) for Dutch, Magno-Caldognetto *et al.* (1978) for Italian; Fujisaki *et al.* (1979) for Japanese; Thorsen (1978) for Danish; Svetozarova (1975) for Russian.

For the correlation between closed and open meanings and falls and rises, see Cruttenden (1981b). For falls and rises as innate, see Lieberman (1967).

For intonational change, see Bolinger (1964b) and Fónagy (1979).

For early vocal development, see Cruttenden (1979), Oller (1980) and Stark (1980).

For early mimicry, see Nakazima (1962).

For jargon intonation, see Peters (1977).

For early words with yoked pitch patterns, see Halliday (1975).

For the early presence of fall v. rise, see Leopold (1947 : 255).

For some meanings of rises on first words, see Wells, Montgomery and MacLure (1979).

For chronological development of tones, see Crystal (1979).

For early nucleus placement, see Wieman (1976).

For the late development of intonation comprehension, see Cruttenden (1974, 1985).

6
Conspectus

In this chapter a brief look is taken at other prosodic and paralinguistic features with which intonation interacts and at the relationship of intonation to other media, i.e. writing and gesture; the chapter ends with an overview of the present 'state-of-the-art' in intonational studies.

6.1 Prosodic, paralinguistic, and extralinguistic

These three terms (like the terms 'stress' and 'accent') have been used in a variety of ways by linguists (quite apart of course from the use of 'prosodic' as a term in the study of poetic metre); I shall therefore take up a little space to explain my use of the terms. Both prosodic and paralinguistic refer to vocal effects which are used to convey meaning. Prosodic features are suprasegmental, i.e. they are co-occurrent with sequences of segmental phonemes and of words. Some prosodic features are more obviously describable in terms of a system, intonation itself being the prime example of such a feature: there is a system of contrasting nuclear tones in a language and moreover this system clearly interacts with a central linguistic system like sentence-type. Other prosodic features are less easy to describe in terms of a system. It is, for example, less easy to describe a system of tempo: for one thing, different rates of utterance form a gradient from very fast to very slow; for another, it is not easy to relate meanings systematically to variations of speed. Paralinguistic effects, as opposed to prosodic features, are interruptive rather than co-occurrent: those effects commonly called vocalisations fall into this category, e.g. [bβ] as the articulation of a shiver, or ⟋⟍ as a wolf whistle. Lastly, the term 'extra-linguistic' refers to various co-occurrent features and interruptive effects which have no conventional meaning but which are conditioned by factors over which the speaker has no immediate control. Some of these may be physical, e.g. sex, age, body-build; and some simply habitual, e.g. a particular speaker may habitually speak at a faster tempo than other speakers of his language. In addition some of these habits may be language-specific, e.g. speakers of one language may habitually speak at a faster tempo than speakers of another language. Some phonetic features and effects may be used both prosodically or paralinguistically on the one hand, and extralinguistically on the other, e.g. females generally use a higher pitch than males, which is extralinguistic; but both males and females may use a higher register for certain meanings in certain situations, which is prosodic. I shall have little more to say about the extralinguistic occurrence of features and effects.

6.1.1 Prosodic features

The boundary between segments and prosodic features (or 'prosodies') has been drawn differently by different phonological theories. Phonetic features like nasalisation and vowel harmony have been treated by the majority of linguists as part of the segmental phonemic description, e.g. the fact that the vowel in *mass* is nasalised for most speakers is treated as an assimilatory effect whereby a nasal consonant affects an adjacent vowel. But some phonological theories would wish to extract features like nasalisation and say that they are represented on an independent tier which is then mapped onto whole linguistic units like syllables or morphemes or words. In other words they treat such features as prosodic. So palatalisation is said to be a feature of syllables in Russian, pharyngealisation of syllables in Arabic, and vowel harmony of words in Turkish. This sort of phonological approach is particularly associated with two theoretical approaches to phonology, the one actually called prosodic phonology, and the other called autosegmental phonology (which was briefly touched on in chapter 3, section 3.8.1 above). This is not the place to get into detailed arguments about the merits of one phonological theory as opposed to those of another; but one thing which should be pointed out is that all the features which have traditionally been regarded as suprasegmental and prosodic, e.g. intonation, rhythm, tempo and voice-quality, are potentially mapped onto units larger than a single word, whereas features like vowel-harmony and nasalisation, even though they extend over more than one segment, rarely extend beyond word-boundaries. (Nasalisation may of course be extralinguistic, i.e. it may be a habitual characteristic of a speaker's voice.) I am limiting my discussion here to features which potentially extend over more than one word.

Apart from accent and intonation, there are at least four features which can be used prosodically as well as extralinguistically: loudness, tempo, rhythmicality, and voice-quality. Loudness is one of the exponents (although generally the least consistent one) of accented syllables, but it can also be used over larger stretches of utterance: we may shout, for example, when we are angry; and we usually speak more softly when we are inserting a parenthetic remark (as well as using a lower key – see chapter 4, section 4.5 above). Tempo and rhythmicality (i.e. emphasising the rhythm of an utterance) may be similarly varied. The average tempo of a British English speaker has generally been estimated to be around six syllables per second; but we will frequently speak at a faster tempo when we are excited (as well as often using a higher register) and we may use an accelerating tempo as we became more excited. Listen for example, to a horse race commentary, or a soccer commentator during the build-up to a goal. In the case of voice quality, a considerable amount of information is available, both as regards phonatory and articulatory detail, and as regards linguistic uses. Voice quality divides into supra-laryngeal settings of the mouth and tongue, and laryngeal settings (or phonation types) involving the vocal cords or the larynx as a whole. Both supralaryngeal and laryngeal settings are principally extralinguistic, i.e. a constellation of features of voice quality is typical of a particular speaker. But voice qualities, and especially phonation types, are also used prosodically to convey linguistic meaning, e.g. creaky voice often indicates boredom or resignation. More commonly, particular phonation types are considered appropriate to certain situations, e.g. breathy voice is often described as 'bedroom voice', whispery voice as 'library voice', and lowered larynx voice as 'sepulchral voice'. Moreover a particular phonation type is often associated with a particular tone, e.g. rise-fall is frequently accompanied by breathy voice to give a 'conspiratorial' meaning.

6.1.2   Paralinguistic effects

As defined above, these are interruptive rather than co-occurrent. The most common interruptive effect, i.e. pause, has already been dealt with in chapter 3, sub-section 3.2.1, where it was shown to be one of the potential markers of intonation-group boundaries, but frequently used also when a speaker is hesitant. In the latter case it is especially likely to be a filled pause; filled, that is, by some combination of [ʔ] [m] and [ə] in R.P., but by other sounds in other dialects and languages. There is another class of interruptive effects which should probably be classed as extralinguistic; effects like crying, sobbing, laughing, and giggling, which seem to be more or less universal, although custom in different cultures may decree that one or another of these effects is taboo or appropriate in certain situations. There are, however, many other effects which certainly convey conventional meanings, and which may often be language-specific, or limited only to certain languages; these effects are often called 'vocalisations'. They may involve single phonemes or sequences of phonemes of the language, e.g. [ʃ:] for 'be quiet', [kɔ:] for 'amazement', and French [bz] or [bʒ] for 'irritation'; or they may involve sounds or sequences which are not part of the core phonetic inventory of the language, e.g. [pɸ] for 'contempt' (cf. [pɸ:] for 'I am only just surviving the pressure'), [pst] for attention-getting, and [fçu] for heat. Vocalisations frequently involve non-pulmonic airstreams, e.g. [ʮ] for 'irritation' or 'naughty', [ʘ] for 'gee-up' and [k̃x'] for 'shooting' (little boys' favourite sound). They may even involve sounds which are not transcribable by any current transcription system, e.g. an ingressive interdental fricative for hurt, ingressive creaky voice for a snort, or a deep breath plus long exhalation for a sigh. In many African languages a class of words known as ideophones is often described; ideophones seem to be the near-equivalent of what have so far been described as vocalisations, although they include rather more onomatopoeic sequences and reduplications; like vocalisations they often involve sounds (and pitches, since most African languages are tone languages) outside the phonemic inventory of the language concerned. Some examples from Shona are: [ɗiɗiɗi] (on a constant high pitch) ('walking fast'); [tkwiriri] (on high-mid-mid) 'staring in amazement'; and [ŋwi:] (with high-fall) 'being silent'.

Of most interest in a book on intonation are those vocalisations which depend principally on a precise sequence of pitches or pitch movements (the 'intonational idioms' mentioned in chapter 4, section 4.4). Such intonational idioms may be associated with lexical items, or with particular non-lexical sequences of sounds, or with whistling or coughing. Mothers say *all gone* to their babies on the pitch sequence ⌐•— , while there are a large number of vocalisations involving [ə] [ʔ] and [h] which have fixed pitch patterns, e.g. [ʔəʔə] ⌐•◞ 'There's no chance of that'; [ʔoʔou] ⌐•— 'Something bad is happening'; and [ʔəhə] •—◝ 'So that's what's happening'. A cough is obviously closely related to a glottal stop and a glottal fricative, so it is not surprising that some vocalisations are typically produced as coughs, e.g. •◝ (usually made with closed lips) as an attention-getter. Whistles of course are an alternative to the vocal cords as a way of producing pitch but do not allow the imposition of an articulatory posture: already mentioned has been the wolf whistle ◞◝ ; a reversed wolf whistle is another attention-getter, as is the sequence ⌐•— , which was characterised as a stylised fall-rise in subsection 4.4.4.3 above.

6.2   **Intonation and punctuation**

Since punctuation is the preserve of the literate and since the literate in any language tend to know at least something about grammar but little or nothing about intonation, punctuation is generally prescribed according to grammatical rule rather than to mirror intonation. For many uses of punctuation indeed there is no intonational equivalent, e.g. spaces between words and the use of apostrophe for possessives and for elision. In other cases there are clear correlations between punctuation and intonation, e.g. a pair of commas will often indicate a parenthesis or a parenthetical type of structure like a non-restrictive relative, and in such a case the pair of commas will often correlate with the boundaries of a separate intonation-group, e.g.

Carl Basset, who was expected to win, actually only came second.

Punctuation generally serves two purposes: it may delimit, as in the last example, or it may specify, like the apostrophe for possession or various diacritics for the specification of syllables which take word-stress (this latter not of course in English). In both uses (delimitation and specification) there are areas, as already remarked, which involve regular correlations between punctuation and intonation. In such areas there are strong indications that popular usage (if unimpeded by grammarians' and publishing houses' prescriptions) will tend towards letting intonation take over from grammar as the major determiner of punctuation. For example, the four delimitative marks, comma, semi-colon, colon, and full stop (also called period), are used to indicate different syntactic and/or semantic links, but all of them regularly indicate that an intonation-group boundary will occur at that point (not necessarily a pause – remember that intonation-group boundaries are not always marked by a pause – see chapter 3, section 3.2). But there are certain positions where a group boundary commonly occurs but where a delimitative punctuation mark is proscribed and in these positions popular usage often uses a comma where it is not supposed to be used. In particular this applies to the boundary between the subject and predicate of a clause. In chapter 4, section 4.2, we saw that the subject of a clause is commonly given a separate intonation-group in English when it is contrastive or when it is long (principally by postmodification). Here are two such examples with inappropriately punctuated versions underneath:

ᵛPercy /didn't appˋrove of the idea/but his ᵛwife/was ˋvery keen
Percy, didn't approve of the idea but his wife, was very keen
The ᵛfirst batsman to get a thousand runs in May/was Denis
　　ˋCompton
The first batsman to get a thousand runs in May, was Denis Compton

In both examples, the commas are proscribed by rule but nevertheless were inserted by the writer: newspapers and personal letters very commonly show commas in this position.

An area of specification where punctuation is at least as closely related to intonation as to grammar in English is sentence-type. Yes/no interrogatives and wh interrogatives are regularly marked with the question mark in place of the full stop; both types of interrogatives may take a falling or a rising tone. But the question mark is also regularly (and in this case allowably) used following declarative questions and echoes; these regularly take a high-rise tone. The conclusion in this case is that the question mark correlates most closely with sentence function whether marked by grammar or by intonation. Much the same applies to the use of the exclamation mark; it is used to indicate a function and the syntactic form of the utterance may or may not be in the syntactic form of an exclamative, cf.

> What an idiot I've been!
> Isn't she stupid!

But here the correlation is not only with function but also consistently with intonation: the exclamation mark indicates a falling tone almost without exception.

Notice that while intonation-group boundaries are fairly regularly marked in some way and differences in tone are at least implied in the use of the question and exclamation marks, there is (at least in English and probably universally) no usual marking of nucleus placement. Sometimes capitalisation, or italicisation, or underlining, or (as in this book) bold type, is used for this purpose (particularly in the case of contrastive nuclei) but such devices are frowned upon when used other than occasionally. Rather, it is expected that we use other focussing devices in written language (e.g. clefting).

6.3 **Intonation and gesture**

While the links between intonation and punctuation apply, of course, only to literate societies, the links between intonation and gesture are of an altogether more primitive sort. That intonation is a unique part of language is clearly demonstrated from experiments in dichotic listening. In this sort of experimentation similar auditory material is fed to the two ears and the listener shows a preference for the material presented to one ear. For language generally, for tone in tone languages, and even for consonant-vowel nonsense syllables, an advantage is shown for the right ear, which involves the left hemisphere of the brain; whereas a left ear (right hemisphere) advantage is shown for intonation, along with music and general environmental noises. So it is not surprising that in a large majority of cases of acquired language disorders, and even in cases of severe phonological or grammatical disorder, intonation is unaffected. In those few cases in which intonation **is** affected, patients may well have gestural problems as well. This suggests a close connection between intonation and gesture.

Chapter 5 concluded that there are certainly universal tonal tendencies in languages: falls or lower tones are associated with closed meanings while rises or higher tones are associated with open meanings. There are also tendencies for certain gestures to be associated with each of these types. The most obvious relation is with a lowering or raising movement of the head: it takes considerable practice to be able to produce a rising pitch as the head is lowered or *vice versa*. Other common correlations with rising tones include eyebrows lifted, head inclined forward, raised shoulders, lengthy eye contact, hands lifted and/or palms upwards. All of this suggests that there is some sort of similar instinctual underpinning to both intonation and gesture: rising tones and related gestures all involve an increase in tension whereas falling tones and related gestures all involve a decrease in tension.

6.4   State-of-the-art

The study of intonation is at a point from which there is likely to be significant and consistent progress in the next decade or two. Six areas can be identified in which work is likely to be concentrated: the bringing together of work from these six areas will constitute the beginnings of a theory of intonation:

(i) the assignment of intonation-groupings and nucleus placement basically on syntactic grounds (although not in the simplistic ways which have been proposed in the past), but with readjustment rules which take account of the discourse environment and which also allow for an element of speaker choice;

(ii) the establishment of a set of tones to constitute the set of tones in the intonational lexicon of an individual language, together with the set of features which vary the tones (e.g. accent range). The precise set ultimately to be preferred will be that which gives the best combined solution to (iii)–(v) below; it is likely that the tones will have a dual formal representation: contours, to which the abstract meanings of (iii) are attached, but also sequences of levels, which are specified for each contour, because this makes possible a simpler statement of the realisational rules in (v);

(iii) the semantics involved in a set of abstract meanings to be matched to the set of tones in an intonational lexicon. It is not yet even clear what sorts of meanings are involved;

(iv) the pragmatics involved in the choice of tone and in the interaction between the abstract meanings of the tones and other levels of meaning (lexical, grammatical, gestural) to produce local meanings;

(v) the realisation rules involved in mapping the tones from the intonational lexicon onto varying stretches of segments which have pre-assigned stresses (by an earlier operating phonological theory – perhaps a metrical theory) and nucleus placements (by (i) above);

(vi) the comparative study of the proceeding five areas to refine our intonational typology and our knowledge of universals.

A start has been made in all six areas and I hope that this book makes some small contribution to the advancement, synthesis, and promulgation of our knowledge of intonation. It is an exciting time for intonationists.

Sources and further reading
For prosodic and paralinguistic features, see Crystal and Quirk (1964) and Crystal (1969a).
For prosodic phonology, see Firth (1948), Lyons (1962), and Sommerstein (1977).
For autosegmental phonology, see van der Hulst and Smith (1982).
For voice quality, see Catford (1977), and Laver (1980).
For non-lexical pitch patterns, see Luthy (1983).
For a description of English punctuation, see Appendix III of Quirk *et al.* (1972).
For intonation and gesture generally, see Bolinger (1983) and Chapter 11 of Bolinger (forthcoming).
For hemispheric processing of language, see Blumstein and Cooper (1974).

REFERENCES

Agard, F. B. and di Pietro, R. J. (1965). *The sounds of English and Italian.* Chicago: University of Chicago Press.

Akmajian, A. (1979). *Aspects of the grammar of focus in English.* New York: Garland.

Allan, K. (1984). 'The component functions of the high rise terminal contour in Australian declarative sentences.' *Australian Journal of Linguistics*, 4, 19–32.

Allerton, D. J. and Cruttenden, A. (1974). 'English sentence adverbials: their syntax and their intonation in British English.' *Lingua*, 34, 1–30.

Allerton, D. J. and Cruttenden, A. (1976). 'The intonation of medial and final sentence adverbials in British English.' *Archivum Linguisticum*, 7, 29–59.

Allerton, D. J. and Cruttenden, A. (1978). 'Syntactic, illocutionary, thematic and attitudinal factors in the intonation of adverbials.' *Journal of Pragmatics*, 2, 155–88.

Allerton, D. J. and Cruttenden, A. (1979). 'Three reasons for accenting a definite subject.' *Journal of Linguistics*, 15, 49–53.

Armstrong, L. E. and Ward, I. C. (1926). *Handbook of English intonation.* Leipzig and Berlin: Teubner. Second edition (1931). Cambridge: Heffer.

Bailey, C-J. N. (1978). *Systems of English intonation with gradient models.* Bloomington: Indiana University Linguistics Club.

Berinstein, A. E. (1979). 'A cross-linguistic study: the perception and production of stress.' *UCLA Working Papers in Phonetics*, 47. Los Angeles: UCLA Phonetics Laboratory.

Berman, A. and Szamosi, M. (1972). 'Observations on sentential stress.' *Language*, 48, 304–25.

Bierwisch, M. (1966). 'Regeln für die Intonation deutscher Sätze.' *Studia Grammatica*, 7, 99–201.

Bilton, L. (1982). 'A note on Hull intonation.' *Journal of the International Phonetic Association*, 12, 30–5.

Bing, J. M. (1979a). 'Up the noun phrase: another stress rule.' In E. Engdal and M. Stein (eds.), *Papers presented to Emmon Bach by his students.* Amherst: University of Massachusetts.

Bing, J. M. (1979b). *Aspects of English prosody.* Unpublished Ph.D. dissertation, University of Massachusetts.

Bing, J. M. (1980). 'Intonation and the interpretation of negatives.' *Cahiers Linguistiques d'Ottawa* NELS, 10, 13–23.

References

Blumstein, S. and Cooper, W. E. (1974). 'Hemispheric processing of intonation contours.' *Cortex*, 10, 148–58.

Bolinger, D. L. (1947). Review of K. L. Pike, *Intonation of American English*. *American Speech*, 22, 134–6.

Bolinger, D. L. (1958). 'A theory of pitch accent in English.' *Word*, 14, 109–49.

Bolinger, D. L. (1961). *Generality, gradience, and the all-or-none*. The Hague: Mouton.

Bolinger, D. L. (1964a). 'Around the edge of language: intonation.' *Harvard Educational Review*, 34, 282–93. Reprinted in D. L. Bolinger (ed.), *Intonation*.

Bolinger, D. L. (1964b). 'Intonation as a universal.' In H. G. Lunt (ed.), *Proceedings of the ninth international congress of linguists*. The Hague: Mouton.

Bolinger, D. L. (1972a). 'Accent is predictable (if you're a mind reader).' *Language*, 48, 633–44.

Bolinger, D. L. (ed.) (1972b). *Intonation*. Harmondsworth: Penguin.

Bolinger, D. L. (1978). 'Intonation across languages.' In J. P. Greenberg, C. A. Ferguson and E. A. Moravcsik (eds.), *Universals of human language*. Volume 2: *Phonology*. Stanford: Stanford University Press.

Bolinger, D. L. (1981). *Two kinds of vowels, two kinds of rhythm*. Bloomington: Indiana University Linguistics Club.

Bolinger, D. L. (1983). 'Intonation and gesture.' *American Speech*, 58, 156–74.

Bolinger, D. L. (1985). 'Two views of accent.' *Journal of Linguistics*, 21, 79–123.

Bolinger, D. L. (forthcoming). *Intonation and its parts*. Volume 1. Stanford: Stanford University Press.

Boomer, D. S. (1965). 'Hesitation and grammatical encoding.' *Language and Speech*, 8, 148–58.

Bowen, J. D. (1969). *Beginning Tagalog*. Berkeley: University of California Press.

Boyanus, S. C. (1955). *Russian pronunciation*. London: Lund Humphries.

Brazil, D. (1975). *Discourse intonation*. University of Birmingham: Department of English.

Brazil, D. (1978). *Discourse intonation II*. University of Birmingham: Department of English.

Brazil, D. C., Coulthard, M. R. and Johns, C. (1980). *Discourse intonation and language teaching*. London: Longman.

Brend, R. M. (1975). 'Male-female intonation patterns in American English.' In B. Thorne and N. Henley (eds.), *Language and sex: difference and dominance*. Rewley, Mass.: Newbury House.

Bresnan, J. (1971). 'Sentence stress and syntactic transformations.' *Language*, 47, 257–82.

Brown, G. (1983). 'Intonation, the categories *given/new* and other sorts of knowledge.' In A. Cutler and D. R. Ladd (eds.), *Prosody: models and measurements*. Berlin: Springer-Verlag.

Brown, G., Currie, K. L. and Kenworthy, J. (1980). *Questions of intonation*. London: Croom Helm.

Brown, G. and Yule, G. (1983). *Discourse analysis*. Cambridge: Cambridge University Press.

Brown, P. and Levinson, S. (1978). 'Universals in language usage: politeness phenomena.' In E. N. Goody (ed.), *Questions and politeness: strategies in social interaction*. Cambridge: Cambridge University Press.

Canepari, L. (1977). 'The dialect of Venice.' *Journal of the International Phonetic Association*, 6, 67–76.

Catford, J. C. (1977). *Fundamental problems in phonetics*. Edinburgh: Edinburgh University Press.

Chafe, W. L. (1974). 'Language and consciousness.' *Language*, 50, 111–33.

Chafe, W. L. (1976). 'Givenness, contrastiveness, definiteness, subjects, topics, and point of view.' In C. N. Li (ed.), *Subject and topic*. New York: Academic Press.

Chang, N-C. T. (1958). 'Tones and intonation in the Chengtu dialect (Szechuan, China).' *Phonetica*, 2, 59–84. Reprinted in D. L. Bolinger (ed.), *Intonation*.

Chapallaz, M. (1979). *The pronunciation of Italian*. London: Bell and Hyman.

Chomsky, N. (1971). 'Deep structure, surface structure, and semantic interpretation.' In D. D. Steinberg and L. A. Jakobovits (eds.), *Semantics: an interdisciplinary reader in philosophy, linguistics, and psychology*. Cambridge: Cambridge University Press.

Chomsky, N. and Halle, M. (1968). *The sound pattern of English*. New York: Harper and Row.

Clayre, I. F. C. S. (1973). 'The phonemes of Sa'ban: a language of Highland Borneo.' *Linguistics*, 100, 26–46.

Cohen, A. and Hart, J. 't (1967). 'On the anatomy of intonation.' *Lingua*, 19, 177–92.

Collier, R. and Hart, J. 't (1981). *Cursus Nederlandse intonatie*. Leuven: Acco.

Cooper, W. E. and Sorensen, J. M. (1977). 'Fundamental frequency contours at syntactic boundaries.' *Journal of the Acoustic Society of America*, 62, 683–92.

Coustenoble, H. and Armstrong, L. (1934). *Studies in French intonation*. Cambridge: Heffer.

Cruttenden, A. (1974). 'An experiment involving comprehension of intonation in children from 7 to 10.' *Journal of Child Language*, 1, 221–32.

Cruttenden, A. (1979). *Language in infancy and childhood*. Manchester: Manchester University Press.

Cruttenden, A. (1981a). *The intonation of English sentences with special reference to sentence adverbials*. Unpublished Ph.D. thesis, University of Manchester.

Cruttenden, A. (1981b). 'Falls and rises: meanings and universals.' *Journal of Linguistics*, 17, 77–91.

Cruttenden, A. (1984). 'The relevance of intonational misfits.' In D. Gibbon and H. Richter (eds.), *Intonation, accent, rhythm*. Berlin: de Gruyter.

Cruttenden, A. (1985). 'Intonation comprehension in ten-year-olds.' *Journal of Child Language*, 12.

Crystal, D. (1969a). *Prosodic systems and intonation in English*. Cambridge: Cambridge University Press.

Crystal, D. (1969b). 'A forgotten English tone: an alternative analysis.' *Le Maître Phonétique*, 132, 34–7.

Crystal, D. (1975). 'Prosodic features and linguistic theory.' In D. Crystal, *The English tone of voice*. London: Edward Arnold.

References

Crystal, D. (1979). 'Prosodic development.' In P. Fletcher and M. Garman (eds.), *Language acquisition: studies in first language development*. Cambridge: Cambridge University Press.

Crystal, D. and Davy, D. (1969). *Investigating English style*. London: Longman.

Crystal, D. and Quirk, R. (1964). *Systems of prosodic and paralinguistic features in English*. The Hague: Mouton.

Cunningham, U. (1983). 'Aspects of the intonation of Spanish.' *Nottingham Linguistic Circular*, 12, 21–54.

Davy, D. (1968). *A study of intonation and analogous features as exponents of stylistic variation, with special reference to a comparison of conversation with written English read aloud*. Unpublished M.A. thesis, University of London. Cited in Crystal (1969a).

Delattre, P. (1972). 'The distinctive function of intonation.' In D. L. Bolinger (ed.), *Intonation*.

Dik, S. *et al.* [sic] (1980). 'On the typology of focus phenomena.' *Leids Taalkundig Bulletin GLOT* 3, 41–74.

Dogil, G. (1980). 'Focus marking in Polish.' *Linguistic Analysis*, 6, 221–45.

Edelsky, C. (1979). 'Question intonation and sex roles.' *Language in Society*, 8, 15–32.

Egerod, S. (1966). 'A statement on Atayal phonology.' In B. Shin, J. Boisselier and A. B. Griswold (eds.), *Essays offered to G. H. Luce. Artibus Asiae*, Supplement 23, Volume 1.

Essen, O. von (1956). *Grundzüge der hochdeutschen Satzintonation*. Düsseldorf: Henn.

Fairbanks, G. and Pronovost, W. (1939). 'An experimental study of the pitch characteristics of the voice during the expression of emotions.' *Speech Monographs*, 6, 87–104.

Fintoft, K., Mjaavatn, P. E., Møllergård, E. and Ulseth, B. (1978). 'Toneme patterns in Norwegian dialects.' In E. Gårding, G. Bruce and R. Bannert (eds.), *Nordic prosody: papers from a symposium*. Lund University: Department of Linguistics.

Firbas, J. (1980). 'Post-intonation-centre prosodic shade in the modern English clause.' In S. Greenbaum, G. Leech and J. Svartvik (eds.), *Studies in English linguistics for Randolph Quirk*. London: Longman.

Firth, J. R. (1948). 'Sounds and prosodies.' *Transactions of the Philological Society*. Oxford: Blackwell. Reprinted in J. R. Firth (1951), *Papers in Linguistics 1934–51*. London: Oxford University Press.

Fónagy, I. (1978). 'A new method of investigating the perception of phonetic features.' *Language and Speech*, 21, 34–49.

Fónagy, I. (1979). 'Structure et aspects sociaux des changements prosodiques.' In E. Fischer-Jørgensen, J. Rischel and N. Thorsen (eds.), *Proceedings of the ninth international congress of phonetic sciences*. Volume 2. University of Copenhagen: Institute of Phonetics.

Fox, A. (1969). 'A forgotten English tone.' *Le Maître Phonétique*, 131, 13–4.

Fox, A. (1970). 'The forgotten tone: a reply.' *Le Maître Phonétique*, 134, 29–31.

Fox, A. (1973). 'Tone sequences in English.' *Archivum Linguisticum* (New Series), 4, 17–26.

Fox, A. (1982). 'Remarks on intonation and "Ausrahmung" in German.' *Journal of Linguistics*, 18, 89–106.

Fox, A. (1984). *German intonation: an outline*. Oxford: Clarendon Press.

Fries, C. C. (1964). 'On the intonation of "yes-no" questions.' In D. Abercrombie, D. B. Fry, P. A. D. MacCarthy, N. C. Scott and J. L. M. Trim (eds.), *In honour of Daniel Jones*. London: Longman.

Fromkin, V. A. (1972). 'Tone features and tone rules.' *Studies in African Linguistics*, 3, 47–76.

Fromkin, V. A. (ed.) (1978). *Tone: a linguistic survey*. New York: Academic Press.

Fry, D. B. (1955). 'Duration and intensity as physical correlates of linguistic stress.' *Journal of the Acoustical Society of America*, 27, 765–8.

Fry, D. B. (1958). 'Experiments in the perception of stress.' *Language and Speech*, 1, 126–52.

Fuchs, A. (1980). 'Accented subjects in "all-new" sentences.' In G. Brettschneider and Ch. Lehmann (eds.), *Wege zur Universalienforschung (Festschrift für Hans-Jakob Seiler)*. Tübingen: Gunter Narr.

Fuchs, A. (1984). '"Deaccenting" and "default accent".' In D. Gibbon and H. Richter (eds.), *Intonation, accent, and rhythm: studies in discourse phonology*. Berlin: de Gruyter.

Fudge, E. (1984). *English word-stress*. London: George Allen and Unwin.

Fujisaki, M., Hirose, K. and Ohta, K. (1979). 'Acoustic features of the fundamental frequency contours of declarative sentences.' *Annual Bulletin of the Research Institute of Logopedics and Phoniatrics, University of Tokyo*, 13, 163–72.

Garde, P. (1968). *L'Accent*. Paris: Presses Universitaires de France.

Garde, P. (1973). 'Principles of the synchronic description of stress.' In E. Fudge (ed.), *Phonology*. Harmondsworth: Penguin.

Gårding, E. (1977a). 'The importance of turning points for the pitch patterns of Swedish accents.' In L. M. Hyman (ed.), *Studies in stress and accent*. Southern California Occasional Papers in Linguistics No. 4. Los Angeles: University of Southern California.

Gårding, E. (1977b). *The Scandinavian word accents*. Travaux de L'Institut de Linguistique de Lund, XI. Lund University: Department of Linguistics.

Gårding, E. (1979). 'Sentence intonation in Swedish.' *Phonetica*, 36, 207–15.

Gårding, E. (1981). 'Contrastive prosody: a model and its applications.' *Studia Linguistica*, 35, 146–65.

Gårding, E. (1983). 'A generative model of intonation.' In A. Cutler and D. R. Ladd (eds.), *Prosody: models and measurements*. Berlin: Springer-Verlag.

Garro, L. and Parker, F. (1982). 'Some suprasegmental characteristics of relative clauses in English.' *Journal of Phonetics*, 149–61.

Gibbon, D. (1976). *Perspectives of intonation analysis*. Bern: Lang.

Giegerich, H. J. (1984). *Relating to metrical structure*. Bloomington: Indiana University Linguistics Club.

Giegerich, H. J. (1985). *Metrical phonology and phonological structure: English and German*. Cambridge: Cambridge University Press.

Goldman-Eisler, F. (1958). 'The predictability of words in context and the length of pauses in speech.' *Language and Speech*, 1, 226–31.

References

Goldman-Eisler, F. (1972). 'Pauses, clauses, sentences.' *Language and Speech*, 15, 103–13.

Goyvaerts, D. L. and Pullum, D. K. (eds.). (1975). *Essays on the sound pattern of English*. Ghent: Story-Scientia.

Guéron, J. (1980). 'On the syntax and semantics of PP extraposition.' *Linguistic Inquiry*, 11, 637–78.

Gussenhoven, C. (1983a). 'Focus, mode, and the nucleus.' *Journal of Linguistics*, 19, 377–417. Reprinted in Gussenhoven (1984).

Gussenhoven, C. (1983b). *A semantic analysis of the nuclear tones of English*. Bloomington: Indiana University Linguistics Club. Reprinted in Gussenhoven (1984).

Gussenhoven, C. (1984). *On the grammar and semantics of sentence accents*. Dordrecht: Foris.

Gussenhoven, C. (1985). 'The intonation of George and Mildred: post-nuclear generalizations.' In C. Johns-Lewis (ed.), *Intonation in discourse*. London: Croom Helm. Reprinted in Gussenhoven (1984).

Guy, G. R. and Vonwiller, J. (1984). 'The meaning of an intonation in Australian English.' *Australian Journal of Linguistics*, 4, 1–17.

Haldenby, C. (1959). *Intonation in Lincolnshire dialect*. Unpublished M.A. dissertation, University of Leeds.

Halliday, M. A. K. (1967). *Intonation and grammar in British English*. The Hague: Mouton.

Halliday, M. A. K. (1970). *A course in spoken English: intonation*. London: Oxford University Press.

Halliday, M. A. K. (1975). *Learning how to mean*. London: Edward Arnold.

Halliday, M. A. K. and Hasan, R. (1976). *Cohesion in English*. London: Longman.

Hart, J. 't and Cohen, A. (1973). 'Intonation by rule: a perceptual quest.' *Journal of Phonetics*, 1, 309–27.

Hart, J. 't and Collier, R. (1975). 'Integrating different levels of intonation analysis.' *Journal of Phonetics*, 3, 235–55.

Hart, J. 't and Collier, R. (1978). 'A course in Dutch intonation.' *Annual Progress Report, Institute for Perception Research*, Eindhoven, 13, 31–5.

Haugen, E. and Joos, M. (1952). 'Tone and intonation in East Norwegian.' *Acta Philologica Scandinavica*, 22, 41–64. Reprinted in D. L. Bolinger (ed.), *Intonation*.

Heringer, J. and Wolontis, M. (1972). 'Focus in Finnish.' *Papers from the Eighth Regional Meeting, Chicago Linguistic Society*, 152–61.

Hirst, D. (1977). *Intonative features: a syntactic approach to English intonation*. The Hague: Mouton.

House, J. (1983). 'Nucleus and focus: a pilot study.' *Speech, Hearing, and Language: Work in Progress*. University College, London: Department of Phonetics and Linguistics.

Householder, F. W. (1965). *Basic course in Azerbaijani*. Bloomington: Indiana University Press.

Huckin, T. N. (1977). *An integrated theory of English intonation*. Unpublished Ph.D. dissertation, University of Washington.

Hulst, H. van der and Smith, N. (1982). *The structure of phonological representations*. Part I. Dordrecht: Foris.

Iivonen, A. (1978). 'Is there interrogative intonation in Finnish?' In E. Gårding, G. Bruce and R. Bannert (eds.), *Nordic prosody: papers from a symposium*. Lund University: Department of Linguistics.

Isačenko, A. V. and Schädlich, H-J. (1966). 'Untersuchungen über die deutsche Satzintonation.' *Studia Grammatica*, 7, 7–67. Translated by J. Pheby as *A model of standard German intonation*. (1970). The Hague: Mouton.

Jackendoff, R. S. (1972). *Semantic interpretation in generative grammar*. Harvard, Mass.: MIT Press.

Jarman, E. and Cruttenden, A. (1976). 'Belfast intonation and the myth of the fall.' *Journal of the International Phonetic Association*, 6, 4–12.

Jassem, W. (1952). *The intonation of conversational English*. Warsaw: La Société des Sciences et des Lettres.

Johns-Lewis, C. (ed.) (forthcoming). *Intonation in discourse*. London: Croom Helm.

Jones, D. (1909). *The pronunciation of English*. Second edition (1914). Third edition (1950). Fourth edition (1956). Cambridge: Cambridge University Press.

Jones, D. (1918). *An outline of English phonetics*. Second edition (1922). Third edition (1932). Ninth edition (1960). Leipzig: Teubner. Third and subsequent editions: Cambridge: Heffer.

Jones, D. and Ward, D. (1969). *The phonetics of Russian*. Cambridge: Cambridge University Press.

Kenning, M.-M. (1979). 'Intonation systems in French.' *Journal of the International Phonetic Association*, 9, 22–30.

Key, M. R. (1972). 'Linguistic behaviour of male and female.' *Linguistics*, 88, 15–31.

Kingdon, R. (1958a). *The groundwork of English intonation*. London: Longman.

Kingdon, R. (1958b). *The groundwork of English stress*. London: Longman.

Knowles, G. (1974). *Scouse: the urban dialect of Liverpool*. Unpublished Ph.D. thesis, University of Leeds.

Knowles, G. (1978). 'The nature of phonological variables in Scouse.' In P. Trudgill (ed.), *Sociolinguistic patterns in British English*. London: Edward Arnold.

Kohler, K. J. (1977). *Einführung in die Phonetik des Deutschen*. Berlin: Erich Schmidt Verlag.

Ladd, D. R. (1977). *The function of the A rise accent in English*. Bloomington: Indiana University Linguistics Club.

Ladd, D. R. (1978). 'Stylized intonation.' *Language*, 54, 517–39.

Ladd, D. R. (1979a). 'Light and shadow: a study of the syntax and semantics of sentence accent in English.' In L. R. Waugh and F. van Coetsem (eds.), *Contributions to grammatical studies: semantics and syntax*. Leiden: Brill.

Ladd, D. R. (1979b). *Basic bibliography of English intonation*. Bloomington: Indiana University Linguistics Club.

Ladd, D. R. (1980). *The structure of intonational meaning*. Bloomington: Indiana University Press.

Ladd, D. R. (1981). 'On intonational universals.' In T. Myers, J. Laver and J. Anderson (eds.), *The cognitive representation of speech*. Amsterdam: North Holland.

References

Ladd, D. R. (1983). 'Phonological features of intonational peaks.' *Language*, 59, 721–59.

Ladefoged, P. (1975). *A course in phonetics*. New York: Harcourt Brace Jovanovich.

Lakoff, G. (1972). 'The global nature of the nuclear stress rule.' *Language*, 48, 285–303.

Laver, J. (1980). *The phonetic description of voice quality*. Cambridge: Cambridge University Press.

Leben, W. R. (1976). 'The tones of English intonation.' *Linguistic Analysis*, 2, 67–107.

Lee, W. R. (1956). 'English intonation: a new approach.' *Lingua*, 5, 345–71.

Lee, W. R. (1980). 'A point about the rise-endings and the fall-endings of yes/no questions.' In L. R. Waugh and C. H. van Schooneveld (eds.), *The melody of language: intonation and prosody*. Baltimore: University Park Press.

Leed, R. L. (1968). 'The intonation of yes/no questions in Serbo-Croatian.' *Slavic and East European Journal*, 3, 330–6.

Lehiste, I. (1970). *Suprasegmentals*. Cambridge, Mass.: MIT Press.

Lehiste, I. (1977). 'Isochrony reconsidered.' *Journal of Phonetics*, 5, 253–63.

Lehman, C. (1977). 'A re-analysis of discourse: stress in discourse.' *Papers from the Thirteenth Regional Meeting, Chicago Linguistic Society*, 316–24.

Leopold, W. F. (1947). *Speech development of a bilingual child: a linguist's record*. Volume 2: *Sound learning in the first two years*. Evanston, Illinois: Northwestern University Press.

Lewis, J. W. (1970). 'The tonal system of remote speech.' *Le Maître Phonétique*, 134, 31–6.

Lewis, J. W. (1977). *Phonetic readings in current English*. Berlin: Cornelsen and Oxford University Press.

Liberman, M. and Pierrehumbert, J. (1982). 'Intonational invariance under changes in pitch-range and length.' Preprint. Cambridge, Mass.: Bell Laboratories.

Liberman, M. and Prince, A. (1977). 'On stress and linguistic rhythm.' *Linguistic Inquiry*, 8, 249–336.

Liberman, M. and Sag, I. (1974). 'Prosodic form and discourse function.' *Papers from the Tenth Regional Meeting, Chicago Linguistic Society*, 416–27.

Lieberman, P. (1967). *Intonation, perception and language*. Cambridge, Mass.: MIT Press.

Loveday, L. (1981). 'Pitch, politeness, and sexual role: an exploratory investigation into the pitch correlates of English and Japanese politeness formulae.' *Language and Speech*, 24, 71–89.

Luthy, M. J. (1983). 'Nonnative speakers' perception of English "nonlexical" intonation signals.' *Language Learning*, 33, 19–36.

Lyons, J. (1962). 'Phonemic and non-phonemic phonology.' *International Journal of American Linguistics*, 28, 127–33.

McClure, J. D. (1980). 'Western Scottish intonation: a preliminary study.' In L. R. Waugh and C. H. van Schooneveld (eds.), *The melody of language: intonation and prosody*. Baltimore: University Park Press.

McConnell-Ginet, S. (1978). 'Intonation in a man's world. *Signs: Journal of Women in Culture and Society*, 3, 541–59.

McGregor, R. L. (1980). 'The social distribution of an Australian English intonation contour.' *Working Papers*, Vol. 2, No. 6, 1–26. Macquarie University; School of English and Linguistics.

Magno-Caldognetto, E., Ferrero, F. E., Lavagnoli, C. and Vagges, K. (1978). 'Fø contours of statements, yes-no questions, and wh-questions of two regional varieties of Italian.' *Journal of Italian Linguistics*, 3, 57–68.

Martin, Ph. (1978). 'Questions de phonosyntaxe et de phonosémantique en français.' *Linguisticae Investigationes*, 2, 93–125.

Martin, S. E. (1952). 'Morphophonemics of standard colloquial Japanese.' *Language* 28, *Language Dissertation* 47.

Maw, J. and Kelly, J. (1975). *Intonation in Swahili*. London: School of Oriental and African Studies.

Miller, J. and Tench, P. (1981). 'Aspects of Hausa intonation, 1: utterances in isolation.' *Journal of the International Phonetic Association*, 10, 45–63.

Mol, H. and Uhlenbeck, E. M. (1956). 'The linguistic relevance of intensity in stress.' *Lingua*, 5, 205–13.

Moulton, W. G. (1962). *The sounds of English and German*. Chicago: University of Chicago Press.

Nakazima, S. (1962). 'A comparative study of the speech developments of Japanese and American English in childhood.' *Studia Phonologica*, 2, 27–39.

Nash, R. and Mulac, A. (1980). 'The intonation of verifiability.' In L. R. Waugh and C. H. van Schooneveld (eds.), *The melody of language: intonation and prosody*. Baltimore: University Park Press.

Nespor, M. and Vogel, I. (1983). 'Prosodic structure above the word.' In A. Cutler and D. R. Ladd (eds.), *Prosody: models and measurements*. Berlin: Springer-Verlag.

Newman, S. (1946). 'On the stress system of English.' *Word*, 2, 171–87.

Nooteboom, S. G. and Terken, J. M. B. (1982). 'What makes speakers omit pitch accents?' *Phonetica*, 39, 317–36.

Oakeshott-Taylor, J. (1984). 'Factuality and intonation.' *Journal of Linguistics*, 20, 1–21.

Oates, J. M. and Dacakis, G. (1983). 'Speech pathology considerations in the management of transsexualism – a review.' *British Journal of Disorders of Communication*, 18, 139–51.

Obolensky, S., Panah, K. Y. and Nouri, F. K. (1963). *Persian basic course*. Washington D.C.: Center for Applied Linguistics.

O'Connor, J. D. and Arnold, G. F. (1961). *Intonation of colloquial English*. Second edition (1973). London: Longman.

Ohala, J. (1978). 'Production of tone.' In V. A. Fromkin (ed.), *Tone: a linguistic survey*. New York: Academic Press.

Oller, D. K. (1979). 'Syllable timing in Spanish, English, and Finnish.' In H. Hollien and P. Hollien (eds.), *Current issues in the phonetic sciences*. Amsterdam: John Benjamins.

Oller, D. K. (1980). 'The emergence of the sounds of speech in infancy.' In

References

G. H. Yeni-Komshian, J. F. Kavanagh and C. A. Ferguson (eds.), *Child phonology.* Volume 1 *Production.* New York: Academic Press.

Pakosz, M. (1982). 'Intonation and attitude.' *Lingua*, 56, 153–78.

Palmer, H. E. (1922). *English intonation, with systematic exercises.* Cambridge: Heffer.

Pellowe, J. and Jones, V. (1978). 'On intonational variability in Tyneside speech.' In P. Trudgill (ed.), *Sociolinguistic patterns in British speech.* London: Edward Arnold.

Peters, A. M. (1977). 'Language learning strategies: does the whole equal the sum of the parts?' *Language*, 53, 560–73.

Pheby, J. (1975). *Intonation und grammatik im deutschen.* Berlin: Akademie-Verlag.

Pierrehumbert, J. (1979). 'The perception of fundamental frequency declination.' *Journal of the Acoustical Society of America*, 66, 363–9.

Pierrehumbert, J. (1980). *The phonology and phonetics of English intonation.* Unpublished Ph.D. thesis, Massachusetts Institute of Technology.

Pike, K. L. (1945). *The intonation of American English.* Ann Arbor: University of Michigan Press.

Pike, K. L. (1948). *Tone languages.* Ann Arbor: University of Michigan Press.

Prince, E. F. (1981). 'Toward a taxonomy of given-new information.' In P. Cole (ed.), *Radical pragmatics.* New York: Academic Press.

Quirk, R., Duckworth, A. P., Rusiecki, J. P. L. and Colin, A. J. T. (1964). 'Studies in the correspondence of prosodic to grammatical features in English.' In H. G. Lunt (ed.), *Proceedings of the ninth international congress of linguists.* The Hague: Mouton.

Quirk, R., Greenbaum, S., Leech, G. and Svartvik, H. (1972). *A grammar of contemporary English.* London: Longman.

Roach, P. (1982). 'On the distinction between "stress-timed" and "syllable-timed" languages.' In D. Crystal (ed.), *Linguistic controversies: essays in linguistic theory and practice in honour of F. R. Palmer.* London: Edward Arnold.

Rohrer, F. (1952). *Untersuchungen zur Intonation der Dialekte von Dorset, Gloucester, Westmorland, Yorkshire, Lincoln, and Norfolk.* Gutenberg: Kessler.

Romportl, M. (1973). 'On the synonymy and homonymy of means of intonation.' In M. Romportl, *Studies in phonetics.* The Hague: Mouton.

Sachs, J., Lieberman, P. and Erickson, D. (1973). 'Anatomical and cultural determinants of male and female speech.' In R. W. Shuy and R. W. Fasold (eds.), *Language attitudes: current trends and prospects.* Washington: Georgetown University Press.

Sadock, J. M. and Zwicky, A. M. (1985). 'Speech act distinctions in syntax.' In T. Shopen (ed.), *Language typology and syntactic description.* Volume 1. Cambridge: Cambridge University Press.

Scherer, K. R. (1981). 'Speech and emotional states.' In J. K. Darby (ed.), *Speech evaluation in psychiatry.* New York: Grune and Stratton.

Schmerling, S. F. (1974). 'A re-examination of "normal stress".' *Language*, 50, 66–73.

Schmerling, S. F. (1976). *Aspects of English sentence stress.* Austin: University of Texas Press.

Schooneveld, C. H. van (1961). *The sentence intonation of contemporary standard Russian*. The Hague: Mouton.

Schubiger, M. (1958). *English intonation: its form and function*. Tübingen: Niemeyer.

Schubiger, M. (1965). 'English intonation and German modal particles – a comparative study.' *Phonetica*, 12, 65–84. Reprinted in D. L. Bolinger (ed.), *Intonation*.

Schubiger, M. (1980). 'English intonation and German modal particles II – a comparative study.' In L. R. Waugh and C. H. van Schooneveld (eds.), *The melody of language*. Baltimore: University Park Press.

Selkirk, E. O. (1984). *Phonology and syntax: the relation between sound and structure*. Cambridge, Mass.: MIT Press.

Sharp, A. E. (1958). 'Falling-rising intonation patterns in English.' *Phonetica*, 2, 127–52.

Sinclair, J. McH. and Brazil, D. (1982). *Teacher talk*. Oxford: Oxford University Press.

Smith, N. and Wilson, D. (1979). *Modern linguistics: the results of Chomsky's revolution*. Penguin: Harmondsworth.

Sommerstein, A. H. (1977). *Modern phonology*. London: Edward Arnold.

Sorensen, J. M. and Cooper, W. E. (1980). 'Syntactic coding of fundamental frequency in speech perception.' In R. A. Cole (ed.), *Perception and production of fluent speech*. Hillsdale, NJ: Erlbaum.

Stark, R. E. (1980). 'Stages of speech development in the first year of life.' In G. H. Yeni-Komshian, J. F. Kavanagh, and C. A. Ferguson (eds.), *Child phonology*. Volume 1. *Production*. New York: Academic Press.

Stockwell, R. P. (1972). 'The role of intonation: reconsiderations and other considerations.' In D. L. Bolinger (ed.), *Intonation*.

Stockwell, R. P. and Bowen, J. D. (1965). *The sounds of English and Spanish*. Chicago: University of Chicago Press.

Svetozarova, N. D. (1975). 'The inner structure of intonation contours in Russian.' In G. Fant and M. A. A. Tatham (eds.), *Auditory analysis and the perception of speech*. New York: Academic Press.

Swadesh, M. (1946). 'Chitimacha.' In H. Hoijer (ed.), *Linguistic structures of native America*. New York: Viking Fund Publications in Anthropology.

Sweet, H. (1878). *Handbook of phonetics*. Oxford: Clarendon Press.

Sweet, H. (1892). *A primer in phonetics*. Oxford: Clarendon Press.

Taglicht, J. (1982). 'Intonation and the assessment of information.' *Journal of Linguistics*, 18, 213–30.

Taglicht, J. (1984). *Message and emphasis: on focus and scope in English*. London: Longman.

Tarone, E. S. (1976). 'Aspects of intonation in Black English.' *American Speech*, 48, 29–36.

Thomas, D. (1975). 'Chrau intonation.' In R. M. Brend (ed.), *Studies in tone and intonation*. Basel: Karger.

Thompson, H. S. (1980). *Stress and salience in English: theory and practice*. Palo Alto Research Center: Xerox.

Thompson, I. (1981). *Intonation practice*. Oxford: Oxford University Press.

References

Thorsen, N. (1978). 'An acoustical analysis of Danish intonation.' *Journal of Phonetics*, 6, 151–75.

Thorsen, N. (1983). 'Two issues in the prosody of standard Danish.' In A. Cutler and D. R. Ladd (eds.), *Prosody: models and measurements*. Berlin: Springer-Verlag.

Topping, D. M. (1969). 'A restatement of Chamorro phonology.' *Anthropological Linguistics*, 11, 62–78.

Trager, G. L. and Smith, H. L. Jnr. (1951). *An outline of English structure*. Washington: American Council of Learned Societies.

Trim, J. L. M. (1959). 'Major and minor tone-groups in English.' *Le Maître Phonétique*, 112, 26–9.

Trim, J. L. M. (1964). 'Tonetic stress-marks for German.' In D. Abercrombie, D. B. Fry, P. A. D. MacCarthy, N. C. Scott and J. L. M. Trim (eds.), *In honour of Daniel Jones*. London: Longman.

Trim, J. L. M. (1970). 'Some continuously variable features in British English intonation.' In *Proceedings of the tenth international congress of linguistics, 1967*. Bucharest: Éditions de l'Académie de la République Socialiste de Roumanie.

Ultan, R. (1978). 'Some general characteristics of interrogative systems.' In J. H. Greenberg, C. A. Ferguson and E. A. Moravcsik (eds.), *Universals of human language*. Volume 4: *Syntax*. Stanford: Stanford University Press.

Umeda, N. (1982). '"F_o declination" is situation-dependent.' *Journal of Phonetics*, 10, 279–90.

Vaissière, J. (1983). 'Language-independent prosodic features.' In A. Cutler and D. R. Ladd (eds.), *Prosody: models and measurements*. Berlin: Springer-Verlag.

Vanderslice, R. and Ladefoged, P. (1972). 'Binary suprasegmental features and transformational word-accentuation rules.' *Language*, 48, 819–38.

Vanvik, A. (1966). *A phonetic-phonemic analysis of the dialect of Trondheim*. Oslo: Oslo University Press.

Varga, L. (1984). 'Hungarian sentence prosody: an outline.' *Folia Linguistica*, 17, 117–51.

Walker, J. (1787). *The melody of speaking delineated*. London: Printed for the Author. Reprinted by The Scholar Press, Menston, Yorks (1970).

Wells, G., Montgomery, M. and MacLure, M. (1979). 'Adult-child discourse: outline of a model of analysis.' *Journal of Pragmatics*, 3, 337–80.

Wells, J. C. (1982). *Accents of English*. Volume 3: *Beyond the British Isles*. Cambridge: Cambridge University Press.

Wells, R. S. (1945). 'The pitch phonemes of English.' *Language*, 21, 27–39.

Welmers, W. E. (1973). *African language structures*. Berkeley: University of California Press.

Wieman, L. A. (1976). 'Stress patterns in early child language.' *Journal of Child Language*, 3, 283–6.

Wilde, H. O. (1938). *Der Industrie-Dialekt von Birmingham: Intonation and Sprachvariante: Tonbewegung, Lautqualität, und Lautquantität*. Studien zur Englischen Philologie, 94. Halle: Niemeyer.

Williams, C. E. and Stevens, K. N. (1972). 'Emotion and speech: some acoustical correlates.' *Journal of the Acoustical Society of America*, 52, 1238–50.

Williamson, K. (1979). 'Sentence tone in some southern Nigerian languages.'

In E. Fischer-Jørgensen, J. Rischel and N. Thorsen (eds.), *Proceedings of the ninth international congress of phonetic sciences*, Volume 2, 424–30.

Wilson, D. and Sperber, D. (1979). 'Ordered entailments: an alternative to pre-suppositional theories.' In C-K On, and D. Dineen (eds.), *Syntax and semantics*. Volume 11: *Presuppositions*. New York: Academic Press.

SUBJECT INDEX

Page references in **bold** *refer to main discussions*

abstract meanings, of tones, 98, 115–19,
    123, 125, 131, 168–9, 184
  vs. local meanings, 98, 101
accent
  degree of stress/accent, 21–3, 52
  vs. stress, 16–17
  see also pitch accent, nucleus, nucleus
    placement, pre-nuclear pitch accent
accent d'insistance, in French, 22–3
accent range, **52–5**, 120–2
  and accented function words, 49
  and autosegmental intonation, 64
  and declination, 127
  related to key and register, **52–5**, 129, 130
  and meaning, 98, 115, **120–2**, 123
  and paratones, 135
  and style, 135
  and the three-tone approach, 118
  as a tonal feature, **120–2**, 131, 183
  and the two-tone approach, 116
Accents I and II, in Swedish, 11
acoustic correlates, of main prosodic
    features, **2–8**, 16, 48
  of length, 2
  of loudness, 3
  and perception, 4, 5, **6–7**, 16
  of pitch, 3–4
  relative importance of, 16, 48
acquisition, of intonation, 171–4
adjectives, word-stress in, 19
adverbials
  and choice of tune, 43, 50, **102–5**, 112,
    124
  clause initial, 50, 76, 112
  in French, 149
  in German, 161
  and intonational sandhi, 43, 86
  and intonation-grouping, 43, **76–7**, 83,
    112, 124, 125
  limiting vs. reinforcing, **103–4**, 114, 160,
    168, 169
  in Portuguese, 149
  sentence final and unaccented, 29, 83, 84,
    87, 89, 95

African (tone) languages, 9, 84, 128, 180,
    189
age (of speaker) and intonation, 134–6, 170,
    177
agreement and disagreement, 97–8, 101–2,
    112, 113–14, 168
all gone, 172, 180
all-new sentences, 81, 82, 95
  see also broad focus, normal stress
all-or-none vs. gradient distinctions, 100,
    120–2
American English, dialectal variation
    within, 142
American (G.A.) English vs. British (R.P.)
    English *see* British R.P. vs. American
    G.A.
Amerindian, influence on Mexican Spanish,
    170
anacrusis
  as intonation-group boundary markers,
    24, 39, 41
  pitch of, 22, 41
  and rhythm, 24–5, 26, 39
antepenultimate rule, the, 19, 21
any, 110
appeal, meaning of fall-rise, 101–2
appearance and disappearance, verbs of, 83
apposition, and intonation-grouping, 78
Arabic
  pharyngealisation in, 178
  stress-timing in, 25
articulatory correlates, *see* physiological
    correlates
Atayal, 144
attitudinal meanings of intonation, 10, 96,
    97, 99–115 (*passim*), 117, 141
  vs. discoursal meanings, 97–8
  across languages, 10, 55, 156
auditory analysis, vs. instrumental analysis, 6
Australian English
  casual high-rise in, 103, 134, 135–6
  and de-attituding, 170
  dialectal variation in, 142, 143
  intonational change in, 103, 135–6, 143

Subject index

feet
  in metrical phonology, 33
  in the stress-timing theory, 24
final lexical item rule, 82–7 (*passim*), 91
finishing point, 60, 102, 120, 122
Finnish
  broad and narrow focus in, 147, 150
  declarative questions in, 162
  word-stress in, 17–18
fixed word-stress vs. no fixed word-stress
    languages, 17–18
floor, in the Swedish model, 151
focus, intonational, 80–95
  broad focus, **82–7**, 94–5
  cross-linguistic, 147–50, 167
  narrow focus, **87–8**, 88–94, 95, 131: and
      contrast, *see* contrastivity; in echoes,
      92–3; in insists, 93–4; across languages,
      147–50
  and new vs. old information, 88–94
  in the three-tone approach, 117
  see also normal stress, nucleus placement
focusing devices (apart from intonation)
  grammatical, 80, 81, 147–9
  across languages, 149–50
  lexical, 80
formal style, vs. casual style, 134
French
  accent d'insistance, 23
  biased questions in, 165
  declaratives in, 158, 159
  degrees of stress/accent in, 22–3
  exclamatives and imperatives in, 166
  immobile nucleus in, 147
  intonation-groups in, 146–7, 149
  narrow focus in, 149
  syllable-timing in, 23, 25
  vocalisations in, 180
  wh questions in, 165
  word-stress in, 17
fronting, and intonation-groups, 77–8
full-vowel timing, **25–6**, 33, 34
full-rise, 60
function words
  accent on, 49, 61, 93–4
  vs. content words, 82, 87, 89–90
  vowels in, 21
functions of intonation, **75–133**, 153–4
fundamental frequency
  and age of speaker, 136
  and declination, 126–7, 167
  and generative intonation, 72
  and key/register, 129–30
  and perceived pitch, **4–5**
  and sex, 136
  and stressed vs. unstressed syllables, 50

Ganda, characteristic tone in, 8, 9

General American vs. R.P., *see* British R.P.
    vs. American G.A.
generative intonation, 67–72
generative phonology, 17, **26–30**
generative stress rules, **26–30**
German
  biased questions in, 165
  declaratives in, 159, 161
  declarative questions in, 162
  imperatives in, 166
  intonation-groups in, 146, 160
  jumps vs. glides in, 54
  narrow focus in, 148–9
  pre-nuclear pitch movements in, 167
  reduced vowels in, 23
gesture, and intonation, 182–3, 184
given information, *see* new and old
    information
Glasgow English, 138, 139, 141
glides
  across dialects, 138, 139
  vs. jumps, 53–4
  in various tones, 48–54 (*passim*)
gradient, vs. all-or-none distinctions, 100,
    120–2
grammar, relations to intonation,
    sentence-type vs. tone, 96–7, 99–112
        (*passim*), 113–14
grammatical framework, for intonational
        comparison
  between dialects, 137–8
  between languages, 144–5, 156–7
grammatical items, vs. lexical items, *see*
    function words vs. content words
Grebo, yes/no questions in, 162
Greek (modern)
  word-stress in, 18
  yes/no questions in, 161
Greenlandic, yes/no questions in, 161
greetings, and cultural convention, 169
grids,
  in metrical phonology, 32–3
  in the Swedish model, 151–2

habit, vs. meaning, 105, 119, 177–8
Hausa, biased questions in, 165
Hawaiian, declaratives in, 158
heads (as pre-nuclear tunes), 62, 65
hesitation phenomena, 38, 41, 42
High (word accent, in Swedish model), 151,
    152
high-falling tone
  contours of, 46, 56, 57, 59, 63, 100, 121
  meanings and uses of: abstract meanings,
      115–19 (*passim*); local meanings, 56,
      93, 96, 99–102, 121; vs. low-fall, 47,
      52, 53, 96, 99–100
  tonal sequences involving, 112

Subject index

Swahili, sentence non-final groups in, 160
Swedish
limited use of lexical tone in, 11, 13, 14,
141, 149
suspension of declination in yes/no
questions, 163–4
Swedish model, for tonal analysis, **151–2**,
153, 154, 155
syllabic boundaries
problems of determining, 2
transcription of, xiv
syllable-timing, theory of, 23, **24–5**
syntactic constituents
in generative phonology, 27
hierarchy of accentability of, 87
and intonation-grouping, 10, 21, **75–80**,
96–7, 99–111 (*passim*), 167
across languages, 145–7, 156–7
in metrical phonology, 33
and nucleus placement, 80–8 (*passim*)
and pauses, 37
and universals, 167
see also adverbials, subjects, etc.
Szechuanese
intonation in, 11
lexical tone in, 8

Tagalog
imperatives in, 166
intonation-groups (sentence non-final) in,
160
requests in, 166
wh questions in, 165
tag questions
and intonation-grouping, 78
across languages, 165
and nuclear tone, 97, 106–7, 112, 114,
115, 165, 168
tag response questions
and falling tones, 100, 114
and rising-falling tones, 101, 114
Tamil
declaratives in, 157, 158
high register in, 55, 130
teenagers, Australian and American, 134,
135, 136
Telugu, wh questions in, 165
templates, in metrical phonology, 33
tempo
and anacrusis, 24, 39–40
as a prosodic feature, 7, 177, 178, **179**
tense, and the fall-rise, 113
terminal junctures, in contours analyses, 45,
46, 47, 48, 57, 58
termination, in the two-tone approach, 116
tertiary stress
in connected speech, 21–2, 52
in generative phonology, 28–30 (*passim*)

Thai
lexical tone in, 15
surprise and doubt in, 159
theme, vs. rheme, 77
three-tone analysis of intonation, **117–19**,
123–5 (*passim*)
timing, in the Swedish and Dutch models,
154
tonal features, **119–28**, 131
accent range, 120–2
complexity, 122–5
declination and downstep, 126–8
stylisation, 125–6
see also under separate entries
tonal features approaches to intonation,
119–20
tonal universals, **168–9**
see also universals in intonation
tones (1), lexical
vs. intonation, **8–9**
use of in intonation languages, 11–12
see also tone languages
tones (2), nuclear, *see* nuclear tones
tone-groups, 35
see also intonation-groups
tone languages, **8–9**
characteristic tone in, 8–9, 14
focusing devices in, 80
vs. intonation languages, 9–10
vs. pitch accent languages, 12–14
Tone-Linking Rule, in autosegmental
intonation, 65, 66
tone units, 35
see also intonation-groups
tonetics, defined, 58
tonetic-stress marks, xiii–xiv, 47, 58,
60, 62
tonic, 49
see also nucleus
topic (1), vs. comment, 77
see also nucleus placement
topic (2), of paratones, 129
topicalisation, and intonation groups, 77–8,
79
topic markers, 147
top line declination, 126, 129, 163, 167–8
top line resetting, 127, 167
trailing tone, in generative intonation, 68,
69, 70
transcriptions, interlinear tonetic and
tonetic-stress marking, xiii–xiv
for other systems, see under the two-tone
approach, the Dutch model, etc
transformational accounts of nucleus
placement, 85
transglottal pressure, and declination, 168
transitional probability, and pause, 37
tune-text association rules, 64, 67

AUTHOR INDEX